FROM THE FIRST ISSUE OF *F&SF*, Fall, 1949:

"To readers we will offer the best of imaginative fiction from obscure treasures of the past to the latest creations in the field, from the chill of the unknown to the comedy of the known-gone-wrong. In short, the best of fantasy. . . ."

FROM THE INTRODUCTION BY THEODORE STURGEON:

"*F&SF* retains its special magic . . . its editors . . . have each in turn maintained that special enchantment as laid down and launched by (Tony) Boucher and (Mick) McComas . . . There is an indescribably and completely unique feeling when one sits down to read, or to write for, the magazine."

FROM THE PREFACE BY ANNETTE McCOMAS:

"I hope that the material chosen for this book—the stories, articles, poems, and above all, the correspondence—will recreate as vividly as possible the very special flavor that these two editors generated as a team. That flavor seems to me to be compounded of integrity, quality, extraordinary wit, and curiously enough, a deep sense of personal kindness. If the reader can taste some of this flavor in what follows, I rest content."

ALAS, BABYLON by Pat Frank
BABEL-17 by Samuel R. Delany
THE BEGINNING PLACE by Ursula Le Guin
A CANTICLE FOR LEIBOWITZ by Walter Miller, Jr.
CENTURY'S END by Russell M. Griffin
DARKWORLD DETECTIVE by J. Michael Reaves
DHALGREN by Samuel R. Delany
DRAGON LENSMAN by David A. Kyle
THE EINSTEIN INTERSECTION by Samuel R. Delany
THE EUREKA YEARS: Boucher and McComas's The Magazine
    of Fantasy and Science Fiction 1949–54
FANTASTIC VOYAGE by Isaac Asimov
THE GATES OF HEAVEN by Paul Preuss
GOSH! WOW! edited by Forrest J. Ackerman
HELLSTROM'S HIVE by Frank Herbert
THE HEROES OF ZARA KEEP by Guy Gregory
HONEYMOON IN HELL by Fredric Brown
THE HUMANOID TOUCH by Jack Williamson
JEM by Frederik Pohl
THE JEWELS OF APTOR by Samuel R. Delany
A LIFE IN THE DAY OF . . . AND OTHER SHORT STORIES
    by Frank Robinson
LORD VALENTINE'S CASTLE by Robert Silverberg
MAN PLUS by Frederik Pohl
MATHEW SWAIN: HOT TIME IN OLD TOWN by
    Mike McQuay
MOCKINGBIRD by Walter Tevis
NOVA by Samuel R. Delany
QUAS STARBRITE by James R. Berry
SLOW TO FALL DAWN by Stephen Leigh
SONG OF SORCERY by Elizabeth Scarborough
STEEL OF RAITHSKAR by Randall Garrett and
    Vicki Ann Heydron
A STORM UPON ULSTER by Kenneth Flint
SUNDIVER by David Brin
TALES OF NEVERYON by Samuel R. Delany
TIME STORM by Gordon Dickson
TRITON by Samuel R. Delany
THE WINDHOVER TAPES: AN IMAGE OF VOICES by
    Warren C. Norwood

THE
EUREKA
YEARS

Boucher and McComas's
The Magazine of Fantasy and Science Fiction
1949–54

edited by Annette McComas

BANTAM BOOKS
TORONTO · NEW YORK · LONDON · SYDNEY

THE EUREKA YEARS

A Bantam Book / June 1982

ACKNOWLEDGMENTS

"The Model of a Science Fiction Editor" *(poem) by Anthony Boucher, copyright 1952 by Anthony Boucher. Reprinted by permission of Curtis Brown, Ltd.* "The Hurkle is a Happy Breast" *by Theodore Sturgeon, copyright 1949 by Theodore Sturgeon, copyright renewed © 1976 by Theodore Sturgeon.* "The Exiles" *by Ray Bradbury, copyright 1950 by Fantasy House.* "Minister Without Portfolio" *by Mildred Clingerman, copyright 1951 by Fantasy House.* "Gavagan's Bar: Elephas Frumenti" *by L. Sprague deCamp and Fletcher Pratt, copyright 1950 by Fantasy House, Inc., copyright renewed © 1977 by L. Sprague deCamp.* "Come on, Wagon" *by Zenna Henderson, copyright 1951 by Fantasy House. Reprinted by permission of Curtis Brown, Ltd.* "Of Time and Third Avenue" *by Alfred Bester, copyright 1951 by Mercury Press, Inc., copyright renewed © 1976 by Alfred Bester.* "Dress of White Silk" *by Richard Matheson, copyright 1951 by Fantasy House, copyright renewed © 1979 by Richard Matheson. Reprinted by permission of Harold Matson Company, Inc. Excerpt from "Epitaph Near Moonport" by Sherwood Springer, copyright 1954 by Fantasy House.* "The Boy Next Door" *by Chad Oliver, copyright 1951 Fantasy House.* "Not With a Bang" *by Damon Knight, copyright 1950 by Fantasy House, copyright renewed © 1977 by Damon Knight.* "Oh Ugly Bird" *by Manly Wade Wellman, copyright 1951 by Fantasy House.* "Skiametric Morphology and Behaviorism of Ganymedeus Sapiens" *by Kenneth R. Deardorf, copyright 1951, 1952 by Fantasy House.* "Letters to the Editor" *by Ron Goulart, copyright 1952 by Fantasy House.* "Foundation of S.F. Success" *(poem) by Isaac Asimov, copyright 1954 by Fantasy House.* "The Other Inauguration" *by Anthony Boucher, copyright 1953 by Fantasy House. Reprinted by permission of Curtis Brown, Ltd.* "When Half Gods Go" *by Poul Anderson, copyright 1953 by Fantasy House.* "Little Movement" *by Philip K. Dick, copyright 1952 by Fantasy House. Reprinted by permission of the author and the author's agents, Scott Meredith Literary Agency, Inc., 845 Third Avenue, New York, N.Y. 10022.* "The Naming of Names" *by Herman Mudgett, copyright 1953 by Fantasy House. Reprinted by permission of Curtis Brown, Ltd.* "The Last of the Spode" *by Evelyn E. Smith, copyright 1953 by Fantasy House, copyright renewed © 1981. Reprinted by permission of the author and Harry Morrison, Inc., her agents.* "Flies" *by Isaac Asimov, copyright 1953 by Fantasy House.* "Listen" *by Gordon R. Dickson, copyright 1952 by Fantasy House.* "The Devil and Simon Flagg" *by Arthur Porges, copyright 1954 by Fantasy House.* "Limerick" *by Herman W. Mudgett, copyright 1953 by Fantasy House. Reprinted by permission of Curtis Brown, Ltd.* "Brave New Word" *by J. Francis McComas, copyright 1954 by Fantasy House.* "Mousetrap" *by Andre Norton, copyright 1954 by Fantasy House. Reprinted by permission of Larry Sternig Literary Agency.* "Cat" *by R. Bretnor, copyright 1953 by Fantasy House.* "I've Got a Little List" *(poem) by Randall Garrett, copyright 1953 by Fantasy House. Reprinted by permission of Blackstone Literary Agency.*

ISBN 0-553-20673-7

Published simultaneously in the United States and Canada

PRINTED IN THE UNITED STATES OF AMERICA

0 9 8 7 6 5 4 3 2 1

To you
Richard Lupoff and Phyllis Boucher White
From Me
With Love and Thanks

TABLE OF CONTENTS

Introduction

McComas and Boucher; Boucher and McComas . . . magic names from a magic time. Mick and Tony. That they are no longer with us is a prime example of what I call bad scripting.

J. F. McComas was a big man, broad, hearty, generous and warm. There was an immense vitality about him; he laughed well and was all the things a good companion ever has to be. I met him on my first trip to the West Coast, where I stayed with him and his lovely wife Annette in a really beautiful house in the Bay area. Mick took me to dinner on Fisherman's Wharf for my very first abalone steak. I shall never forget it, for I have never seen its like since. It covered most of the plate; it was thick as your thumb, tender as tears, and was covered by a sauce produced by the culinary analogue of Claude Debussy. He had a fine English automobile and work that he liked, and he was glad he was alive, and so was I.

Tony was A. P. White, author of H. H. Holmes, reviewer and critic of detective and mystery stories, and Anthony Boucher, author/editor/critic of science-fiction and fantasy, and conductor of "Golden Voices," a long-running radio series on opera, of which his knowledge was encyclopedic and his taste faultless. He carried on all these activities more or less simultaneously, which had to mean reading close to three hundred books a year and countless manuscripts, as well as riding herd on all the business of publishing a manuscript and preparing his radio series; yet I never saw the man hurried or burdened or unwilling to settle back and generate that special kind of Conversation which I find so rare, where the capital C is called for because in it, things get *said* rather than just talked. I never saw him without time to play poker all night long, or to party endlessly with his friends, or to listen with a saint's patience to one's personal woes. I have had the thought that he had a special arrangement with Time Itself to be able to do all these things so well and so unhurriedly, and that may explain why he was with us for so little of it.

The Magazine of Fantasy, as it was first called, was launched with a big bang in the ballroom of a New York hotel. The announcement and invitation came via Western Union, a fine long yellow sheet (and damn the expense) describing what and where, time and place, and please reply collect. I wired my reply full rate and at almost equal length, paying for it not because I could afford it or even because anyone might notice, but because it made me feel good. And I went, and it was impressive, because Everybody-Who-Was-Anybody was there. I happened to be beside the podium when Basil Rathbone was introduced, and heard him ask someone next to him, "What's this about? Eh? Eh?"

"Poe and all that," said the someone.

"Ah," said Mr. Rathbone and got up to the mike and said how pleased he was to be here; then he recited *Annabel Lee,* took his ovation, and off.

And I went home and wrote a story for Tony and Mick, and it appeared in Vol. I, No. 1, which makes me happy to this day.

There were three magazines for the fantasy/science-fiction freak in those days (well, there were more, but these three mattered most) John Campbell's *Astounding,* a newcomer, Horace Gold's *Galaxy,* and *F&SF.* Not its full title; just *F&SF. Astounding* has been likened to *Popular Science* of its day, *Galaxy* to *The Saturday Evening Post, F&SF* to *Harper's* and *The Atlantic Monthly.* More briefly, nuts-and-bolts stories, general fiction stories, and real good writing—all, of course, in the fantasy/science-fiction category. The first two, in that Golden Age, usually made money or broke even. *F&SF* was always able, just barely, able to keep one nostril above high-water mark and sometimes had to hold its breath for months at a time. For most of that time—and this remarkable fact holds true even to this day in the early eighties—writers and editors and artists were paid less than they could have gotten elsewhere; and that is a definition of love. And the magazine retains its special magic; its editors Robert Mills, Avram Davidson, Joe and then Ed Ferman, have each in turn maintained that special enchantment as laid down and launched by Boucher and McComas, and I know I speak for many others beside myself when I say that there is an indescribably and completely unique feeling when one sits down to read or to write for the magazine. It's the echo of Mick's explosive "Hey!" of approval, and of some special syllable of Tony's, sung, not said, still thrumming in the cosmos, even for those who never knew them.

I shall close with what, to me, is the definitive Boucher anecdote.

The editors had asked me for a story and had, in time, pressed a little by telling me there was a slot for it in the upcoming issue, but it had to be in by such-and-such. Finding just the right story to tell wasn't easy, and the calendar and then the clock began to run awfully fast, and finally I sat down with my head as blank as the paper and started to put out words more or less at random, until some thirty sleepless, eatless, even coffeeless hours had gone by. Somehow I got it into the mail and then fell over sidewise. In due course I convalesced, and sat down to read my carbon.

I was horrified. I felt that the manuscript was too long, the story too thin, and the whole thing totally unprofessional and unworthy of the magazine.

I tottered to the typewriter and banged out (as I remember) five single-spaced pages saying all the above in much greater detail, begging the editors to fill my slot with someone else's story, pleading for advice as to how to fix this one if it could be fixed, or giving me some sort of plot or idea or spring-board for another story that I could get out in the next four weeks before deadline. All but weeping, I fired this moany missive off to California.

By return mail I got the only airmail, special delivery *post card* I have ever seen. It read:

Dear Ted:
   I love you.
   You write such beautiful stories.
                    Tony

—Theodore Sturgeon

Preface

They were an unusual team of editors, Boucher and McComas. In their nine years together from 1945 to 1955, four getting the magazine launched and five as coeditors of the magazine, they created a special aura that pervaded the realm of both writers and readers of imaginative fiction. They were not only respected and admired but also really loved both for themselves and their product. Perhaps a few personal memories will help the reader flesh out the men and their times. I wish they were around to do this book themselves. I'd like to re-create in this book, as far as I can, the unique quality which made both themselves and their magazine so distinctive. Here is a brief glimpse of who and what they were.

When the notion for editing a magazine of fantasy first evolved, Mick and I were living in Santa Monica Canyon, and Tony Boucher (A. P. White to us) lived with his wife and family in Berkeley, California. Since Mick was a publisher's representative and traveled the whole Western territory, he was in Northern California often, while I was not. So I never really heard the true beginnings back in 1945–1946. What I got was snitches and snatches, and I do not think I took the notion at all seriously.

We all met at U.C. Berkeley back in the 30's—I mean AP, his wife Phyllis (then Phyllis Price), Mick, and me. We were all in Little Theatre—either writing plays, directing plays, or acting in plays. We became close friends then, when we were very late teenish. We shared meals, football games, poker games. Later, our skimpy, early married income brackets held us together as we swapped economy menus and suggestions for how to get along on practically nothing a month.

As AP became established as a writer and critic, his *nom de plume* of Anthony Boucher began to overshadow his "birth" name, and he became almost exclusively Anthony or Tony Boucher (except to a few of us). Phyllis learned to answer to "Mrs. White," "Mrs. Holmes" (another writing alias), and primarily "Mrs. Boucher." I was responsible for Mick's nickname. He so hated his first name (Jesse) and didn't think much of Francis either. Since he was predominately Irish by birth, and in appearance and attitudes, Mick seemed a natural!

The Whites (Bouchers) became long-distance neighbors in the Los Angeles area, from about 1938 to 1941. We had all married that year: Phyllis and AP in May 1938 and Mick and I in November. The White-Bouchers returned to their beloved Bay area and Berkeley, but their stay in "the South," as we call Southern California out here, was certainly active. One of the most delightful features of those years was participation in the Mañana Literary Society. Bob Heinlien, then dwelling in the hills of Laurel Canyon near Hollywood, formed this "club" and generously used his own residence as headquarters. It wasn't really a club; it was more an excuse for getting together kindred souls who loved in-depth conversations on fantasy and science-fiction. Bob, when in the mood, would invite writers and would-be writers for talk about stories they were all going to write "some day," and for the consumption of "Dago Red" wine ($1.00 a gal!), the telling of jokes, swapping of information on magazine publishers and markets, and the like.

The club parties were a lot of fun. They became a haven for every visiting published (and frequently unpublished) science-fiction writer. Visitors and parties went together. Some of the locals and visitors included Henry Kuttner, C. L. Moore, L. Sprague de Camp, L. Ron Hubbard, Cleve Cartmill, Arthur K. Barnes, Leigh Brackett, and Willy Ley, Jack Williamson, and various and sundry wives and girl friends.

Shaggy Dog stories were big in those days, and these people seemed to have an absolute genius for telling them. They were unbelievably attenuated, length being part of their so-called fascination. Mick was famous for his "Bengal Bicycle Club" story. He did it very well. It was naturally very long and a constant request at the club parties. AP's specialty was original limericks, mostly amusingly risqué and wonderfully clever. He was blessed with a photographic memory and could repeat hundreds of other people's limericks, too. Later, a number of the limericks appeared in a private printing, called *Unexpurgated*, distributed only to friends. My copy disappeared a long time ago. It must be a priceless collector's item for some, however. The club provided some very merry times, in spite of the threats of war hanging over our heads.

Both Mick and Tony (I can't keep saying AP) had been caught up in the literature of fantasy, science-fiction, horror, and the supernatural since boyhood. They also shared an equally intense interest in true crime and mystery fiction. Both ultimately became reviewers in both these fields for large city newspapers. Mick, from the beginning, demonstrated a real flair for high-caliber editing. He wrote true crime articles and published two anthologies on famous real life murders. By 1945 he was involved in editing, along with Ray Healy, the classic anthology, *Adventures in Time and Space* which is still available in paperback.* The idea of editing an imaginative fiction magazine was a natural for him.

Tony Boucher's original foray into writing was in the mystery field. He had published seven mystery novels by 1945. His novel *Rocket to the Morgue* deals considerably with the activities of the Mañana Literary Society and discusses science-fiction theory and writing of the 1940's. The novel was originally published under his pseudonym of H. H. Holmes. Actually he turned away from novel writing to composing short stories for the mystery and imaginative fiction fields by 1942, since it furnished a more immediate return in feeding and housing a wife and two little sons. Tony Boucher has been referred to by many of his contemporaries as a "Renaissance" man, because he was so talented in so many different areas. For years, for instance, he had his own radio program on opera locally, in Berkeley, with a dedicated, large following.

I would like to be able to describe the actual way that these two old friends came up with their notion for a national magazine, but I really don't know, and neither does Phyllis. I do remember their mutual delight in compiling lists for their own entertainment of marvelous, obscure or overlooked, fantasy, horror, and science-fiction stories. Sometimes they drew up lists of the best for the year in various categories in the imaginative fiction and nonfiction fields. They corresponded with and spent time with a large number of writers

---

* Ballantine Books edition, 3rd printing, Dec., 1979.

and editors already active in fantasy and science fiction. It must somehow have all fallen together and sparked the germination of their plan for a "different" type of magazine. Originally, you will note in the first letter to Mr. Lawrence Spivak of Mercury Publications in 1946, they were thinking of a magazine of fantasy and horror stories. Between January and March of 1946, they selected material for a first issue for submission. I do remember the long distance telephone calls—which neither could afford—the never-ending stream of correspondence, the excitement or despondency caused by replies from New York, and the various labors of Hercules that were involved in setting up the final choices.

None of us, I think, quite grasped what a monumental job the production of the magazine would become, even when we once grasped the astonishing idea that there was going to be at least one issue of the magazine. The responsibility of producing a monthly national magazine is difficult under any circumstances. When one considers that this was not a full-time job for either editor—each had other large responsibilities—and that distance from the publisher created many hardships and delays, it becomes even more amazing that the magazine could ever evolve and survive. Add to that the particular temperaments of the two gentlemen, both fascinated wholly by quality and willing to go to any lengths to help create it, and the amount of work becomes colossal. The wives of these two gentlemen became almost horrified at the seemingly endless amount of patience displayed by their spouses, laboring over relentless numbers of rewrites, writing loving personal letters to encourage writers, answering every piece of mail. There the editors sat, typing hour after hour, letters of encouragement to women writers to enter a male-dominated field, congratulations to writers for the comic and incongruous pieces which they adored, doling out advice to writers about how to get novels published, how to protect manuscript rights, how to settle disputes with publishers. These letters, of course, did not include their lively and continuous correspondence with author-friends about such topics as religion or mathematics, for instance, (Tony) or Indians, folklore, and the Civil War (Mick). Phyllis tells a lovely ancedote about receipt of mail at their residence which acted also as the magazine office. When the magazine first started, the editors were in a state of glory as the mail brought one day their first unsolicited manuscript! They were really in business. About four weeks later they received a call from the Berkeley post office informing them that a special mail sack was being created especially for them. Mail was arriving in fantastic numbers. There were suddenly 80 to 120 manuscripts a week, to say nothing of the stream of letters. The editors' joy soon subsided to the level of dogged patience. The flow of mail never diminished in their years together.

By the time Phyllis and I really began to take this whole project seriously, (it rather sneaked up on us), we had become file clerks, cataloguers, subeditors and typists. Then we *really* knew something was happening. It was called WORK.

Nonetheless, those years were a fascinating time. We met so many remarkable people. We went to and gave so many fun parties. We got so much pleasure from seeing the project grow and prosper. And we glowed that our husbands were the very first to edit a national magazine from the West Coast. Quite a feat!

I hope that the material chosen for this book—the stories, articles, poems, and above all, the correspondence—will re-create as vividly as possible the very special flavor that these two editors generated as a team. That flavor seems to me to be compounded of integrity, quality, extraordinary wit, and curiously enough, a deep sense of personal kindness. If the reader can taste some of this flavor in what follows, I rest content.

Annette Peltz McComas

Autobiographies

The following material is written by each editor in response to the request of L. Sprague de Camp for biographical material for his book. It seems fitting that each tell his background up to October 1952 in his own words.

Biographical data on me: (Anthony Boucher)
Born Oakland, Calif., Aug. 21, 1911, Education: Pasadena J. C. 1929/30; U.S.C. 1930/32, B.A. '32; U.C. (Berkeley) 1932/34, M.A. '34. Military service: none. Scientific or technical experience or training: none. (But a pretty eye for spotting boners in MSS.)

My M.A. was in German. My thesis, with the ringing title of THE DUALITY OF IMPRESSIONISM IN RECENT GERMAN DRAMA, was (at least as of 1934) the shortest master's thesis in the university's history.

No "other and previous occupations": just writing, reviewing, editing.

Writings: 7 mystery novels, best known being THE CASE OF THE BAKER STREET IRREGULARS by Anthony Boucher (Simon & Schuster, 1940); ROCKET TO THE MORGUE by H. H. Holmes, recently republished as by A. B.* (Duell, Sloan & Pearce, 1942). Edited 2 detective fiction anthos and 1 fact-crime antho. Edited with McComas THE BEST FROM FANTASY AND SCIENCE FICTION (Little, Brown; 1st series 1952; 2nd series 1953). Many shorts, novelets, articles—detective fiction, f&fs, fact-crime, criticism—reprinted in 33 anthologies (as of the moment—doubtless more by the time your book appears). Several hundred radio plays (SHERLOCK HOLMES, GREGORY HOOD, etc). Translated many stories

*A.B.—Anthony Boucher.

1

of Georges Simenon, Thomas Narcojac, Pierre Boileau, Jorge Luis Borges, Antonio Helú, etc.

Reviewing: Formerly mystery reviewer of S.F. *Chronicle* & EQMM, now of *N.Y. Times Book Review*. MWA Edgar award for best U.S. criticism 1945, 1950. Formerly science-fantasy reviewer of S.F. *Chronicle* & Chi *Sun-Times*, now (as H.H. Holmes) of N.Y. *Herald Tribune Book Review*.

I first adopted the Boucher name (my grandmother's maiden name) because as White I was being an unsuccessful playwright and I thought I'd keep the mystery novels separate. By now things have reached a point where I really feel pseudonymous and incognito if I'm going about as White. No particular point in legal change of name since I can use Boucher legally anyway. I've even testified as an expert witness in court under that name; and I have a joint checking account with myself. My bank is uncomfortable, but cannot find anything technically wrong with the idea.

Yes, the Bouchers were French-Irish.

Anthony Boucher (William Anthony Parker White "AP.") became sole editor of *The Magazine of Fantasy and Science Fiction* in the Fall of 1954 and left the magazine in 1958. He died in Oakland, California on April 29, 1968.

Jesse Francis McComas: (Now to myself, always an interesting subject.)

Born: Kansas City, Missouri, June 9, 1910.
Many previous occupations: working in bridge and tunnel construction, too many years with an oil company, plus newspaper and radio writing. Also a little bit of professional acting, very hammy. In 1941 I entered the publishing business, working as a salesman and editorial representative. Spent two years in New York City with Random House. Came back to the Coast in 1944 and worked for a while as editorial representative for the Pacific Coast for Henry Holt and Company. During that time I also sold for Simon and Schuster and

am now Northern California sales manager and general editorial representative.

I haven't done much writing of my own, my talent seems to be in raising Hell with other people's efforts. However, I have done what my partner graciously calls the historically definitive Anthology of Science Fiction, with Raymond J. Healy, ADVENTURES IN TIME AND SPACE. Have also done with AP the two BESTS from the magazine.

Right now I am also doing Science Fiction reviewing for the *New York Times Book Review*. Since we took over the Mercury magazine TRUE CRIME DETECTIVE I have gotten interested in writing True Crime (always one of my hobbies) and our current issue has a piece of mine on capital punishment in the United States.

Education: Berkeley High School and the University of California. The depression caught up with me and I never was graduated from the latter, and really haven't missed the degree.

Military Service: I was once in the California National Guard, when their physical requirements were not too rigid. A bad knee they passed upon kept me out of the army during World War II.

Yes, I, too, am Irish. My ancestors came to this country just in time to tote a musket with great enthusiasm, if with no especial distinction, against the odious British. However, this prejudice has disappeared with the generations and while we do not necessarily approve of everything they do, "some of my best friends are English."

Scientific or technical training—none unless you want to call experience as radio announcer, manager, and acting both before the microphone and before an unwilling audience technical training. I do have a pretty fair knowledge of American History, can part of the time hold my own with Fletcher* in arguing about the Civil War. I think that is about it.

J. Francis McComas (Mick) resigned from his editorship in the Fall of 1954. He died in Fremont, California on April 19, 1978.

*Fletcher Pratt

The Birth
and
the Growth

Mick and A.P. were friendly with that half of Ellery Queen known as Fred Dannay* who was in charge of *Ellery Queen's Mystery Magazine,* published by the American Mercury, Inc. under the leadership of Lawrence Spivak. The magazine was flourishing in 1945 when Boucher and McComas began inquiring of Dannay whether he would be interested in lending his name to a sister magazine that would be devoted to fantasy, supernatural and horror themes. They suggested themselves as editors of such a possible publication. Dannay wrote to them saying that he would not like to participate in a project which bore his name when in truth he knew almost nothing about the genres. However, he wrote, he would recommend they contact Mr. Lawrence Spivak in New York and present their idea directly to him. The magazine could resemble EQMM closely in format, and he, Dannay, would be glad to give them a glowing reference before they contacted Mr. Spivak.

The contact was made, and in January 1946, the two aspirants met with Mr. Spivak in New York. Spivak was interested and suggested that they assemble material for a test issue. After a feverish interval of hard work exploring and considering material in a general atmosphere of great ebullience, they finally sent a letter to Lawrence Spivak dated March 11, 1946.

Dear Mr. Spivak:

When the writer and Mr. Anthony Boucher were in New York in January; we discussed with you the founding of a magazine, similar in publishing policy to ELLERY QUEEN'S MYSTERY MAGAZINE, but containing short

---

*The other half, Manfred E. Lee (Manny), also a good friend, was later to enlist the services of Boucher as a collaborator on the Ellery Queen radio show.

stories of the fantasy, supernatural, or ghost genre. At that time you expressed considerable interest in the idea and suggested that we assemble material for a test issue.

Since our return to California we have done just that. For the hitherto unpublished part of the magazine, we have lined up "off-the-trail" stories by Raymond Chandler, S. Guy Endore, Dorothy B. Hughes, Philip MacDonald, H. F. Heard and/or Stuart Palmer. I think you will agree that that is certainly a top-flight group of selling names! Both Chandler and Endore have a trunkful of our type of manuscripts, unpublished for lack of a proper market. We could certainly count on them to be regular contributors.

For the reprint section we have such authors as M. R. James, H. R. Wakefield, John Dickson Carr, Fitz-James O'Brien, Robert Bloch and H. P. Lovecraft.

Editorially speaking, we would have a short general introduction, introducing the whole field to the general reader and a brief comment on each story.

We have now reached the limit of independent action and need clarifying advice from you as to matters of payment, publication date, etc. Our own opinion is that writers of the stature of Chandler and Hughes will hardly be content with less than two cents a word. For reprints not in public domain we can hardly pay less than one cent a word. We understand those are approximately the rates with which EQMM started.

As for ourselves, we believe that we should operate on a minimum plus a percentage, but that can be discussed after the test issue has been run and the success or failure of the venture determined.

We have not yet settled upon a name for the magazine. Any suggestions from your own wisdom and experience would be deeply appreciated.

A general letter from you, outlining your opinion and policy on the above and any other matters pertinent to the initial issue would enable us to settle all editorial details and forward to you the contents of the first issue. Settlement of details with authors on this more positive basis would permit us to have all material ready for an early Fall publication date—or earlier if you deem it adviseable.

Both Mr. Boucher and I enjoyed meeting you in New

York and we venture to hope it will have begun a mutually profitable association.

   With kindest personal regards.

Sincerely,

J. Francis McComas

   As Boucher later wrote to L. Sprague de Camp, the gestation of the magazine was considerably longer than that of the elephant (a mere two years) since it was a full three years before the first issue appeared. A letter of agreement was signed in August of 1946 with a dismissal of the whole contract if the first issue was not published by March of 1947. Joseph Ferman, general manager of Mercury Publications, renewed the contract at that time with a promise to try for a publication date within the year. Reasons for delay were based on a decline at that time in newsstand sales in general. It is difficult to project the mercurial mood changes of Boucher and McComas as encouragement and delays replaced one another. They wanted desperately to edit this magazine. They were convinced they had a unique and needed approach. Consider, for instance, the dizzy elation when they received the following letter from Joe Ferman.

23 September 1947

Dear Mr. McComas:

   We are now considering publishing the first issue of FANTASY AND HORROR—A Magazine of Weird and Fantastic Stories—before the end of this year.

   Will you be good enough to send along the complete material for the first issue including an introduction for the magazine as a whole as well as the brief editorial notes at the beginning of each story. The artwork for the cover is completely finished and I think we can make a decision on the publication as soon as we hear from you.

   I am enclosing herewith a list of the stories that were bought and paid for (four original stories and two reprints).

   Kind regards.

Sincerely,

[*J. Ferman*]

STORIES TO BE PURCHASED FOR "THE MAGAZINE
   OF FANTASY AND TERROR"
ORIGINAL STORIES AT $100:
PRIVATE—KEEP OUT
by Philip MacDonald, Laguna Beach, California
SEEK AND YE SHALL FIND
by Stuart Palmer, Baraboo, Wisconsin
RINGS ON HIS FINGERS
by Cleve Cartmill, Saint Enterprises, Los Angeles, CA
REVIEW COPY
by H. H. Holmes, %Willis Kingsley Wing, NY
REPRINTS AT $50:
MEN OF IRON
by Guy Endore, Los Angeles, California
PERSEUS HAD A HELMET
by Richard Sale, Paul Reynolds, NY

The would-be editors pulled themselves together, donned
their masks of dignity and restraint and returned this reply to
Joe Ferman.

5 October 1947

Dear Joseph Ferman:
   Tony Boucher and I are forwarding under separate cover
the material you requested. With some minor changes and
complications. Inasmuch as this letter has considerable
comment on all this, I'd like to abandon business formality
and list these items numerically. So, with your approval—
1) We enclose therewith a general introduction to the
   magazine (and ourselves) to be signed by Mr. Spivak.
   Length about 350–500 words.
2) We enclose therewith brief (very brief) editorial notes
   on the stories themselves.
3) Now for the copy itself: We enclose therewith of the
   stories you've listed as purchased.
4) Lacking are:
        New: SEEK AND YE SHALL FIND, by Stuart
        Palmer
        Reprint: MEN OF IRON, by Guy Endore
   Some time ago the authors of these requested their

return for minor revisions. Since the pub date of the
magazine was so vague, we haven't rushed the boys.
However, they've been wired and these two purchased
stories will be in your hands, plus our own editorial
notes, by the end of the week.

5) We also enclose a table of contents, suggesting the
order in which we think the stories would appear to
their best advantage.

6) On this table, in addition to the purchased stories, you
will notice two additional opuses—both also enclosed.
These are:

THE LOST ROOM, by Fitz-James O'Brien—a
very little known reprint. In public domain.

IN THE DAYS OF OUR FATHERS, by Winona
McClintic—a new story by a new author for which
the standard rate of $100 should be paid.

In your letter of Sep 23, you gave us no final word on
the length of the magazine. However, our discussions and
contract called for a magazine of approximately 128 pages
(EQMM format) or about 50,000 words. The purchased
material comes to 34,000 words. So these two new stories
seem to fill out the gap.

As for the stories themselves: The O'Brien most ably
demonstrates the magazine's policy (like that of EQMM)
of rediscovering and reprinting lost classics. O'Brien's
WHAT WAS IT? and THE DIAMOND LENS are known—
because over-anthologized—to every reader of the fantastic and supernatural. THE LOST ROOM is completely
forgotten and, we think, better than either of the other
two.

IN THE DAYS OF OUR FATHERS best illustrates
another phase of our policy (again like EQMM)—that of
seeking out and publishing new writers. While Miss
McClintic is new, she is fully qualified to stand along with
Stuart Palmer, Richard Sale, and the rest.

If this first test issue is to typify the magazine as
projected, we feel strongly that it should include these
fine and unfamiliar specimens of the very old and the
very new. If there's any reason why they should not be
included, will you so advise us? Needless ·to say, we

look forward to it with somewhat feverish excitement. And we do thank you, personally, for your kind cooperation.

Kindest regards,

Tony Boucher and Mick McComas

Now, they felt, things were, at last, going to happen. It was Elation Time once again. On November 10, 1947 this letter from Ferman took care of that bit of High and reduced them again to General Gloom.

Dear Mick and Tony:

I'm afraid we shall have to postpone, at least temporarily, publication of FANTASY AND HORROR. I know how terribly disappointed both of you will be, but we are convinced that it is best to wait until there's a better opportunity to make it a really successful publication. The newsstand situation on digest-size and pocketbooks has not improved much, except occasionally in a very spotty way. We are experimenting, however, with 35¢ books in the Jonathan Press series and on ELLERY QUEEN'S MYSTERY MAGAZINE. If this becomes feasible on a national basis, perhaps we can test FANTASY AND HORROR at 35¢ sometime early next year. I have the figures on Avon FANTASY for the first two issues in twelve important cities from New York to St. Louis and it doesn't add up to much.

You know, of course, that the extension of our first agreement carried only to the end of this year and if you feel that it might be better for you and for the publication to make some other arrangements, by all means do so. However, I am hoping that you will agree with us that it is best to wait until the situation appears a little clearer.

Larry Spivak sends his regards.

J.F.

This kind of seesawing is not good for the nerves or the temper. However, they felt they were too close to success not to agree, albeit unhappily, that it would be best to wait for a "clearer situation."

The next glimmer of encouragement didn't materialize with any real meaning until they received the following in February of 1949. That was a wait of over a year, and they had really tasted of despair.

9 February 1949

Dear Tony:

We have been discussing again the possibility of testing a one-shot of FANTASY AND HORROR.

Do you feel that we would be diluting the spirit and quality of the magazine too much if a science-fiction story was used in each issue?

Also, do you think we might add a story with a little more sex in it—or possibly a story with more sex in the title than in the story?

I assume you have a copy of the Table of Contents of the first issue as originally planned, but if not let me know and I shall be glad to send a copy both to you and to Mick.

Kind regards.

Sincerely,

Joe

This very prompt answer speaks for itself.

12 February 1949

Dear Joe:

We're delighted (as we hardly need to say) at the prospect of a one-shot trial on FANTASY & HORROR.

And we're very warm toward the idea of regularly including at least one science-fiction story. In fact, we'd been planning from the first to slip in borderline science-fiction from time to time. The borderline between science-fiction—look, let's save typing and call it stf—and fantasy (and even horror) is a difficult one to draw; the best of science-fiction has or could have a very strong appeal to the fantasy reader. The routine gadget-story type of stf or the Interplanetary Horse Opera we wouldn't be using; they're passé by now anyway among the stf-mags which cater to the sort of audience we hope to attract. And intelligent adult stf would in no wise "dilute the spirit" of fantasy-&-horror.

For the first issue, we feel that a stf story should be an original. Up to now, the cream of the mature crop, the kind of stuff we would like to reprint in a mag like ours, has appeared chiefly in ASTOUNDING; and you know how much chance we'd have of getting reprint rights from Street & Smith. But we know many of the authors who have made S&S's reputation, and particularly several who are also known to broader reaches of the reading public.

If you want to buy another original at $100 the first issue, we can guarantee securing a good stf story by a good name. Let us know definitely, and we'll make arrangements.

Now we come to Sex. (McComas leers over my shoulder—AB) We gather that your reason for bringing this up is the commercial success of the Avon FANTASY READER. Their approach on this has been, as you've probably gathered, strictly a deceptive hocuspocus. An occasional story does have a sex slant (of the somewhat slavering and obvious pulp kind); but even that never remotely lives up to the cover.

We're afraid that deliberately *trying* to get sex in could be a very bad idea. If an editor starts looking for a sexy story or an author is asked to produce one, the result is apt to be either purely unprintable or simply in questionable taste. We're all for sex where it is a natural and well-integrated part of a fantasy story; we'd like to feel that our editorial standards in that respect could be far more liberal than those of, say, Street & Smith. But we're doubtful about going out hunting for it.

With warm regards from both of us.

Sincerely,

J. F. McComas
Anthony Boucher

Joe Ferman hastened to write and agree with the editors in their attitude toward the use of S-E-X in the magazine. Their bias was toward L-O-V-E. They actually did open the field to the idea that it wasn't unmanly or un-science-fictionish to include some true emotional interplay between men and women in this genre. However they weren't adverse to a little lasciviousness either if it unfolded at the level of their literary standards.

The next word from Joe made it all seem a little more real and possible.

10 May 1949

Dear Mick:

We are planning now for the publication of the first issue of Fantasy in late Summer or early Fall.

I am a little dubious about the title and I'm inclined now to use something like the following:

The Magazine of
FANTASY

(then at the bottom, the following:)

A Selection of the Best Stories of Fantasy and Horror,
Both New and Old

I look forward to hearing from you soon. Meanwhile, we are going ahead with preparation of the material for the cover.

Joe Ferman

Naturally, the editors agreed heartily and cordially. (In my opinion it would have had to be a dreadful title to have elicited a less delighted response.)

13 May 1949

Dear Joe:

Tony and I heartily approve of the new title. It's less "pulpish" than the other—avoiding the use of the world "terror" will eliminate the risk of frightening off women readers—who love light fantasy but—alack!—scare easily. Then, too, not using "terror" will keep us from the atten-

tion of these self-appointed guardians of the public weal—
vigilante groups in all-too-many communities who have
taken over censorship of the newsstands.

Cordially,

Mick

With the release of the following publicity piece in early
August 1949, Boucher and McComas finally felt secure. The
first experimental issue was going to happen at last.

FOR IMMEDIATE RELEASE:
"The Magazine of Fantasy," a new publication in the
fantasy and science-fiction field, will be launched October
16th by Lawrence Spivak, publisher of The American
Mercury. J. Francis McComas and Anthony Boucher, two
well-known fantasy and science-fiction writers, will co-edit
the new periodical.
The new magazine will be an anthology of the best
fantasy stories new and old. Volume One, Number One,
will include stories by Stuart Palmer, Philip MacDonald,
Theodore Sturgeon, Guy Endor and Richard Sale.
The new technique of four-color photography combined
with four-color artwork will be used on the cover of
"Fantasy." The magazine will be the same size and format as Ellery Queen's Mystery Magazine, another American Mercury publication, and will sell for 35¢.

Once having decided on the plunge, Mercury Publications
determined to bring the infant into the world with a royal
christening party. On August 5, Joe Ferman wrote that plans
were crystallizing. He said in part "we plan a luncheon at
The Waldorf on October 6 sponsored by a committee (suggested name 'Centennial Anniversary Committee on the Fantasy Story—commemorating the 100th anniversary of the death
of Edgar Allan Poe, one of the great fantasy writers of all
time.'). We need your advice for the name of the committee. . . . You (Mick) and Tony Boucher will act as co-
chairmen, and we will invite in your name, 15 or 20 outstanding authors, critics, publishers or readers to act on this
committee." Extensive press coverage was planned including

the wire services, the local newspapers and radio time. Ironically after three years of waiting, Joe ended this letter, "Time is of the essence. How soon can we get your suggestions for the name of the committee, the committee members and the Poe Story?" (To be specially printed and distributed as a "favor" at the luncheon.)

It all sounded very glamorous and exciting. As events fell out, McComas was required to go on his Fall sales trip as a publisher's representative precisely on the dates when he should have been in New York. Boucher faced a severe dilemma. He and his young family lived exclusively on his earnings as an author and critic. At this particular time, the pickings were very scant. He didn't have the money to go to New York! The editors had no intention of making this fact known to the publishers. Mick borrowed from Simon and Schuster in New York in the form of "added" expense money for his sales trip, and Tony Boucher accepted the invitation to chair the luncheon, promising to repay Mick, which he, of course, did in time.

On September 8, Mercury sent out 30 copies of the telegram which follows, of which 25 accepted the invitation to serve on the committee. Among those who accepted were John Dickson Carr, Groff Conklin, Frederic Dannay, Basil Davenport, Boris Karloff, Murray Leinster, Willy Ley, Lewis Padgett, Theodore Sturgeon, and Basil Rathbone.

WILL YOU JOIN POE CENTENNIAL FANTASY AND SCIENCE-FICTION COMMITTEE WHICH WE ARE ORGANIZING TO MARK THE 100TH ANNIVERSARY OF THE DEATH OF EDGAR ALLAN POE, ONE OF THE WORLD'S GREATEST WRITERS OF FANTASY AND SCIENCE-FICTION? AN INVITATIONAL LUNCHEON WILL BE HELD OCTOBER 6 AT THE WALDORF ASTORIA TO COMMEMORATE THE DATE AND TO MARK THE LAUNCHING OF A NEW FANTASY ANTHOLOGY PERIODICAL. YOUR ACCEPTANCE CARRIES WITH IT NO OBLIGATION OF TIME, EFFORT OR MONEY. BY DOING SO YOU WILL HONOR POE'S CONTRIBUTION TO AN IMPORTANT PHASE OF AMERICAN CULTURAL LIFE AND FOCUS PUBLIC ATTENTION ON THE VALUE OF FANTASY AND SCIENCE-FICTION IN THE WORLD TODAY. PLEASE WIRE COLLECT.

LAWRENCE SPIVAK
ANTHONY BOUCHER
J. FRANCIS MC COMAS
570 LEXINGTON AVENUE, N.Y., N.Y.

The editors chose Poe's "Masque of the Red Death" as the story to be used. An edition of 150 copies was issued "to commemorate the 100th Anniversary of the death of Edgar Allan Poe, and to mark the first issue of a Fantasy and Science Fiction Anthology periodical, edited by Anthony Boucher and J. Francis McComas." I wonder which collectors have these now.

The feeling of the occasion itself comes across best in an excerpted version from the text of Allen Prescott's radio report over WJZ in New York on October 7, 1949:

Yesterday I went to a luncheon for Edgar Allan Poe. Its purpose was to launch a new fantasy and science-fiction quarterly entitled the "Magazine of Fantasy." I must say that it's the most entertaining launching I've attended in a long while.

Well, everyone directed his remarks to the point, and managed to be interesting along the way. The point was that the science-fiction authors and those who write fantasy imagine actualities long before the scientists make them a fact. For instance, in speaking of Mr. Poe's work, Doctor Willy Ley, the international authority on rockets and interplanetary space travel—a limited occupation—pointed out that Poe's best contribution to science-fiction, while a hoax, contained prophesies that have now come true. In 1884 Poe evolved a stunt with the New York Sun by announcing that a steerable balloon had crossed the Atlantic Ocean. That was in 1884. He followed this by an alleged journal supposedly written by Mr. Mason, the inventor, on the trip over the Atlantic. The details were quite wonderful, but I haven't time for them here. However the ship was supposed to have arrived 75 hours after take-off. It so happens that 75 hours was the usual crossing time of the airship Hindenberg almost a century later. He wrote that at high altitudes the sky appeared nearly black and that stars were visible, but the sea still appears concave. Not only that, but Mr. Poe mentioned ice flakes on the envelope of the airship which made him the first to guess at what we now call icing conditions in flying.

"The Magazine of Fantasy" people were very bright in getting Basil Rathbone for the master of ceremonies. Not only was he charming in that capacity but he contributed a bit of his own magic by reading Poe's poem, Annabelle Lee. I think you had better all look at "The Magazine of Fantasy" so we can be ready for what's going to happen tomorrow.

It is appropriate, I feel, to include a small excerpt from the Introduction to Volume I, Issue 1, Fall 1949 of *The Magazine of Fantasy*. Remember that its title would be changed in Issue 2 to its present title. The introduction is ostensibly written by Lawrence E. Spivak, publisher, of *Meet the Press* fame. Surely everyone is aware that such writings are, to put it modestly, "helped" by the editors?

. . . publishers have begun to realize the existence of a human demand which cannot be ignored. In the past few years some two dozen anthologies of fantasy stories have been published. Tales long buried in forgotten "pulps" are appearing in book form. A dozen or more novels of the supernatural have recently made their debuts. There must be a public demand!
. . . In this new periodical, The Magazine of Fantasy, *I hope to satisfy every aspect of that demand for the finest available material in stories of the supernatural. I hasten to point out that by "the supernatural" I mean all of the world of fantasy, from the thrilling to the chilling, from the comic to the cosmic—*
To authors who have long wished to try their hand at this sort of thing and found the usual markets closed to such experiments, let me assure you that the latch-string is out and the welcome-mat freshly dusted. Send us your material. There is no formula. Just make your efforts sufficiently out of this world to contradict the laws of man's *logic—while adhering firmly to a freshly-created logic of their own.*
To readers we will offer the best of imaginative fiction, from obscure treasures of the past to the latest creations in the field, from the chill of the unknown to the comedy of the known-gone-wrong. In short, the best of fantasy and horror.

LAWRENCE E. SPIVAK,
Publisher

It is interesting to observe the shift to a small number of science-fiction stories and quite shortly thereafter to a healthy portion of the contents, as it became apparent that the reading public preferred this genre to straight fantasy or the supernatural—the more science fiction, the bigger the sales, it seemed.

Launching a magazine in style is one thing, but granting permission to the editors to move beyond the experimental first issue to a second issue is quite another. The infant remained in the incubator hovering between life and death until Joe Ferman sent a wire to each editor on November 7, 1949, and followed it up with a letter.

8 November 1949

Dear Tony:

The confirming carbon of last night's wire is enclosed. I am sure you both will be delighted to know that we can go ahead with the second issue at once.

We plan of course, to change the title to The Magazine of FANTASY and SCIENCE-FICTION as discussed, and I assume you will be putting in a higher proportion of science-fiction.

Cordially,

Joe

It looked as if the magazine had a real chance now. The editors even got permission to buy ahead for a third and fourth issue (publication dates unknown). Naturally, they began now to live for the day when the magazine would go bi-monthly at least—and perhaps someday in the unknown future, even MONTHLY.

27 January 1950

Dear Larry [Spivak]

We'd like to express our deep appreciation of what a beautiful job you and the whole Mercury outfit have done on the second issue of F&SF.

You've given us a production that puts the magazine in

a class quite outside of competition from any of its rivals; and we only hope that we can succeed in making the same distinction editorially.

Gratefully,

Mick

To give you an idea of some of the unexpected quirks of the trade, consider the unusual aspects of this case of plagiarism! Worries of editors extended from anxieties over distribution to problems of dealing with different varieties of plagiarisms.

26 April 1950

Dear Joe:

First item in this letter concerns itself with the most curious case of plagiarism yet to come our way. Curious, because it involves of all things—the labelling of phono-graph records. We are sending you under separate cover a phonograph record (2 sides of jazz by the Dave Brubeck trio) trademarked "Fantasy." The lettering of the word fantasy is an exact duplication of Mr. Salter's design and lettering of the word as used on our cover. Believe me, it's more than a reasonable facsimile! Manufacturer is The Circle Record Co., 654 Natoma St., San Francisco.

Obviously, this hasn't much effect on the magazine, but it does seem some kind of infringment on Mr. Salter's (and subsequently, the firm's) rights. So . . . the evidence will be in your hands soon.

Best,

Mick

Note the emphasis on the net sales of the magazine. Publishers are not in the business primarily to gladden the hearts of science-fiction and fantasy buffs. The editors were beginning to feel secure, however. Bi-monthly publication was to become a reality.

9 May 1950

Dear Tony and Mick:

In a few weeks we expect to have the final royalty report ready on the first issue of FANTASY. I think we will probably show about 57,000 net sale. Not as good perhaps as you and we were led to expect, but still not bad.

We are still planning to go bi-monthly after the 4th issue, so that #5 will be published in October; #6 in December, and bi-monthly thereafter.

Thanks for sending along the Fantasy record mentioned in your letter of April 26. We will see what can be done about that.

Kind regards.

Sincerely,

[*Joe Ferman*]

This letter, which is self-explanatory, seemed to me extraordinarily interesting since it deals with the editors as writers of fiction, salable to other markets in the same field.

16 October 1950

Dear Joe:

The situation which RPM [Robert P. Mills, General Manager] says you'd like explained is one that it just never occurred to me needed any explanation—that is, my selling to other markets. It seems inevitable to me that my editor would sell elsewhere when possible—A) because he wants (or should want) editing (which of course doesn't quite apply here, since I have McComas); B) because his readers are apt to think he's showing favoritism toward himself . . . and possibly also think that he couldn't sell elsewhere.

We did use a story of mine in #1 because A) it was hard to line up contents for that 1st issue; B) there wasn't at that time a comparable market for it. And we then set between ourselves a policy that either of us could submit a story to the magazine, in which case the other became pro tem sole editor.

The picture's different now—there are at least 3 other markets paying decent rates for class material. And our inventory is such that we can't buy all the stories we want from other people and have no intention of laying out some of that precious money on our own stuff.

Your question as to whether we don't pay enough is hard to answer. It isn't really a part of this problem—I recently did, for all of this complex of reasons, sell a story to OTHER WORLDS for less than we'd pay for it. But you might like to know our payment position in respect to the rest of the specialized field:

From a writer's point of view, no pulp magazine pays "enough." But as this field goes we're all right. Most of them pay less than we do, or if they pay as much they take all rights, or at least more rights than we. The only competitor that tops us in pay is GALAXY—which pays $100 or 3¢ a word, whichever is greater, for first rights only. Since GALAXY also has high editorial quality and prestige, it will probably in time (if writers and agents have sense) see most things before we do. (We also think that we and GALAXY are the 2 mags most likely to outlive the bubble-pricking which is bound to come soon.)

Incidentally, it's common custom for editors to take in each other's washing. We've published one (extremely successful) story by Damon Knight (ed. of Hillman's new untitled mag); we've rejected a couple from Horace Gold of GALAXY but will undoubtedly be publishing him later; and various other "rivals" have submitted stories to us.

Hope all this answers the question—and I very much hope there isn't any worry in your mind as to its being unwise for me to appear elsewhere. Seems to me it simply helps build the Boucher name and maybe lure new readers to us.

I'm feeling very gleeful today—just sold a story to ESQUIRE for approximately 15¢ a word!

Best,

[*Tony*]

Publishers sometimes ask questions which seem downright ignorant and baffling to their editors. Publishers, of course, do not claim to be the experts that their editors are presumed to be. The following letter demonstrates this situation fairly well:

8 October, 1951

Dear Joe:

RPM [Bob Mills] has passed along to us your query on the advisability of a) getting some of the bigger names of the field to contribute to the magazine, and b) paying higher rates for same.

This puts us in a small quandary. We have had as continuing contributors most of the top names in fantasy and/or science fiction. Poul Anderson, Alfred Bester, R. Bretnor, L. Sprague de Camp and Fletcher Pratt, Charles L. Harness, Damon Knight, Fritz Leiber, Richard Matheson, A. E. Van Vogt—to name the first rate men published in BEST OF S F, 1951, have all appeared in the mag. At our regular rates. Not once, but, usually, several times.

Bob Heinlein sent us a story which we (along with 6 or 7 other editors) rejected. He's promised us any others, although his short story output is small. Ray Bradbury has promised us first crack at any fantasy rejected by the slicks. (Obviously, we can't compete with *their* rates!) Henry Kuttner, a personal friend of AB's, is doing no shorts, but has promised us first look at any produced after he finishes his current novel. We have rejected what few Frederic Brown stories we've seen and same have wound up in WEIRD TALES.

In short, Joe, neither Tony nor myself feel that we're missing any "names." Actually, our big fan acclaim has been given to the "unknowns" we've discovered. Our readers look to us, not for a routine job by an old pro, but for something juicy by the veriest rookie! We think readers usually buy a mag for its—*feel*, it's *tone;* only seldom do they break their habits and get a mag simply because it has an author listed on the cover that doesn't, as a rule, appear in said mag. And because we represent most everyone in the field, that doesn't apply to us.

Really, like EQMM, we've made names—Richard Matheson, Idris Seabright, H. Nearing Jr, etc. etc.

In conclusion, we'd say that we're getting all the names

in the field. So we don't think rates should be increased for any specific author, just to get him or her within our pages. But we dó hope that someday circulation will permit a general raise in our basic payment.

With best regards.

[*Mick*]

On the inside of the cover of MF&SF for September 1952 Boucher and McComas made their proud announcement inaugurating a policy still currently in effect under the present publisher and editor of the magazine, Edward L. Ferman, son of Joe Ferman. The editors wrote in part:

"With this issue, F&SF steps up from bi-monthly to monthly publication, and thus we achieve the goal that was bright before us when we commenced publication as a quarterly in 1949. Of course, we are well aware that all of this has been possible solely because of the fine support you readers have accorded us from the beginning, and gratefully, we'll continue our efforts to please you—redouble them in fact! In line with this policy, we intend to increase the proportion of science fiction, as many of you have requested. . . . If you have any other suggestions, or any complaints, let us know—we want to hear them."

ANTHONY BOUCHER   *J. FRANCIS MC COMAS*

It wasn't all smooth sailing, of course, from then on, but now they acted and moved from a well-rooted base, with the feeling that their magazine was just as important, just as frequent, just as much admired as the other giants in the field. They had carried through a difficult project and had proven that a national magazine of merit could emanate from the West Coast, ending forever the myth that you've Got to be in New York to make it!

Let me culminate this short survey of how the magazine happened to be with a quotation written to the editors by Basil Davenport of Book-of-the-Month. He was forwarding to them a reprint suggestion for a "lost" Dickens story that turned out to be wonderful, and he followed with a general comment. The editors were particularly pleased with Davenport's comment because they felt that he knew more about fantasy than any other professional critic of their acquaintance.

Here is what Basil Davenport wrote to them:

"I should be proud and happy to make a contribution, even at second hand, to F&SF, in return for the pleasure it has given me. It is a small compliment to say it is the best in the field, for there is nothing else in that precise field, that offers works of pure imagination, humorous as well as horrific, but it is hard to imagine that any other could be as good."

In 1954 major changes came about in the publication of MF&SF. Because of health and personal problems, Mick would, with deep regret, turn over full reins of editorship to Tony Boucher in September 1954. Earlier, in June of that year, Lawrence Spivak wrote the following letter which summed up those years very well indeed.

3 June 1954

Dear Tony:

I know Joe has kept you informed about our negotiations and has I am sure told you that I have sold my stock in all our publications and that he is now owner, publisher and President.

I cannot leave the publications without telling you and Mick how much my association with you has meant, even though our personal contacts have been much too infrequent. I had a high regard for you, before you came with us and my regard for you and Mick went up at a rapid rate as I came to know your work better. It is always such a pleasure to work with people of high character and literary integrity. I think both of you have made an outstanding contribution in the field of fantasy and science fiction and I know it is going to be recognised by an ever-widening audience as the years go by.

Cordially,

Lawrence E. Spivak

You will find three parodies of Gilbert and Sullivan origin in this book: Boucher, Asimov and Randall Garrett, G&S enthusiasts, all.

The Model Of A Science Fiction Editor

I am the very model of a modern s f editor.
My publisher is happy, as is each and every creditor.
I know the market trends and how to please the newsstand purchaser;
With agents and name authors my relations can't be courteouser.
I've a clever knack of finding out what newsmen want to write about
And seeing that their stories spread my name in black and white about.
I've a colleague to be blamed for the unpleasant sides of bossery,
And I know the masses never quite get tired of flying saucery.
In short in matters monetary, social and promotional,
I am the very model of a pro s f devotional.

I've a pretty taste in literature and know the trends historical
From Plato down to Bradbury in order categorial.
I can tell a warp in space from one that's purely in chronology,
And every BEM I publish has his own strange teratology.
I make my writers stress the small scale human problems solely
Because the sales are better and you might be picked by Foley.
I can stump the highbrow critics with allusions to Caractacus
A ploy that I've perfected by a plentitude of practicus.
In short in matters cultural, esthetical and liter'y
I run the very model of a tru s f outfittery.

Now if I had a smattering of knowledge scientifical,
If I were certain "terrene" didn't simply mean "terrifical,"
If I could tell a proton from a neutron or a neuron,
How your weight on Mars will vary from the planet that now you're on,
If I knew enough to know why Velikovsky is nonsensic
And why too close a Shaver can make even hardened fen sick,
If I'd read what men have learned from other planets' spectranalysis,
In short, if I could tell the future Wonderland from Alice's,
I might in logic, insight and inspired extrapolation
Produce the very model of ideal s f creation.

ANTHONY BOUCHER

The Letters
and
the Stories

The collection of correspondence from THE MAGAZINE OF FANTASY & SCIENCE FICTION under the editorship of Boucher and McComas is part of the Mercury Press Collection donated to Syracuse University by Joseph W. Ferman. The collection is contained in forty-odd file boxes. The letters written by the editors are contained in manila folders, each representing a two-week period—e.g., January 1–15 1950. The letters received by the editors are contained in folders, alphabetically arranged. Those writers who were well-known got folders to themselves. Lesser lights are filed under "Ab-to-Ba" type folders. The process of selection of the correspondence finally chosen for this book represents the winnowing down and excerpting of some 2,000 letters originally chosen from the five-year period to the modest number contained herein. In addition to editing out with considerable regret some delightfully amusing or especially informative material because it had not exact relevance to the stories or focus chosen for the anthology, the letters which do appear have almost all without fail been pared down, edited, and shortened. However, not a word has been added that does not belong to the original authors. The selections which have been removed have been mainly personal trivia, almost libelous references or detailed discussions of stories not relevant to this collection. Sometimes salutation names have been changed, mainly for the comfort of the salutees.

It has been my wish to keep the flavor of the actual flow of editorial operations by leaving the material in letter form, using the actual dates of the letters, if not always the actual names. Sometimes there is a hint of contemporary events, politics, or flying saucers, etc.

To me, the most attractive aspect of the exchange of letters is its projection of an aura of warmth and intimacy. The Boucher-McComas personalities and those of their writers come to keep company with the reader.

Sturgeon-Editors Correspondence

14 April 1949

Dear Mr. Sturgeon:

The idea, in brief, is a magazine to do for short fantasy what EQMM has done for the short mystery—revive neglected gems and create a fresh market for high-caliber new material.

We had planned to go easy on leading the fantasy reader around to science-fiction, and had lined up our first issue without any out-and-out stf. But the publisher, presumably with an ear to the ground and a straw to the wind, has decided that we should have one pure stf item—not routine gadget stuff or wild space-opera, but stf with human values, literacy and humor—to say nothing of all the other qualities that I spread myself on when reviewing WITHOUT SORCERY.

You begin to get the pitch: We'd like a Sturgeon stf short. Length approximately 3500–6000.

Editorial policy: very broad. We're willing to go as far off formula as any writer wants, provided he makes a good story. And we'll use a leetle more sex than other stf markets—if it's integrated.

Sincerely,

Anthony Boucher

23 April 1949

Dear Tony Boucher,

A thousand times yes, you get your story, and soon. I'll do my utmost to have it for you by May 1.

It sounds fine. It sounds like what I've been looking for for years. I started to write at the same time UNKNOWN was born, and became a stf writer by default. I'd rather write fantasy than anything else, and I can't because I can't market it and I have to eat. If my joy is mixed by anything at all here, it's because of the resurgence of that old bugaboo—I'd *much* rather be known as a fantaisist than a stf writer. But I'm still glad you want something from me for the book, and you'll get the best I can do.

I've never lost hope that some day there would be the kind of outlet I need for the stuff I like best to write, and from your letter I think that maybe there's going to be one.

Many sincere thanks.

Theodore Sturgeon

25 April 1949

Dear Tony Boucher,

Here's the HURKLE and I hope you like it.

I have another story in mind about Lirht and its gwiks and hurkles. This one concerns the gwik Hvov, who was an anti-religionist fanatic, dedicated to the destruction of the symbol of a certain sect. This symbol was two hollow cylinders joined at the top, and the destruction was always confined to the symbol, never to anything it might contain. When Hvov was exiled from Lirht through space-time, he arrived on earth and found himself surrounded by people wearing the detested symbol on their nether limbs. He built a radiating incunabulator coupled to a defriction lens and proceeded to dissolve the hated things wherever he found them.

Cordially,

Theodore Sturgeon

13 May 1949

Dear Ted:

To round out the family acquaintanceship, I hereby introduce you to co-editor, J. F. McComas, who will continue the report. . . .

Taking over, I cannot tell you how much AB and myself

enjoyed your sardonic job. Naturally, we have accepted it and it will be a pleasure to have the name of Sturgeon on the first (of *many*, we hope, we hope!) cover of our magazine.

Being the kind of writer you are, we hope you will feel that you have a personal stake in the mag's success, so if you have any publicity angles on it's launching, we'd be very pleased to hear about them.

A special line to thank you for your prompt handling of Boucher's request. Such lovely service in meeting a deadline is a rare treat for such agonised editors as we are at present.

A few details that might interest you: Current shift of opinion is a new title, as thus:

The Magazine Of
F A N T A S Y

(then at the bottom of the cover)
A Selection of the Best Stories of Fantasy and Horror,
Both New and Old.

A good title, we think.

Again our thanks and our hopes that this starts a good editor-writer relationship!

Cordially,

J. Francis McComas

Such sober-minded individuals as the British Astronomer Royal keep telling us that life cannot exist on such-and-such a planet because conditions there would not support life as we know it. The writers of science fiction prefer to believe that the Creator is too versatile to be restricted to our familiar nitrogen metabolism, and like to speculate on the literally unearthly forms of life that may exist elsewhere. Theodore Sturgeon, whose book WITHOUT SORCERY *has been one of the critically best received ventures in recent fantasy publishing, has here speculated so delightfully on the nature of* hurkles *that you may almost find yourself wishing that the astonishing ending were factually true.*

Anthony Boucher
J. F. McComas

The Hurkle Is A Happy Beast
By Theodore Sturgeon

This is Earth, and it once was horrible with wars, and murders, and young love in the spring. It would be today, but for a man of principle, a man of action. So gather around me, and hear about how it began. It began on Lirht.

Lirht is either in a different universal plane or in another island galaxy. Perhaps these terms mean the same thing. The fact remains that Lirht is a planet with three moons (one of which is unknown) and a sun.

Lirht is inhabited by gwik, its dominant race, and by several less highly developed species which, for purposes of this narrative, can be ignored. Except, of course, for the hurkle. The hurkle are highly regarded by the gwik as pets, in spite of the fact that a hurkle is so affectionate that it can have no loyalty.

The prettiest of the hurkle are blue.

Now, on Lirht, in its greatest city, there was trouble, the nature of which does not matter to us, and a gwik named Hvov, whom you may immediately forget, blew up a building which was important for reasons we cannot understand. This event caused great excitement, and gwik left their homes and factories and strubles and streamed toward the center of town, which is how a certain laboratory door was left open.

In times of such huge confusion, the little things go on. During the "Ten Days That Shook the World" the cafes and theaters of Moscow and Petrograd remained open, people fell in love, sued each other, died, shed sweat and tears; and some of these were tears of laughter. So on Lirht, while the decisions on the fate of the miserable Hvov were being formulated, gwik still fardied, funted, and fupped. The great central hewton still beat out its mighty pulse, and in the anams the corsons grew. . . .

Into the above-mentioned laboratory, which had been left open through the circumstances described, wandered a hurkle kitten. It was very happy to find itself there; but then, the hurkle is a happy beast. It prowled about fearlessly—it could become invisible if frightened—and it glowed at the legs of the tables and at the glittering, racked walls. It moved sinuously, humping its back and arching along the floor. Its front and rear legs were stiff and straight as the legs of a chair; the middle pair had two sets of knees, one bending forward, one back. It was engineered as ingeniously as a scorpion, and it was exceedingly blue.

Occupying almost a quarter of the laboratory was a huge and intricate machine, unhoused, showing the signs of development projects the galaxies over—temporary hookups from one component to another, cables terminating in spring clips, measuring devices standing about on small tables near the main work. The kitten regarded the machine with curiosity and friendly intent, sending a wave of radiation outward which were its glow, or purr. It arched daintily around to the other side, stepping delicately but firmly on a floor switch.

Immediately there was a rushing, humming sound, like small birds chasing large mosquitos, and parts of the machine began to get warm. The kitten watched curiously, and saw, high up inside the cluster of coils and wires, the most entrancing muzziness it had ever seen. It was like heat-flicker over a fallow field; it was like a smoke-vortex; it was like red neon lights on a wet pavement. To the hurkle kitten's senses, that red-orange flicker was also like the smell of catnip to a cat, or anise to a terrestrial terrier.

It reared up toward the glow, hooked its forelegs over a

busbar—fortunately there was no ground potential—and drew itself upward. It climbed the transformer to power-pack, skittered up a variable condenser—the setting of which was changed thereby—disappeared momentarily as it felt the bite of a hot tube, and finally teetered on the edge of the glow.

The glow hovered in midair in a sort of cabinet, which was surrounded by heavy coils embodying tens of thousands of turns of small wire and great loops of bus. One side, the front, of the cabinet was open, and the kitten hung there fascinated, rocking back and forth to the rhythm of some unheard music it made to contrast this sourceless flame. Back and forth, back and forth it rocked and wove, riding a wave of delicious, compelling sensation. And once, just once, it moved its center of gravity too far from its point of support. Too far—far enough. It tumbled into the cabinet, into the flame.

One muggy, mid-June day a teacher, whose name was Stott and whose duties were to teach seven subjects to forty moppets in a very small town, was writing on a blackboard. He was writing the word Madagascar, and the air was so sticky and warm that he could feel his undershirt pasting and unpasting itself on his shoulder-blades with each round "a" he wrote.

Behind him there was a sudden rustle from the moist seventh-graders. His schooled reflexes kept him from turning from the board until he had finished what he was doing, by which time the room was in a young uproar. Stott about-faced, opened his mouth, closed it again. A thing like this would require more than a routine reprimand.

His forty-odd charges were writhing and squirming in an extraordinary fashion, and the sound they made, a sort of whimpering giggle, was unique. He looked at one pupil after another. Here a hand was busily scratching a nape; there a boy was digging guiltily under his shirt; yonder a scrubbed and shining damsel violently worried her scalp.

Knowing the value of individual attack, Stott intoned, "Hubert, what seems to be the trouble?"

The room immediately quieted, though diminished scrabblings continued. "Nothin', Mister Stott," quavered Hubert.

Stott flicked his gaze from side to side. Wherever it rested, the scratching stopped and was replaced by agonized control. In its wake was rubbing and twitching. Stott glared, and idly thumbed a lower left rib. Someone snickered. Before he could identify the source, Stott was suddenly aware of an intense itching. He checked the impulse to go after it, knotted his jaw, and swore to himself that he wouldn't scratch as long as he was out there, front and center. "The class will—" he began tautly, and then stopped.

There was a—a *something* on the sill of the open window. He blinked and looked again. It was a translucent, bluish cloud which was almost nothing at all. It was less than a something should be, but it was indeed more than a nothing. If he stretched his imagination just a little, he might make out the outlines of an arched creature with too many legs; but of course that was ridiculous.

He looked away from it and scowled at his class. He had had two unfortunate experiences with stink bombs, and in the back of his mind was the thought of having seen once, in a trick-store window, a product called "itching powder." Could this be it, this terrible itch? He knew better, however, than to accuse anyone yet; if he were wrong, there was no point in giving the little geniuses any extra-curricular notions.

He tried again. "The cl—" He swallowed. This itch was . . . "The class will—" He noticed that one head, then another and another, were turning toward the window. He realized that if the class got too interested in what he thought he saw on the window sill, he'd have a panic on his hands. He fumbled for his ruler and rapped twice on the desk. His control was not what it should have been at the moment; he struck far too hard, and the reports were like gunshots. The class turned to him as one; and behind them the thing on the window sill appeared with great distinctness.

It was blue—a truly beautiful blue. It had a small spherical head and an almost identical knob at the other end. There were four stiff, straight legs, a long sinuous body, and two central limbs with a boneless look about them. On the side of the head were four pairs of eyes, of graduated sizes. It teetered there for perhaps ten seconds, and then, without a sound, leapt through the window and was gone.

Mr. Stott, pale and shaking, closed his eyes. His knees trembled and weakened, and a delicate, dewy mustache of perspiration appeared on his upper lip. He clutched at the desk and forced his eyes open; and then, flooding him with relief, pealing into his terror, swinging his control back to him, the bell rang to end the class and the school day.

"Dismissed," he mumbled, and sat down. The class picked

up and left, changing itself from a twittering pattern of rows to a rowdy kaleidoscope around the bottle-necking doorway. Mr. Stott slumped down in his chair, noticing that the dreadful itch was gone, had been gone since he had made that thunderclap with the ruler.

Now, Mr. Stott was a man of method. Mr. Stott prided himself on his ability to teach his charges to use their powers of observation and all the machinery of logic at their command. Perhaps, then, he had more of both at his command—after he recovered himself—than could be expected of an ordinary man.

He sat and stared at the open window, not seeing the sun-swept lawns outside. And after going over these events a half-dozen times, he fixed on two important facts:

First, that the animal he had seen, or thought he had seen, had six legs.

Second, that the animal was of such a nature as to make anyone who had not seen it believe he was out of his mind.

These two thoughts had their corollaries:

First, that every animal he had ever seen which had six legs was an insect, and

Second, that if anything were to be done about this fantastic creature, he had better do it by himself. And whatever action he took must be taken immediately. He imagined the windows being kept shut to keep the thing out—in this heat—and he cowered away from the thought. He imagined the effect of such a monstrosity if it bounded into the midst of a classroom full of children in their early teens, and recoiled. No; there could be no delay in this matter.

He went to the window and examined the sill. Nothing. There was nothing to be seen outside, either. He stood thoughtfully for a moment, pulling on his lower lip and thinking hard. Then he went downstairs to borrow five pounds of DDT powder from the janitor for an "experiment." He got a wide, flat wooden box and an electric fan, and set them up on a table he pushed close to the window, and then he sat down to wait, in case, just in case the blue beast returned.

When the hurkle kitten fell into the flame, it braced itself for a fall at least as far as the floor of the cabinet. Its shock was tremendous, then, when it found itself so braced and already resting on a surface. It looked around, panting with fright, its invisibility reflex in full operation.

The cabinet was gone. The flame was gone. The laboratory with its windows, lit by the orange Lirhtian sky, its ranks of shining equipment, its hulking, complex machine—all were gone.

The hurkle kitten sprawled in an open area, a sort of lawn. No colors were right; everything seemed half-lit, filmy, out-of-focus. There were trees, but not low and flat and bushy like honest Lirhtian trees, but with straight naked trunks and leaves like a portle's tooth. The different atmospheric gases had colors; clouds of fading, changing faint colors obscured and revealed everything. The kitten twitched its cafmors and ruddled its kump, right there where it stood; for no amount of early training could overcome a shock like this.

It gathered itself together and tried to move; and then it got its second shock. Instead of arching over inchworm-wise; it floated into the air and came down three times as far as it had ever jumped in its life.

It cowered on the dreamlike grass, darting glances all about, under, and up. It was lonely and terrified and felt very much put-upon. It saw its shadow through the shifting haze, and the sight terrified it even more; for it had no shadow when it was frightened on Lirht. Everything here was all backwards and wrong way up; it got more visible, instead of less, when it was frightened; its legs didn't work right, it couldn't see properly, and there wasn't a single, solitary malapek to be throdded anywhere. It thought some music; happily, that sounded all right inside its round head, though somehow it didn't resonate as well as it had.

It tried, with extreme caution, to move again. This time its trajectory was shorter and more controlled. It tried a small, grounded pace, and was quite successful. Then it bobbed for a moment, seesawing on its flexing middle pair of legs, and, with utter abandon, flung itself skyward. It went up perhaps fifteen feet, turning end over end, and landed with its stiff forefeet in the turf.

It was completely delighted with this sensation. It gathered itself together, gryting with joy, and leapt up again. This time it made more distance than altitude, and bounced two long, happy bounces as it landed.

Its fears were gone in the exploration of this delicious new freedom of motion. The hurkle, as had been said before, is a happy beast. It curvetted and sailed, soared and somersaulted, and at last brought up against a brick wall with stunning and unpleasant results. It was learning, the hard way, a distinction between weight and mass. The effect was slight but painful. It drew back and stared forlornly at the bricks. Just when it was beginning to feel friendly again. . . .

It looked upward, and saw what appeared to be an opening in the wall some eight feet above the ground. Overcome by a spirit of high adventure, it sprang upward and came to rest on a windowsill—a feat of which it was very proud. It crouched there, preening itself, and looking inside.

It saw a most pleasing vista. More than forty amusingly ugly animals, apparently imprisoned by their lower extremities in individual stalls, bowed and nodded and mumbled. At the far end of the room stood a taller, more slender monster with a naked head—naked compared with those of the trapped ones, which were covered with hair like a mawson's egg. A few moments' study showed the kitten that in reality only one side of the heads was hairy; the tall one turned around and began making tracks in the end wall, and its head proved to be hairy on the other side too.

The hurkle kitten found this vastly entertaining. It began to radiate what was, on Lirht, a purr, or glow. In this fantastic place it was not visible; instead, the trapped animals began to respond with most curious writhings and squirmings and sussurant rubbings of their hides with their claws. This pleased the kitten even more, for it loved to be noticed, and it redoubled the glow. The receptive motions of the animals became almost frantic.

Then the tall one turned around again. It made a curious sound or two. Then it picked up a stick from the platform before it brought it down with a horrible crash.

The sudden noise frightened the hurkle kitten half out of its wits. It went invisible; but its visibility system was reversed here, and it was suddenly outstandingly evident. It turned and leapt outside, and before it reached the ground, a loud metallic shrilling pursued it. There were gabblings and shufflings from the room which added force to the kitten's consuming terror. It scrambled to a low growth of shrubbery and concealed itself.

Very soon, however, its irrepressible good nature returned. It lay relaxed, watching the slight movement of the stems and leaves—some of them may have been flowers—in a slight breeze.

It turned its attention again to the window, wondering what those racks of animals might be up to now. It seemed very quiet up there. . . . Boldly the kitten came from hiding and launched itself at the window again. It was pleased with itself; it was getting quite proficient at precision leaps in this mad place. Preening itself, it balanced on the window sill and looked inside.

Surprisingly, all the smaller animals were gone. The larger one was huddled behind the shelf at the end of the room. The kitten and the animal watched each other for a long moment. The animal leaned down and struck something into the wall.

Immediately there was a mechanical humming sound and something on a platform near the window began to revolve. The next thing the kitten knew it was enveloped in a cloud of pungent dust.

It choked and became as visible as it was frightened, which was very. For a long moment it was incapable of motion; gradually, however, it became conscious of a poignant, painfully penetrating sensation which thrilled it to the core.

The hurkle felt strange, transported. It turned and leapt high into the air, out from the building.

Mr. Stott stopped scratching. Disheveled indeed, he went to the window and watched the odd sight of the blue beast, quite invisible now, but coated with dust, so that it was like a bubble in fog. It bounced across the lawn in huge floating leaps, leaving behind it diminishing patches of white powder in the grass. He smacked his hands, one on the other, and smirking withdrew to straighten up. He had saved the earth from battle, murder and bloodshed, forever, but he did not know that.

And the hurkle kitten?

It bounded off through the long shadows, and vanished in a copse of bushes. There it dug itself a shallow pit, working drowsily, more and more slowly. And at last it sank down and lay motionless, thinking strange thoughts, making strange music, and racked by strange sensations. Soon all its movements ceased, and it stretched out stiffly, motionless.

For about two weeks. At the end of that time, the hurkle, no longer a kitten, was possessed of a fine, healthy litter of just under two hundred young. Perhaps it was the DDT, and perhaps it was the new variety of radiation that the hurkle received from the terrestrial sky, but they were all parthenogenetic females, even as you and I.

And the humans? Oh, we *bred* so! And how happy we were!

But the humans had the slidy itch, and the scratchy itch, and the prickly or tingly or titillative paraesthetic formication. And there wasn't a thing they could do about it.

So they left.

Isn't this a lovely place?

Bradbury-Editors Correspondence

19 September 1949

Dear Ray:

If you will indulge in such fulsome praise of your editors, you will find them asking favors of you. Which, in the main, is what this letter is.

We do very much, very very much, want a Bradbury for the second number. Which brings us to this. While it has its quota of the usual Bradbury good writing, we feel that it isn't distinctive enough, doesn't have enough power to meet the terrifically high standard we will want to set for that problematical second number. Are we correct in assuming that it is a kind of quiet interlude in the Martian chronicle? As such, it is perfect. But, for our follow-up on Vol I, No 1, we need the maximum of excitement, action *on*-stage, rather than off. Do I make us clear?

Perhaps this isn't altogether fair to you. But rule number one of our editorial policy is always to take advantage of our friends. So, forgive us.

Ever,

Mick

28 September 1949

Dear Ray:

Here we go again. . . . we shame-facedly conclude that we, editors of a low-paying mag whose very existence is still a matter of some doubt, are much more critical than editors of huge mags who page $700 for a story.

Briefly, something came right up, smacked us in the face and, after a fine beginning, spoiled THE EXILES for us. That was characterisation of the exiles themselves.
1) Poe is magnificent.

2) Bierce is completely incredible. Can you imagine 'Bitter' Bierce saying, "What will happen to us? God save us?" Rather, he would chortle gleefully over the dilemma and enjoy with complete detachment the futilities of both the invaders and the exiles.

3) You are, for Ray Bradbury, amazingly inaccurate about Hawthorne. Recently published biographies (with which a goodly percentage of our readers are sure to be familiar) indicate that he was anything but a recluse. I quote from Benet's READER'S ENCYCLOPEDIA "His work is marked by symbolism, allegory, frequent use of supernatural themes . . .!"

4) These are minor. Why is Othello listed among Shakespeare's supernatural characters? Why is the Emerald City made the abode of evil spirits? It is a city of goodness and tranquility.

Ever,

Mick

3 October 1949

Dear Mick:

Sorry about THE EXILES. You're right about Bierce and Hawthorne. Put it down to the fact that I've never been a research man in my life, preferring to manufacture my fantasies out of whole cloth. Also, I thought I recalled, smugly, enough about Bierce and Hawthorne. I see I was wrong. How in hell Othello crept in, don't ask. I will defend my use of the Oz Emerald City, though; I thought it a rather ironic place for all the evil people to be living!

Although you mention my bad characterization of Bierce, Hawthorne, et cetera, you never mentioned whether the story as a whole titillated you. If you would like the story rewritten to patch up the holes, you know darn well I would enjoy correcting my own errors. If you like, some time later in the year, I can do a few days work on the story, perhaps for later use by your magazine. This, of course, only if you really *like* the idea. Do you?

Yours,

Ray

7 October 1949

Dear Ray:

Always assuming that there's a second issue, I think that we could be certain that your re-write would meet our objections and could accept THE EXILES for Vol I, No 2.

Who will take the place of Hawthorne?

Please include Bierce, only make him as Bierce was. As for the Emerald City—leave it, I can't argue too much with a guy who's so anxious to do us a favor. How about a one paragraph vignette of HPL* The real HPL, that is—not the saintly wonder man that Augie and Wandreth** have created.

Thanks again on THE EXILES.

Ever,

Mick

*H.P. Lovecraft
**Donald Wandrei

27 October 1949

Dear Ray:

A little more on THE EXILES.

We rather doubt that Thoreau is a good idea—a little too far out of the fantasy pattern.

But we have two suggestions for exiles:

A) Charles Dickens, who does fit the position which you allotted to Hawthorne—a man known for a certain amount of fantasy, which is however a very minor part of his work, either on quantity or on quality.

B) L. Frank Baum—a man who was personally all sunshine and love and who would be hurt and puzzled to find his lightsome fairy tales classed with the products of all the great creators of oogie boogie.

We think that what we mean by the "real" Lovecraft emerges somewhat even from the most idolatrous accounts. See Derleth's HPL: A MEMOIR and the Grant-Hadley RHODE ISLAND ON LOVECRAFT. A curious introvert, frustrated sexually, financially and creatively, ridden by neurotic dreads of cold and fish (and almost morbidly devoted to his one debauchery: ice cream), seeking refuge in thoughts of an Eighteenth Century which he did not understand but created in his own image, compensating in tremendous letter-writing for his failures in personal relations. . . . You could do something nice with him in a few adroit strokes.

Yours,

A. P. [*Tony Boucher*]

27 November 1949

Dear Mick and Tony:

Thanks for the really wonderful carbon of your editorial comment on THE EXILES. Bless you both, and keep you! I really feel very fortunate in having such good and generous friends and editors. I hope I can always please you, and deserve your kind words.

Yours,

Ray

It is difficult to classify the work of Ray Bradbury. There can be no question of his pre-eminence among our younger short story writers. He's the "young" master and that's that. But no two Bradbury fans (ourselves included) can agree on just what type of story Mr. Bradbury tells best. We think The Exiles *gives a simple solution to the problem; he does* everything *well. Here we give you Bradbury humor, bitter, ironic, yet verging on the farcical; Bradbury fantasy-horror, in the macabre efforts of the Exiles to salvage some gloomy dregs of their somber existence, and Bradbury science-fiction-satire, in his grim portrayal of a future earth, surgically aseptic, where men's minds have grown as sterile as the world in which they live. For years Mr. Bradbury has been writing about Mars, until his readers know that planet as well as the devotees of Sinclair Lewis know Zenith. This spring a unified and expanded volume of Bradbury Martiana will appear under the title* THE MARTIAN CHRONICLES—*a book that will undoubtedly be henceforth considered a keystone volume in any science-fiction library. But here is a Martian story not included in those chronicles—a tale from a different dimension of time and thought, a tale which deals at once warmly and chillingly with some of the greatest names in all fantasy—and serves to fix more securely than ever among those great names that of Ray Bradbury.*

Anthony Boucher
J. F. McComas

The Exiles
By Ray Bradbury

Their eyes were fire and the breath flamed out the witches' mouths as they bent to probe the cauldron with greasy stick and bony finger.

> "When shall we three meet again
> In thunder, lightning, or in rain?"

They danced drunkenly on the shore of an empty sea, fouling the air with their three tongues and burning it with their cats' eyes malevolently aglitter:

> "Round about the cauldron go;
> In the poisoned entrails throw!
> Double, double, toil and trouble,
> Fire burn and cauldron bubble!"

They paused and cast a glance about. "Where's the crystal? Where the needles?" "Here!" "Good!" "Is the yellow wax thickened?" "Yes!" "Pour it in the iron mould!" "Is the wax figure done?" They shaped it like molasses adrip on their green hands. "Shove the needle through the heart!" "The crystal, the crystal, fetch it from the tarot bag, dust it off, have a look!"

They bent to the crystal, their faces white.

> "See, see, see. . . . . ."

A rocket ship moved through space from the planet Earth to the planet Mars. On the rocket ship, men were dying.

The captain raised his head, tiredly. "We'll have to use the morphine."

"But, captain . . ."

"You see yourself this man's condition." The captain lifted the wool blanket and the man restrained beneath the wet sheet moved and groaned. The air was full of sulphurous thunder.

"I saw it, I saw it." The man opened his eyes and stared at the port where there were only black spaces, reeling stars, Earth far removed, and the planet Mars rising large and red. "I saw it, a bat, a huge thing, a bat with a man's face, spread over the front port. Fluttering and fluttering, fluttering and fluttering!"

"Pulse?" asked the captain.

The orderly measured it. "130."

"He can't go on with that. Use the morphine. Come along, Smith."

They moved away. Suddenly the floorplates were laced with bone and white skulls that screamed. The captain did not dare look down, and over the screaming he said, "Is this where Perse is?" turning in at a hatch.

A white-smocked surgeon stepped away from a body. "I just don't understand it."

"How did Perse die?"

"We don't know, captain. It wasn't his heart, his brain, or shock. He just—died."

The captain felt the doctor's wrist which changed to a hissing snake and bit him. The captain did not flinch. "Take care of yourself. You've a pulse, too."

The doctor nodded. "Perse complained of pains, needles, he said, in his wrists and legs. Said he felt like wax, melting. He fell. I helped him up. He cried like a child. Said he had a silver needle in his heart. He died. Here he is. We can repeat the autopsy for you. Everything's physically normal."

"That's impossible. He died of *something*."

The captain walked to a port. He smelled of menthol and iodine and green soap on his polished and manicured hands. His white teeth were dentrificed and his ears scoured to a pinkness, as were his cheeks. His uniform was the color of new salt, and his boots were black mirrors shining below him. His crisp crew-cut hair smelled of sharp alcohol. Even his breath was sharp and new and clean. There was no spot to him. He was a fresh instrument, honed and ready, still hot from the surgeon's oven.

The men with him were from the same mould. One expected huge brass keys spiraling slowly from their backs. They were expensive, talented, well-oiled toys, obedient and quick.

The captain watched the planet Mars grow very large in space.

"We'll be landing in an hour on that damned place. Smith? Did you see any bats, or have other nightmares?"

"Yes, sir. The month before our rocket took off from New York, sir. White rats biting my neck, drinking my blood. I didn't tell. I was afraid you wouldn't let me come on this trip."

"Never mind," sighed the captain, "I had dreams, too. In all of my fifty years I never had a dream until that week before we took off from Earth. And then, every night, I dreamed I was a white wolf. Caught on a snowy hill. Shot with a silver bullet. Buried with a stake in my heart." He moved his head toward Mars. "Do you think, Smith, *they* know we're coming?"

"We don't know if there *are* Martian people, sir."

"Don't we? They began frightening us off eight weeks ago, before we started. They killed Perse and Reynolds now. Yesterday, they made Grenville go blind. How? I don't know. Bats, needles, dreams, men dying for no reason. I'd call it witchcraft in another day. But this is the year 2120, Smith. We're rational men. This all can't be happening. But it is. Whoever they are, with their needles and their bats, they'll try to finish all of us."

He swung about. "Smith, fetch those books from my file. I want them when we land."

Two hundred books were piled on the rocket deck.

"Thank you, Smith. Have you glanced at them? Think I'm insane? Perhaps. It's a crazy hunch. At that last moment, I ordered these books from the Historical Museum. Because of my dreams. Twenty nights I was stabbed, butchered, a screaming bat pinned to a surgical mat, a thing rotting underground in a black box; bad, wicked dreams. Our whole crew dreamed of witch-things and were-things, vampires and phantoms, things they *couldn't* know anything about. Why? Because books on such ghastly subjects were destroyed a century ago. By law. Forbidden for anyone to own the grisly volumes. These books you see here are the *last* copies, kept for historical purposes in the locked Museum vaults."

Smith bent to read the dusty titles:

"Tales of Mystery and Imagination, by Edgar Allan Poe. *Dracula,* by Bram Stoker. *Frankenstein,* by Mary Shelley. *The Turn of the Screw,* by Henry James. *The Legend of Sleepy Hollow,* by Washington Irving. *Rappacini's Daughter,* by Nathaniel Hawthorne. *An Occurrence at Owl Creek Bridge,* by Ambrose Bierce. *Alice in Wonderland,* by Lewis Carroll. *The Willows,* by Algernon Blackwood. *The Wizard of Oz,* by L. Frank Baum. *The Shadow Over Innsmouth,* by H. P. Lovecraft. And more! Books by Walter De La Mare, Wakefield, Harvey, Wells, Asquith, Huxley, all forbidden authors. All burned in the same year that Halloween was outlawed and Christmas was banned! But sir, what good are these to us on the rocket?"

"I don't know," sighed the captain, "yet."

The three hags lifted the crystal where the captain's image flickered, his tiny voice tinkling out of the glass:

"I don't know," sighed the captain, "yet."

The three witches glared redly into each other's faces.

"We haven't much time," said one.

"Better warn *Them* up at the House."

"They'll want to know about the books. It doesn't look good. That fool of a captain!"

"In an hour they'll land their rocket."

The three hags shuddered and blinked up at the Emerald City by the edge of the dry Martian sea. In its highest window, a small man held a blood-red drape aside. He watched the wastelands where the three witches fed their cauldron and shaped the waxes. Further along, ten thousand other blue fires and laurel incenses, black tobacco smokes and fir-weeds, cinnamons and bone-dusts rose soft as moths through the Martian night. The man counted the angry, magical fires. Then, as the three witches stared, he turned. The crimson drape, released, fell, causing the distant portal to wink, like a yellow eye.

Mr. Edgar Allan Poe stood in the tower window, a faint vapor of spirits upon his breath. "Hecat's friends are busy tonight," he said, seeing the witches, far below.

A voice behind him said, "I saw Will Shakespeare at the shore, earlier, whipping them on. All along the sea, Shakespeare's army alone, tonight, numbers thousands: the three Witches, Oberon, Hamlet's father, Puck, all, all of them, thousands! Good Lord, a regular sea of people."

"Good William." Poe turned. He let the crimson drape fall shut. He stood for a moment to observe the raw stone room, the black-timbered table, the candle flame, the other man, Mr. Ambrose Bierce, sitting very idly there, lighting matches and watching them burn down, whistling under his breath, now and then laughing to himself.

"We'll have to tell Mr. Dickens now," said Mr. Poe. "We've put it off too long. It's a matter of hours. Will you go down to his home with me, Bierce?"

Bierce glanced up, merrily. "I've just been thinking, what'll happen to us?"

"If we can't kill the rocket men off, frighten them away; then we'll have to leave, of course. We'll go on to Jupiter, and when they come to Jupiter we'll go on to Saturn, and when they come to Saturn we'll go to Uranus, or Neptune, and then on out to Pluto . . ."

"Where then?"

Mr. Poe's face was weary, there were fire-coals remaining, fading in his eyes, and a sad wildness in the way he talked, and a uselessness of his hands and the way his hair fell lankly over his amazing white brow. He was like a satan of some lost dark cause, a general arrived from a derelict invasion. His silky soft black moustache was worn away by his musing lips. He was so small that his brow seemed to float, vast and phosphorescent, by itself, in the dark room.

"We have the advantages of superior forms of travel," he said. "We can always hope for one of their atomic wars, dissolution, the dark ages come again. The return of superstition. We could go back then to Earth, all of us, in one night." Mr. Poe's black eyes brooded under his round and illuminant brow. He gazed at the ceiling. "So they're coming to ruin *this* world, too? They won't leave *anything* undefiled, will they?"

"Does a wolf pack stop until it's killed its prey and eaten the guts? It should be quite a war. I shall sit on the sidelines and be the scorekeeper. So many Earth Men boiled in oil, so many *Mss. Found In Bottles* burnt, so many Earth Men stabbed with needles, so many *Red Deaths* put to flight by a battery of hypodermic syringes—ha!"

Poe swayed angrily, faintly drunk with wine. "What did we do? Be *with* us, Bierce, in the name of God; did we have a fair trial before a company of literary critics? No! Our books were plucked up by neat, sterile, surgeon's pliers, and flung into vats, to boil, to be killed of all their mortuary germs. Damn them all!"

"I find our situation amusing," said Bierce.

They were interrupted by a hysterical shout from the tower stair.

"Mr. Poe! Mr. Bierce!"

"Yes, yes, we're coming!" Poe and Bierce descended to find a man gasping against the stone passage wall.

"Have you heard the news!" he cried, immediately, clawing at them like a man about to fall over a cliff. "In an hour they'll land! They're bringing books with them, *old* books, the witches said!. What're you doing in the tower at a time like this? Why aren't you acting?"

Poe said, "We're doing everything we can, Blackwood. You're new to all this. Come along, we're going to Mr. Charles Dickens' place . . ."

". . . to contemplate our doom, our black doom," said Mr. Bierce, with a wink.

On their way down the stairs they stopped at a heavy door and rapped. A door-plate read: *Mr. H. P. Lovecraft,* and a voice from behind it said, "Come in."

The door was blistering hot to the touch.

"Watch out for the draft!" said Lovecraft, wildly, as they entered and slammed the door. A shudder went through the gaunt frame of the man who sat in a fine antique chair, a quill pen in his thin hand, his coat collar tight up about his neck, his back to a thundering, crackling hearth-fire. The room was so hellish that the candles were melted into tallowy pools. And the fire was so fiercely bright that it was like living in the sun. Lovecraft trembled his chilly hands out to the fire as if the brief opening of the door had let an arctic terror of wind at him. "We can not be too careful," he said. "There are drafts in castles like this. What is it?"

"Come along, we're going to talk to Dickens."

"No, no, I am sorry." Lovecraft hurried to a small icebox which somehow survived this red furnace and brought forth two quarts of ice cream. Emptying these into a large dish he hurried back to his table and began alternately tasting the vanilla ice and scurrying his pen over crisp sheets of writing paper. As the ice cream melted upon his tongue, a look of almost dreamful exultancy dissolved his face; then he sent his pen dashing. "Sorry. Really, I am awfully busy, gentlemen, Mr. Poe, Mr. Bierce. I have so many letters to write."

"But how can that be?" protested Bierce. "You haven't received any letters here."

"That means nothing." The writing man tried another delicate spoonful of the cold treasure. There were six empty vanilla ice-cream boxes piled neatly on the hearth from this day's feasting. And the icebox, in the quick flash they had seen of its interior, contained a good dozen quarts more. "I am writing a letter to Mr. L. Frank Baum, I am quite sure that we shall enjoy a delightful correspondence, once started—"

"But this is *his* castle, the Emerald City, he lives right downstairs," said Poe.

"And then I have a letter I must write to Mr. Samuel Johnson, and Mr. Alexander Pope, and Mr. Machen, and Mr. Coppard, and a thousand others. I do not know when I shall finish. But I shall take the time to help you with Mr. Dickens, nevertheless."

"Will you?"

"Yes." Lovecraft dipped his quill. "I shall write him a letter about this crisis."

"Come on, Edgar," said Bierce, with a laugh.

Poe's eye fell upon a letter. "May I take this along?"

"Of course," said Lovecraft. "I wrote it to you, your name is on it, is it not?"

As they opened the door, Poe and Bierce had a last glimpse of Lovecraft cowering from the cold draft, ice-cream in his terrified mouth, dripping pen in hand.

Bang! The door slammed.

"Remind me to send him a half ton of lobsters," said Poe.

Blackwood was waiting for them.

"Mr. L. Frank Baum was just here," he said. "He wants to see you, Mr. Poe. He's terribly shocked and nervous at the way you've taken over the Emerald City. He doesn't like the cobwebs and bats."

"Tell him to see me later!"

They moved down the echoing throats of the castle, level after dim green level, down into mustiness and decay and spiders and dreamlike webbing. "Don't worry," said Poe, his brow like a huge white lamp before them, descending, sinking. "All along the dead sea tonight I've called the Others. Your friends and mine, Blackwood, Bierce. They're all there. The animals and the old women and the tall men with the sharp white teeth. The traps are waiting, the pits, yes, and the pendulums. The Red Death." Here he laughed quietly. "Yes, even the Red Death. I never thought, no, I never thought the time would come when a thing like the Red Death would actually *be*. But *they* asked for it, and they shall have it!"

"But are we strong enough?" wondered Blackwood.

"How strong is strong? They won't be prepared for us, at least. They haven't the imagination. Those clean young rocket men with their antiseptic bloomers and fish-bowl helmets, with their new religion. About their necks, on gold chains, scalpels. Upon their heads, a diadem of microscopes. In their holy fingers, steaming incense urns which in reality are only germicidal ovens for steaming out superstition. The names of Poe, Bierce, Hawthorne, Blackwood blasphemy to their clean lips."

Outside the castle, they advanced through a watery space, a tarn that was not a tarn, which misted before them like the stuff of nightmares. The air filled with wing sounds and a whirring, a motion of winds and blacknesses. Voices changed, figures swayed at campfires. Mr. Poe watched the needles knitting, knitting, knitting, in the firelight, knitting pain and misery, knitting wickedness into wax marionettes, clay puppets. The cauldron smells of wild garlics and cayennes and saffron hissed up to fill the night with evil pungency.

"Get on with it!" said Poe. "I'll be back!"

All down the empty seashore black figures spindled and waned, grew up and blew into black smokes on the sky. Bells rang in mountain towers and licorice ravens spilled out with the bronze sounds and spun away to ashes.

Over a lonely moor and into a small valley, Poe and Bierce hurried, and found themselves quite suddenly on a cobbled street, in cold, bleak, biting weather, with people stomping up and down stony courtyards to warm their feet; foggy withal, and candles flaring in the windows of offices and shops where hung the Yuletide turkeys. At a distance, some boys, all bundled up, snorting their pale breaths on the wintry air were trilling, "God Rest Ye Merry, Gentlemen—" while the immense tones of a great clock continuously sounded midnight. Children dashed by from the baker's with dinners all asteam in their grubby fists, on trays and under silver bowls.

At a sign which read *Scrooge, Marley and Dickens,* Poe gave the Marley-faced knocker a rap, and from within, as the door popped open a few inches, a sudden gust of music almost swept them into a dance. And there, beyond the shoulder of the man who was sticking a trim-goatee and moustaches at them, was Mr. Fezziwig clapping his hands, and Mrs. Fezziwig, one vast substantial smile, dancing and colliding with other merrymakers, while the fiddle chirped and laughter ran about a table like chandelier crystals given a sudden push of wind. The large table was heaped with brawn and turkey and holly and geese, with mince-pies, suckling-pigs, wreaths of sausages, oranges and apples, and there was Bob Cratchet and Little Dorrit and Tiny Tim and Mr. Fagin himself, and a man who looked as if he might be an undigested bit of beef, a blot of mustard, a crumb of cheese, a fragment of an underdone potato, who else but Mr. Marley, chains and all, while the wine poured and the brown turkeys did their excellent best to steam!

"What do you want?" demanded Mr. Charles Dickens.

"We've come to plead with you again, Charles; we need your help," said Poe.

"Help? Do you think I would help you fight against those good men coming in the rocket? I don't belong here, anyway. My books were burned by mistake. I'm no supernaturalist, no writer of horrors and terrors like you, Poe, you, Bierce, or the others. I'll have nothing to do with you terrible people!"

"You are a persuasive talker," reasoned Poe. "You could go

to meet the rocket men, lull them, lull their suspicions, and then, then we would take care of them.''

Mr. Dickens eyed the folds of the black cape which hid Poe's hands. From it, smiling, Mr. Poe drew forth a trowel.

"The Amontillado?" Mr. Dickens drew back.

"For *one* of our visitors." In his other hand now, Poe showed forth a cap and bells, which jingled softly and suggestively.

"And for the others?"

Poe smiled again, well pleased. "We finished digging the Pit this morning."

"And the Pendulum?"

"Is being installed."

"The Premature Burial?"

"That, too."

"You are a grim man, Mr. Poe."

"I am a frightened and an angry man. I am a God, Mr. Dickens, even as you are a God, even as we all are Gods, and our inventions, our people, if you wish, have not only been threatened, but banished and burned, torn up and censored, ruined and done away with. The worlds we created are falling into ruin. Even Gods must fight!"

"So." Mr. Dickens tilted his head, impatient to return to the party, the music, the food. "Perhaps you can explain why we are here? How did we come here?"

"War begets war. Destruction begets destruction. On Earth, a century ago, in the year 2067, they outlawed our books. Oh, what a horrible thing, to destroy our literary creations that way. It summoned us out of—what? Death? The Beyond? I don't like abstract things. I don't know. I only know that our worlds and our creations called us and we tried to save them and the only saving thing we could do was wait out the century here on Mars, hoping that Earth might overweight itself with these scientists and their doubtings; but now they're coming to clean us out of here, us and our dark things, and all the alchemists, witches, vampires, and were-things that, one by one, retreated across space as science made inroads through every country on Earth and finally left no alternative at all but exodus. You must help. You have a good speaking manner. We need you."

"I repeat, I am not of you, I don't approve of you and the others," cried Dickens, angrily. "I was no player with witches and vampires, and midnight things."

"What of *A Christmas Carol*?"

"Riciculous! *One* story. Oh, I wrote a few others about ghosts, perhaps, but what of that? My basic works had none of that nonsense!"

"Mistaken or not, they grouped you with us. They destroyed your books, your worlds, too. You *must* hate them, Mr. Dickens!"

"I admit they are stupid and rude, but that is all. Good day!"

"Let Mr. Marley come, at least!"

"No!"

The door slammed. As Poe turned away, down the street, skimming over the frosty ground, the coachman playing a lively air on a bugle, came a great coach, out of which, cherry-red, laughing and singing, piled the Pickwickians, banging on the door, shouting *Merry Christmas* good and loud, when the door was opened by the fat boy.

Mr. Poe hurried along the midnight shore of the dry sea. By fires and smokes he hesitated, to shout orders, to check the bubbling cauldrons, the poisons and the chalked pentagrams. "Good!" he said, and ran on. "Fine!" he shouted, and ran again. People joined and ran with him. Here were Mr. Coppard and Mr. Machen running with him now. And there were hating serpents and angry demons and fiery bronze dragons and spitting vipers and trembling witches like the barbs and nettles and thorns and all the vile flotsams and jetsams of the retreating sea of imagination, left on the melancholy shore, whining and frothing and spitting.

Mr. Machen stopped. He sat like a child on the cold sand. He began to sob. They tried to soothe him, but he would not listen. "I just thought," he said. "What happens to us on the day when the *last* copies of our books are destroyed?"

The air whirled.

"Don't speak of it!"

"We must," wailed Mr. Machen. "Now, now, as the rocket comes down, you Mr. Poe, you Coppard, you Bierce, all of you, grow faint. Like wood smoke. Blowing away. Your faces melt. . . ."

"Death. *Real* death for all of us."

"We exist only through Earth's sufferance. If a final edict tonight destroyed our last few works we'd be like lights put out."

Coppard brooded gently. "I wonder who I am. In what Earth mind tonight do I exist? In some African hut? Some hermit,

reading my tales? Is he the lonely candle in the wind of time and
science? The flickering orb sustaining me here in rebellious
exile? Is it him? Or some boy in a discarded attic, finding me,
only just in time! Oh, last night I felt ill, ill, ill to the marrows of
me, for there is a body of the soul as well as a body of the body,
and this soul-body ached in all of its glowing parts, and last
night I felt myself a candle, guttering. When suddenly I sprang
up, given new light! As some child in some yellow garret on
Earth once more found a worn, time-specked copy of me, sneez-
ing with dust! And so I'm given a short respite.''

A door banged wide in a little hut by the shore. A thin short
man, with flesh hanging from him in folds, stepped out and,
paying no attention to the others, sat down and stared into his
clenched fists.

"There's the one I'm sorry for," whispered Blackwood. "Look
at him, dying away. He was once more real than we, who were
men. They took him, a skeleton thought, and clothed him in
centuries of pink flesh and snow-beard and red velvet suit and
black boot, made him reindeers, tinsel, holly. And after centuries of manufacturing him they drowned him in a vat of Lysol,
you might say.''

The men were silent.

"What must it be on Earth?" wondered Poe, "without Christmas? No hot chestnuts, no tree, no ornaments or drums or
candles, nothing; nothing but the snow and wind and the lonely,
factual people . . .''

They all looked at the thin little old man with the scraggly
beard and faded red velvet suit.

"Have you heard his story?"

"I can imagine it. The glitter-eyed psychologist, the clever
sociologist, the resentful, froth-mouthed educationalist, the
antiseptic parents . . .''

"A regrettable situation," said Bierce, smiling, "for the Yuletide merchants who, toward the last there, as I recall, were
beginning to put up holly and sing *Noël* the day before Hallow-
e'en. With any luck at all, this year, they might have started on
Labor Day!''

Bierce did not continue. He fell forward with a sigh. As he lay
upon the ground he had time to say only, "How interesting."
And then as they all watched, horrified, his body burned into
blue dust and charred bones, the ashes of which fled through the
air in black tatters.

"Bierce, Bierce!"

"Gone."

"His last book gone. Someone, on Earth, just now burned it."

"God rest him, nothing of him left now. For what are we but our books, and when those are gone, nothing's to be seen."

A rushing sound filled the sky.

They cried out, terrified, and looked up. In the sky, dazzling it with sizzling fire-clouds, was the Rocket! Around the men on the seashore, lanterns bobbed, there was a squealing and a bubbling and an odor of cooked spells. Candle-eyed pumpkins lifted into the cold clear air. Thin fingers clenched into fists and a witch screamed from her withered mouth:

> "Ship, ship, break fall!
> Ship, ship, burn all!
> Crack, flake, shake, melt!
> Mummy-dust, cat-pelt!"

"Time to go," murmured Blackwood. "On to Jupiter, on to Saturn or Pluto."

"Run away?" shouted Poe in the wind. "Never!"

"I'm a tired old man."

Poe gazed into the old man's face and believed him. He climbed atop a huge boulder and faced the ten thousand gray shadows and green lights and yellow eyes on the hissing wind.

"The powders!" he shouted.

A thick hot smell of bitter almond, civit, cumin, wormseed and orris!

The rocket came down—steadily down, with the shriek of a damned spirit! Poe raged at it! He flung his fists up and the orchestra of heat and smell and hatred answered in symphony! Like stripped tree fragments, bats flew upward! Burning hearts, flung like missles, burst in bloody fireworks on the singed air. Down, down, relentlessly down, like a Pendulum the rocket came! And Poe howled, furiously, and shrank back with every sweep and sweep of the rocket cutting and ravening the air! All the dead sea seemed a pit in which, trapped, they waited the sinking of the dread machinery, the glistening axe; they were people under the avalanche!

"The snakes!"

And luminous serpentines of undulant green hurtled toward

the rocket. But it came down, a sweep, a fire, a motion, and it lay panting out exhaustions of red plumage on the sand, a mile away.

"At it!" shrieked Poe. "The plan's changed! Only one chance! Run! At it! At it! Drown them with our bodies! Kill them!"

And as if he had commanded a violent sea to change its course, to suck itself free from primeval beds, the shirls and savage gouts of fire spread and ran like wind and rain and stark lightning over the sea-sands, down empty river deltas, shadowing and screaming, whistling and whining, sputtering and coalescing toward the rocket which, extinguished, lay like a clean metal torch in the furthest hollow. As if a great charred cauldron of sparkling lava had been overturned, the boiling people and snapping animals churned down the dry fathoms!

"Kill them!" screamed Poe, running.

The rocket man leaped out of their ship, guns ready. They stalked about, sniffing the air like hounds. They saw nothing. They relaxed.

The captain stepped forth last. He gave sharp commands. Wood was gathered, kindled, and a fire leapt up in an instant. The captain beckoned his men into a half circle about him.

"A new world," he said, forcing himself to speak deliberately, though he glanced nervously, now and again, over his shoulder at the empty sea. "The old world left behind. A new start. What more symbolic than that we here dedicate ourselves all the more firmly to science and progress." He nodded crisply to his lieutenant. "The books."

Firelight limned the faded gilt titles: *The Willows, The Outsider, Behold, The Dreamer, Dr. Jekyll and Mr. Hyde, The Land of Oz, Pellucidar, The Land That Time Forgot, A Midsummer Night's Dream*, and the monstrous names of Machen and Edgar Allan Poe and Cabell and Dunsany and Blackwood and Lewis Carroll; the names, the old names, the evil names.

"A new world. With a gesture, we burn the last of the old."

The captain ripped pages from the books. Leaf by seared leaf, he fed them into the fire.

A scream!

Leaping back, the men stared beyond the firelight at the edges of the encroaching and uninhabited sea.

Another scream! A high and wailing thing, like the death of a dragon and the thrashing of a bronzed whale left gasping when the waters of a leviathan's sea drain down the singles and evaporate.

It was the sound of air rushing in to fill a vacuum, where, a moment before, was *something*.

The captain neatly disposed of the last book into the fire.

The air stopped quivering.

Silence.

The rocket men leaned and listened.

"Captain, did you hear it?"

"No."

"Like a wave, sir. On the sea bottom! I thought I saw something. Over there. A black wave. Big. Running at us."

"You were mistaken."

"There, sir!"

"What?"

"See it? There! The City! Way over! That Green City, near the lake! It's splitting in half. It's falling!"

The men squinted and shuffled forward.

Smith stood trembling among them. He put his hands to his head as if to find a thought there. "I remember. Yes, now I do. A long time back. When I was a child. A book I read. A story. Oz, I think it was. Yes, Oz. The Emerald City of Oz . . ."

"Oz? Never heard of it."

"Yes, Oz, that's what it was. I saw it just now, like in the story. I saw it fall."

"Smith!"

"Yes, sir?"

"Report for psychoanalysis tomorrow."

"Yes, sir!" A brisk salute.

"Be careful."

The men tiptoed, guns alert, beyond the ship's aseptic light to gaze at the long sea and the low hills.

"Why," whispered Smith, disappointed, "there's no one here at all, is there? No one here at all."

The wind blew sand over his shoes, whining.

Clingerman-Editors Correspondence

21 March 1951

Mr. Barthold Flos
507 Fifth Ave
New York 17 N Y

Dear Bart:

Just what do you mean by tantalizing us with the statement that Mildred Clingerman "is a *beautiful* but unpublished girl?" Precisely what are you peddling?

In any case, if she remains unpublished long I don't think it'll be our fault. Basically MINISTER WITHOUT PORTFOLIO is very attractive, and a kind of story that we've found has strong popular appeal.

As it is, it doesn't come off as well as it might. A rather slow introduction and it could be cut about in half.

And the ending doesn't seem quite right—a little too blunt for one thing; and the "she envied the woman who had proved herself so useful" is pushing the innocence a little too far.

Can't make any guarantees until we see how she handles the rewrite; but I'd say the chances were pretty good that we might turn her into beautiful but published.

Does your agency furnish phone numbers?

Best,

A. B.

Tucson, Arizona
14 January 1952

Dear Tony,

It was fun seeing my first published story. I couldn't really read it, I found, being strangely overcome with the feeling I was standing on a soapbox addressing strangers and clad only in a tattered nightgown. Not a bit what I expected.

Your more than generous introduction to the story was delightfully fantastic. You should have heard my family trying to snort delicately. Beasts.

Sincerely,

Mildred Clingerman

The F&SF policy of discovering new writers occasionally pays unexpected dividends. When Mildred Clingerman's agent submitted her first story to us, he introduced her as "A beautiful but unpublished girl"; and when later he presented her in person, we awoke with amazement (like the young girl from Peru) to find it was perfectly true. For once we regret our policy of no interior illustrations—but the important thing, to you as to us, is not the beauty of Clingerman's person but the highly attractive quality of her writing. An Arizona housewife with two children, too many cats, a weakness for overimaginative cooking, and a long-suffering husband, she has managed to translate a vast interplanetary theme into small believable domestic terms in a manner we haven't seen equaled since Bill Brown's popular The Star Ducks *(F&SF, Fall, 1950). You'll be seeing more of Mildred Clingerman soon in F&SF—and, we're sure, elsewhere.*

*Anthony Boucher
J. F. McComas*

Minister Without Portfolio
By Mildred Clingerman

Mrs. Chriswell's little roadster came to a shuddering halt. Here was the perfect spot. Only one sagging wire fence to step over and not a cow in sight. Mrs. Chriswell was terrified of cows, and if the truth were told, only a little less afraid of her daughter-in-law, Clara. It was all Clara's idea that her mother-in-law should now be lurking in meadows peering at birds. Clara had been delighted with the birdwatching idea, but frankly, Mrs. Chriswell was bored with birds. They *flew* so much. And as for their colors, it was useless for her to speculate. Mrs. Chriswell was one of those rare women who are quite, quite, color-blind.

"But, Clara," Mrs. Chriswell had pleaded, "what's the point if I can't tell what color they are?"

"Well, but, darling," Clara had said crisply, "how much cleverer if you get to know them just from the distinctive markings!"

Mrs. Chriswell, sighing a little as she recalled the firm look of Clara's chin, maneuvered herself and her burdens over the sagging wire fence. She successfully juggled the binoculars, the heavy bird book, and her purse, and thought how ghastly it was at sixty to be considered so useless that she must be provided with harmless occupations to keep her out of the way.

Since Mr. Chriswell's death she had moved in with her son and his wife to face a life of enforced idleness. The servants resented her presence in the kitchen, so cooking was out. Clara and the snooty nursemaid would brook no interference with the nursery routine, so Mrs. Chriswell had virtually nothing to do. Even her crocheted doilies disappeared magically soon after their presentation to Clara and the modern furniture.

Mrs. Chriswell shifted the heavy bird book and considered rebelling. The sun was hot and her load was heavy. As she toiled on across the field she thought she saw the glint of sun on water. She would sit and crochet in the shade nearby and remove the big straw cartwheel hat Clara had termed "just the thing."

Arrived at the trees, Mrs. Chriswell dropped her burdens and flung the hat willy-nilly. Ugly, ridiculous thing. She glanced around for the water she thought she'd seen, but there was no sign of it. She leaned back against the tree trunk and sighed blissfully. A little breeze had sprung up and was cooling the damp tendrils on her forehead. She opened her big purse and scrambled through the muddle of contents for her crochet hook and the ball of thread attached to a half-finished doily. In her search she came across the snapshots of her granddaughters—in color, they were, but unfortunately Mrs. Chriswell saw them only in various shades of gray. The breeze was getting stronger now, very pleasant, but the dratted old cartwheel monstrosity was rolling merrily down the slight grade to the tangle of berry bushes a few yards away. Well, it would catch on the brambles. But it didn't. The wind flirted it right around the bushes, and the hat disappeared.

"Fiddle!" Mrs. Chriswell dared not face Clara without the hat. Still hanging on to the bulky purse, she got up to give chase. Rounding the tangle of bushes, she ran smack into a tall young man in uniform.

"Oh!" Mrs. Chriswell said. "Have you seen my hat?"

The young man smiled and pointed down the hill. Mrs. Chriswell was surprised to see her hat being passed from hand to hand among three other tall young men in uniform. They were laughing at it, and she didn't blame them. They were standing beside a low, silvery aircraft of some unusual design. Mrs. Chriswell studied it a moment, but, really, she knew nothing about such things. . . . The sun glinted off it, and she realized this was what she had thought was water. The young man beside her touched her arm. She turned towards him and saw that he had put a rather lovely little metal hat on his head. He offered her one with grave courtesy. Mrs. Chriswell smiled up at him and nodded. The young man fitted the hat carefully, adjusting various little ornamental knobs on the top of it.

"Now we can talk," he said. "Do you hear well?"

"My dear boy," Mrs. Chriswell said, "of course I do. I'm not so old as all that." She found a smooth stone and sat down to chat. This was much nicer than birdwatching, or even crochet.

The tall young man grinned and signalled excitedly to his companions. They too put on little metal hats and came bounding up the hill. Still laughing, they deposited the cartwheel in Mrs. Chriswell's lap. She patted the stone by way of invitation, and the youngest looking one of the four dropped down beside her.

"What is your name, Mother?" he asked.

"Ida Chriswell," she said. "What's yours?"

"My name is Jord," the boy said.

Mrs. Chriswell patted his hand. "That's a nice, unusual name." The boy grabbed Mrs. Chriswell's hand and rubbed it against the smoothness of his cheek.

"You are like my Mother's Mother," the boy explained, "whom I have not seen in too long." The other young men laughed, and the boy looked abashed and stealthily wiped with his hands at a tear that slid down his nose.

Mrs. Chriswell frowned warningly at the laughter and handed him her clean pocket handkerchief, scented with lavender. Jord turned it over and over in his hands, and then tentatively sniffed at it.

"It's all right," Mrs. Chriswell said. "Use it. I have another." But Jord only breathed more deeply of the faint perfume in its folds.

"This is only the thinnest thread of melody," he said, "but, Mother Ida, it is very like one note from the Harmony Hills of home!'' He passed the handkerchief all around the circle, and the young men sniffed at it and smiled.

Mrs. Chriswell tried to remember if she had ever read of the Harmony Hills, but Mr. Chriswell had always told her she was lamentably weak in Geography, and she supposed that this was one of her blank spots, like where on earth was Timbuktu? Or the Hellandgone people were always talking about? But it was rude not to make some comment. Wars shifted people about such a lot, and these boys must be homesick and weary of being strangers, longing to talk of home. She was proud of herself for realizing that they were strangers. But there was something. . . . Hard to say, really. The way they had bounded up the hill? Mountain people, perhaps, to whom hills were mere spring-boards to heights beyond.

"Tell me about your hills," she said.

"Wait," Jord said. "I will show you." He glanced at his leader as if for approval. The young man who had fitted her hat nodded. Jord drew a fingernail across the breast of his uniform. Mrs. Chriswell was surprised to see a pocket opening where no pocket had been before. Really, the Air Force did amazing things with its uniforms, though, frankly, Mrs. Chriswell thought the cut of these a bit extreme.

Carefully, Jord was lifting out a packet of gossamer material. He gently pressed the center of the packet and it blossomed out into voluminous clouds of featherweight threads, held loosely together in a weave like a giant spider web. To Mrs. Chriswell's eyes the mesh of threads was the color of fog, and almost as insubstantial.

"Do not be afraid," Jord said softly, stepping closer to her. "Bend your head, close your eyes, and you shall hear the lovely Harmony Hills of home."

There was one quick-drawn breath of almost-fear, but before she shut her eyes Mrs. Chriswell saw the love in Jord's, and in that moment she knew how rarely she had seen this look, anywhere . . . anytime. If Jord had asked it of her, it was all right. She closed her eyes and bowed her head, and in that attitude of prayer she felt a soft weightlessness descend upon her. It was as if twilight had come down to drape itself on her shoulders. And then the music began. Behind the darkness of her eyes it rose in majesty and power, in colors she had never seen, never guessed. It blossomed like flowers—giant forests of them. Their scents were intoxicating and filled her with joy. She could not tell if the blending perfumes made the music, or if the music itself created the flowers and the perfumes that poured forth from them. She did not care. She wanted only to go on forever listening to all this color. It seemed odd to be listening to color, perhaps, but after all, she told herself, it would seem just as odd to me to *see* it.

She sat blinking at the circle of young men. The music was finished. Jord was putting away the gossamer threads in the secret pocket, and laughing aloud at her astonishment.

"Did you like it, Mother Ida?" He dropped down beside her again and patted her wrinkled face, still pink with excitement.

"Oh, Jord," she said, "how lovely . . . Tell me . . ."

But the Leader was calling them all to order. "I'm sorry, Mother Ida, we must hurry about our business. Will you answer some questions? It is very important."

"Of course," Mrs. Chriswell said. She was still feeling a bit dazed. "If I can. . . . If it's like the quizzes on the radio, though, I'm not very good at it."

The young man shook his head. "We," he said, "have been instructed to investigate and report on the true conditions of this . . . of the world." He pointed at the aircraft glittering in the sunlight. "We have traveled all around in that slow machine, and our observations have been accurate. . . ." He hesitated, drew a deep breath and continued. ". . . and perhaps we shall be forced to give an unfavorable report, but this depends a great deal on the outcome of our talk with you. We are glad you stumbled upon us. We were about to set out on a foray to secure some individual for questioning. It is our last talk." He smiled. "And Jord, here, will not be sorry. He is sick for home and loved ones." He sighed, and all the other young men echoed the sigh.

"Every night," Mrs. Chriswell said, "I pray for peace on earth. I cannot bear to think of boys like you fighting and dying, and the folks at home waiting and waiting . . ." She glanced all around at their listening faces. "And I'll tell you something else," she said, "I find I can't really hate anybody, even the enemy." Around the circle the young men nodded at each other. "Now ask me your questions." She fumbled in her purse for her crochet work and found it.

Beside her Jord exclaimed with pleasure at the sight of the half-finished doily. Mrs. Chriswell warmed to him even more.

The tall young man began his grave questionings. They were

very simple questions, and Mrs. Chriswell answered them without hesitation. Did she believe in God? Did she believe in the dignity of man? Did she truly abhor war? Did she believe that man was capable of love for his neighbor? The questions went on and on, and Mrs. Chriswell crocheted while she gave her answers.

At last, when the young man had quite run out of questions, and Mrs. Chriswell had finished the doily, Jord broke the sun-lazy silence that had fallen upon them.

"May I have it, Mother?" He pointed to the doily. Mrs. Chriswell bestowed it upon him with great pleasure, and Jord, like a very small boy, stuffed it greedily into another secret pocket. He pointed at her stuffed purse.

"May I look, Mother?"

Mrs. Chriswell indulgently passed him her purse. He opened it and poured the litter of contents on the ground between them. The snapshots of Mrs. Chriswell's grandchildren stared up at him. Jord smiled at the pretty little-girl faces. He groped in the chest pocket and drew out snapshots of his own. "These," he told Mrs. Chriswell proudly, "are my little sisters. Are they not like these little girls of yours? Let us exchange, because soon I will be at home with them, and there will be no need for pictures. I would like to have yours."

Mrs. Chriswell would have given Jord the entire contents of the purse if he had asked for them. She took the snapshots he offered and looked with pleasure at the sweet-faced children. Jord still stirred at the pile of possessions from Mrs. Chriswell's purse. By the time she was ready to leave he had talked her out of three illustrated recipes torn from magazines, some swatches of material, and two pieces of peppermint candy.

The young man who was the leader helped her to remove the pretty little hat when Mrs. Chriswell indicated he should. She would have liked to keep it, but she didn't believe Clara would approve. She clapped the straw monstrosity on her head, kissed Jord's cheek, waved goodbye to the rest, and groped her way around the berry bushes. She had to grope because her eyes were tear-filled. They had saluated her so grandly as she left.

Clara's usually sedate household was in an uproar when Mrs. Chriswell returned. All the radios in the house were blaring. Even Clara sat huddled over the one in the library. Mrs. Chriswell heard a boy in the street crying "EXTRA! EXTRA!" and the

upstairs maid almost knocked her down getting out the front door
to buy one. Mrs. Chriswell, sleepy and somewhat sunburned,
supposed it was something about the awful war.

She was just turning up the stairs to her room when the snooty
nursemaid came rushing down to disappear kitchenwards with
another newspaper in hand. Good, the children were alone.
She'd stop in to see them. Suddenly she heard the raised voices
from the back of the house. The cook was yelling at somebody.
"I tell you, I saw it! I took out some garbage and there it was,
right over me!" Mrs. Chriswell lingered at the foot of the
stairway, puzzled by all the confusion. The housemaid came
rushing in with the EXTRA edition. Mrs. Chriswell quietly reached
out and took it. "Thank you, Nadine," she said. The housemaid
was still staring at her as she climbed the stairs.

Edna and Evelyn were sitting on the nursery floor, a candy
box between them, and shrieking at each other when their grandmother opened the door. They were cramming chocolates into
their mouths between shrieks. Their faces and pinafores were
smeared with the candy. Edna suddenly yanked Evelyn's hair,
hard. "Pig!" she shouted. "You got three more than I did!"

"Children! Children! Not fighting?" Mrs. Chriswell was
delighted. Here was something she could cope with. She led
them firmly to the bathroom and washed their faces. "Change
your frocks," she said, "and I'll tell you my adventure."

There was only hissing accusals and whispered counter-charges
behind her as she turned her back on the children to scan the
newspaper. Grandmothers, she told herself, have a calming effect
on children. The headlines leapt up at her.

MYSTERIOUS BROADCAST INTERRUPTS PROGRAM ON
ALL WAVE LENGTHS.
UNKNOWN WOMAN SAVES WORLD SAY
MEN FROM SPACE.
ONE SANE HUMAN FOUND ON EARTH.
COOKING, NEEDLEWORK, HOME, RELIGIOUS
INTERESTS SWAY SPACE JUDGES.

Every column of the paper was crowded with the same unin-
telligible nonsense. Mrs. Chriswell folded it neatly, deposited it
on a table, and turned to tie her granddaughters' sashes and tell
her adventure.

". . . And then he gave me some lovely photographs. In

color, he said . . . Good little girls, just like Edna and Evelyn. Would you like to see them?"

Edna made a rude noise with her mouth pursed. Evelyn's face grew saintlike in retaliation. "Yes, show us," she said.

Mrs. Chriswell passed them the snapshots, and the children drew close together for the moment before Evelyn dropped the pictures as if they were blazing. She stared hard at her grandmother while Edna made a gagging noise.

"Green!" Edna gurgled. "Gaaa . . . green skins!"

"Grandmother!" Evelyn was tearful. "Those children are frog-colored!"

Mrs. Chriswell bent over to pick up the pictures. "Now, now, children," she murmured absently. "We don't worry about the color of people's skins. Red . . . yellow . . . black . . . we're all God's children. Asia or Africa, makes no difference. . . ." But before she could finish her thought, the nursemaid loomed disapprovingly in the doorway. Mrs. Chriswell hurried out to her own room, while some tiny worry nagged at her mind. "Red, yellow, black, white," she murmured over and over, "and brown . . . but green . . .?" Geography had always been her weak point. Green . . . Now where on earth . . .?

Trends

Henry Klinger, New York Associate Story editor for Twentieth-Century-Fox, reports that the science fiction trend has caused a revision in Hollywood's classic plot-formula. The new story line runs;

Boy meets girl.
Boy loses girl.
Boy *builds* girl.

Anthony Boucher
J. F. McComas

Sorry, But—
Rejections and Advice

One descriptive phrase has kept recurring as associates and personal friends have described Boucher and McComas—they were many people said, first and foremost, men of good will. An example was their effort in the beginning to answer all manuscript submissions, good or bad, with personal letters. Both remembered the frustration and despair of receiving formal rejection slips themselves. When, rather swiftly, they began to handle around 250 manuscripts a month, they found it humanly impossible to live up to their desire to treat all writers and would-be writers with dignity. They had finally to move to the "Sorry but—" slips followed by a few words for the near-misses, and the formal rejection slip for the impossibles. There were many notable exceptions—any manuscript submitted by a prisoner in any location received personal attention and a letter as encouraging as possible. Again, the Very Young, the ten-to-twenty set, got personal notes from the editors.

The few examples chosen for this small cross section displays a wide variety—from the most sophisticated to the most naive. It certainly displays some of their humor and their sympathy.

The advice, included here, remains exactly appropriate for today's young writers, and I hope they will take note of the "Dutch Uncle" clarity about what's wrong as well as the sensitive encouragement of what's right.

14 December 1949

Dear Mr. Kowkanski:

The trouble is you're trying too hard. You're too intent on showing off. If you like Latin tags, try *ars est celare artem*—which not only indicates that good writing should not be obtrusive and self-conscious, but also conveys in its first four letters precisely where fancy sesquipedalianism gives the reader a pain.

Forget all about influences and imitations. Forget all the

big words you know (and more often, to judge from some of their inept intrusions, don't know). Try telling a story in the English or American language. If you're over 25, this advice probably comes too late; but it's more likely that you're simply going through a phase that often attacks young writers—in which case it's time someone told you bluntly that you're driving up a blind alley.

Further advice: Don't write long introductory letters to editors. It stamps you as an amateur, wastes the editor's time, and cannot possibly affect his decision, which is based solely on the story. And never *never* NEVER send out a MS without enclosing return postage; most editors will simply dump it in the waste basket and God knows why we're more kind-hearted.

We'd be very happy to hear from you again if you ever decide to write like Joe Kowkanski of New Jersey.

Sincerely yours,

A.B.

The editors claimed to have invented the rejection slip with only the words "Sorry, but—" at the beginning. This form provided space for a brief personal note (not always sunny as seen below). Later they added the full formal rejection slip for the utterly hopeless manuscripts, referred to usually as the "slush" (almost always unsolicited and unagented).

Harvey Gorham: SATELLITE NAMED INFINITY

Dear Mr. Gorham.
   Sorry, but if this magazine has a tabu—it's one *violently* against stories wherein protagonist is dead all the time and doesn't know it! We get about 5 such a week.

12 October 1950

Dear Mr. Arnold:
   This is going to be a very lay-it-on-the-line Dutch uncle letter:
   AJAX FROM THE ALLEY was, I think, the first Arnold we saw. It struck us as having a good idea, for all its

flaws, and probably worth discussing later for rewrite possibilities.

In the year since then we've read God knows how many Arnolds—you're probably the most prolific contributor we have. And as a result of this intensive study of Arnolds, we're certain that it's no use talking about a rewrite on AJAX.

You're exceedingly fertile in story-ideas. Many of them are trite and weak; occasionally one is definitely good.

But whether the idea's good or bad, the execution is always at best mediocre. You're turning 'em out so hot and heavy that you don't seem to bother to learn the crudest rudiments of the craft of writing—plot structure, story development, characterization, prose style. And in a year you've shown no growth or improvement.

There aren't any books or courses that'll teach you how to write; but we'd suggest you try some careful analysis of printed stories that you like, figuring out what makes them come off and how they're treated. Then go over your own stuff analytically and observe where and how it differs. Then try thinking about a story and working on it instead of shooting it off fast and whamming into another idea.

Good luck!

A.B.

15 July 1950

Eugene Clement d'Art: THE MAD SCULPTOR
  Sorry, but—
much though we admire Poe, we can't think of a worse model for a modern writer—to get away with his type of heavy elaborate overstatement you have, by God, to *be* Poe.

The Editors

I like the way the following letter enumerates so clearly to the writer the exact kinds of ideas and treatments sought for the magazine.

12 January 1950

Dear Mr. Cowen:

TRAP ON CYBELE is a highly readable story, which should certainly sell somewhere; but it isn't our meat. Strip it of its interplanetary trappings, and it's simply a trite, routine cops-&-robbers story.

We want something fresher, a little different. A new scientific idea, a new plot-twist, a new imaginative concept—anything that isn't simple hack. As a sample of the highly varied kinds of science fiction that appeal to us, see Ted Sturgeon's HURKLE in our first issue or Kris Neville's EVERY WORK INTO JUDGMENT in our second—or see almost any of the stories in such anthologies as the Bleiler-Dikty BEST SCIENCE FICTION 1949 or Judith Merrill's Bantambook SHOT IN THE DARK— to say nothing of my coeditor's ADVENTURES IN TIME & SPACE.

We hope we shall hear from you again with something more distinctive—and possibly including your self-echoing little green men, whom we like.

Sincerely,

A.B.

2 July 1954

Norm Alterer: MR. EMLEE'S LUCK
    Sorry, but—
I rather like this—very neat and logical. But I'm so terribly tired of pact-with-the Devil stories that they have to be not merely good but verging on wonderful.

Regretfully,

The Editors

This straight forward letter to a Very New writer not only spells out the fundamentals but says something very significant about those whom the young writer refers to as "hacks."

17 November 1949

Dear Mr. Lowert:

First a word of warning: 95% of all editors in the business would simply have returned your MS unread, because it was in handwriting. Or rather they wouldn't even have returned it, since no postage was enclosed, but just dumped it in the wastebasket.

If you can't afford to buy a typewriter, then beg, borrow or steal one. Or pay to have your story typed by a professional. Submitting handwritten MSS is a pure waste of time. And ALWAYS enclose return postage, and put your name and address on the story as well as on the cover-letter.

AL'S REVENGE certainly isn't publishable (how many first stories are?): but it's a little hard to say whether or not it shows promise. The idea of a corpse returning after the cement treatment is good and I think new; but the writing, I'm sure you won't be surprised to learn, is very amateurish. The structure's awkward, your characters are just names without personalities, the prose has no individuality.

The hacks that you speak of so scornfully (and incidentally, they do *not* make "comfortable livings") may have little real literary talent, but they do have experience and technique. The only way to get those qualities is by reading a great deal in the fields that interest you, reading critically and trying to observe just how things are put together, how effects are attained; and by writing a great deal, to the point where you begin to see what's wrong with your earlier stuff and how to improve it.

As I say, it's hard to tell from this very fumbling first effort whether you should continue. But if you do decide to, we'd be very happy to see how you're coming along—say about 20 stories from now.

Sincerely yours,

The Editors

This "Sorry but—" went to a well-known agent in the field.

16 March 1950

Sorry but . . . after reading this, A.B. coined the proverb:
One man's turd is another man's turquoise. This disgusting little
piece of scatology is definitely not our turquoise. *McC*

This reply separates personal preference from commercial
possibilities beyond a doubt.

3 April 1950

Dear Mr. Payne:
Since I, too, am a devoted admirer of the creator of
Mssrs. Pickwick and Weller, I'm going to forsake the
usual 'alleybis' of editors and tell you quite frankly why
we cannot use A FRIEND PASSES BY.
While Mr. Boucher and I both found the story wholly
charming, we are both in reluctant agreement that it is too
sentimental and old-fashioned for our readers. An editor
must gauge as accurately as possible the desires of the
majority of his readers (or he soon ceases to be an editor!);
thus, it happens too often that an editor realizes a story he
likes would elicit nothing but an angry clamor from most
of his readers. Such is the present case and both of us
regret it.
May I express my appreciation for a very pleasant half-
hour's reading?

Yours very truly,

J. Francis McComas

I don't know whatever came of the advice that follows. She
had plenty to work on!

1 August 1952

Dear Miss Nayor:
First of all, let me be brutally blunt to say that very few
editors would bother to read a MS as amateurishly submitted as yours. For your future guidance:

Use *black* typewriter ribbon;

Use 8½x11 paper;

For emphasis, use *italics* (indicated in typing by under-lining), not CAPITALS. (For that matter, use less emphasis.)

But I'm glad we are editors who are apt to read anything. We don't see possibilities in FOR EVERY NEED; but THE ROBOT THAT SOLD LIES, awkward though it is, is appealing.

We'd like to see you try a rewrite on this. Since we know nothing about your potential as a writer, we can't make any guarantee on this; it has to be purely speculative.

But we would enjoy seeing a revision along these lines:

A) Pull its length down a little—closer to 1000 words than its present 1300;

B) Cut a good deal of your reiterated exposition, and in its place put in more of the robot's nonsense-logic thoughts, which are fun;

C) Give your Man-Who-Did-Things a name; this allegorical type of label is irritating;

D) Your last page should be a good deal subtler. The theme is good, but it shouldn't be so bluntly stated.

E) We'd like to retitle it THE LITTLEST ROBOT.

Hope you'll feel like trying this. And if you do, please tell us a little about yourself.

A.B.

I was particularly intrigued with this letter; the word-choice is so apt. It is, I think, a splendid critical analysis.

16 May 1950

Dear Mr. W. . . . . . :

If nothing else, politeness limits an editor's criticism of a writer's work. Mere practicality, limitations of time and energy determine just how far an editor should go in criticizing and suggesting revisions of a manuscript. Once in a great while, a badly written story with an inherently great idea forces an editor to forget all those considerations and spew forth an angry, detailed, brutal comment on an author's work.

Such is the case with MR. BURNS.

It is a truly wonderful piece of terror which you have executed probably as badly as possible. I do not mean that you are a bad writer, per se. I do mean that you don't think your ideas through, that your construction is careless, even slipshod, that your plotline is faulty; in brief, you never realize more than the barest minimum of your story idea's potential.

Let us look at what is wrong with MR. BURNS. In the first place, that long cutback beginning with p.3 is structurally an abomination. Your reader loses all the nice feeling he has had developed within him by your first 2 pages, he forgets the thread of the story, and he winds up by still trying to reorient himself while you're busily writing your climax—which, of course, has no effect on the reader whatsoever.

Secondly, you do not give a "why" for this happening. . . . the laws of fantasy justice demand that there be some reason for an executed person having the right (which, in turn, gives him the *ability*) to return for vengeance on the executioner who is, after all, merely an instrument of the law.

Thirdly, you have jammed into a couple of paragraphs that awfulness of Johnny's being the hangman's son. That should be hinted at from the very beginning, built carefully so that its final revelation is logically arrived at. Then, the impact will be at its fullest power. . . . . .

I trust you will pardon my violent tone. But I do hate to see a writer refuse to think through his ideas. Further, I hope you'll work over MR. BURNS . . . and let us see another version. Finally, I hope you'll let your next idea stew in your mind for at least 2 weeks before you begin to write it.

Sincerely,

J. Francis McComas

Finally, the almost-took-it letter, but painstakingly phrased to encourage and stimulate the writer.

29 July 1952

Dear Mr. Franciscus:

If it's any consolation to you in lieu of a check, TOP
SECRET caused a great deal of editorial argument and
necessitated several rereadings.

Final verdict: It's a damned good story, completely
salable . . . and not to us. It's just a smidgin too routine,
unsubtle, conventional, formula, or whatever the proper
word is.

We do want space travel melodrama . . . with a little
more novelty, a little more of the "quality" emphasis on
character rather than the "pulp" stress on pure plot and
action. (You'll understand I'm using "quality" and "pulp"
as descriptive definitions, with no snobbish intent.)

We'd like very much to see more from you, but suggest
that you study the magazine somewhat first. If you haven't
seen it and find it hard to get in Phoenix, let us know and
we'll be glad to send you a few sample back issues.

With your next submissions (soon, I hope), you might
let us know a little about yourself, especially as a writer.

We're positive TOP SECRET will sell elsewhere, and
very fast. Might we suggest a title change? T. S is the title
of a David Grinnell story published by us and very recently anthologized by Groff Conklin.

Cordially,

The Editors

The editors deal with the very young.

13 February 1953

Robert N. Rolfe: THE DEATH CONDEMNED

Certainly, your writing shows a lot of promise but—look!
even your English teacher should know this isn't a *story*. It
has no development, no story line; at best, it would be an
anecdote, a tiny case history in a *book* about the era you
project. Compare this *objectively* to the *stories* Bradbury
has written on the same lines. After some study, I think
you'll realize the vast difference—technically—between
his work and yours.

It's damn' nice to see a 16 yr old thinking as you do. I hope you'll couple that thinking with some sound technique!

Cordially,

The Editors

27 August 1954

Dear Mrs. Sacklow:
Sounds like your bright 17-yr-old is writing without sufficient background reading, so that he's unfortunately duplicating old stuff. The eye-transplant is so very stale I'm 99% sure I wdn't like it even if it were brilliantly done; and the Last Adam theme figures in an awful large percentage of our regular daily rejects. But if he comes up with something brighter, you might try us; we've bought from authors that young, and some of the current Top Names in s f started even younger.

Sincerely,

Anthony Boucher

26 May 1954

Dear Mr. Billet:
B-B-BRAIN isn't for us—not enough development of a concept as old as Capek's R U R; but it's interesting enough to make me take time out to answer your letter:
It's impossible to speak with any certainty, especially on the basis of a single short-story; but I'll make the rash guess that you may "have possibilities as a writer." Chief reason is that you don't, thank God, sound like anybody else; there's an offbeat individuality that's refreshing as an editor wades through MSS. And you've got the good sense not to pad your wordage and not to fall into solid long passages of heavy exposition.
To be completely frank, you don't seem at the moment to be much more than "surprisingly-good-for-15"; but a number of writers, particularly in the science-fantasy field, have begun selling commercially at 16 or 17, and quite

possibly another year or so of practice may get you started. God knows. . . .

As to what you do wrong:

Please, please work very hard on your spelling. I know that a great many professional writers spell badly, but not so badly as, for instance, *tung*.

And *ALWAYS* enclose a stamped addressed return envelope.

Good luck.

Sincerely,

Anthony Boucher

16 January 1950

Dear Mr. J.: Many thanks for your note and permission of 1/14. Don't let your youth scare you. Getting started at an early age is almost a tradition in the modern fantasy field. Ray Bradbury, August Derleth, Isaac Asimov, Theodore Sturgeon—see what company you're in? Good luck.

Sincerely,

The Editors

de Camp/Pratt-Editors Correspondence

30 November 1949

Dear Fletcher [Pratt]:

McComas and I are both extremely gleeful over the Gavagan's Bar stories, and definitely want to introduce that distinguished hangout in our 2d issue. Since that 2d issue is now on its way to press, things are very rush and complicated. What I'm going to do is to present you herewith with a batch of questions to mull over; McComas will be in N Y next week and will see you and collect the answers.

A) Since half the fun of a series is its being a series, and the whole adds up to more than the sum of its parts, we'd like to start this off—as Fred Dannay did a series of Gerald Kersh's— with *two* short samples rather than one longer one. Take the two shortest (which by a happy chance are also the two we like best) and bill them as GAVAGAN'S BAR:
1. Elephas Frumenti
2. The Gift of God

B) We don't believe in unannounced editorial rewrites, so would like to ask permission to tone down a couple of phrases too strong for our family audience.

C) We want to know, to prepare our editorial introduction, whether any other BAR stories have sold and when they're appearing. Of course, we hope we're giving it its debut.

Best,

AB

3 December 1949

Dear Tony:

I'm delighted that you liked the GAVAGAN'S BAR stories, and having talked with Sprague, think the price is okay for the two shorts.

So also are the minor editorial changes you suggest.

Two or three people have expressed a good deal of interest in some of the stories, but in each case it has been a question of wishing to see them when we have completed the careful rewrite necessary on original versions. In no case has this rewrite been done, so you are launching the series. (I may mention, by the way, that the stories sent to you have not been submitted or even mentioned elsewhere.)

As a matter of fact, despite interest elsewhere, we'd rather like to consider, and have you consider, making GAVAGAN'S an exclusively Magazine of Fantasy feature for the reason you give—that the whole is more than the sum of its parts.

Yours,

F. Pratt

L. Sprague de Camp is (or has been) an engineer, lecturer, college instructor and author. Fletcher Pratt is (or has been) an historian (Napoleonic era, American Civil War), a critic, editor and translator. Viewed separately, they seem very orderly, if extraordinarily versatile, citizens. But combine the two, plus a typewriter, and an hilarious disorder ensues. Only Messrs. Pratt and de Camp, working as a team, would have the proper maladjustment to the ordinary for proper reporting of events that occur regularly in Gavagan's Bar, down in Greenwich Village. (Sorry, we don't know the exact address.) Gavagan's is a decent place and its bartender, Mr. Cohan, is a capable enough judge of when a customer has had enough, but even he cannot maintain any order in life. Things just happen—things that shouldn't happen to a—well, an elephant, or a poetess. With these two stories, Elephas Frumenti* and* The Gift of God, *begins the saga of Gavagan's Bar. More of the bewilderments that plague Mr. Cohan's clientele will be served up to you as Messrs. de Camp and Pratt report them to us.*

Anthony Boucher
J. F. McComas

Gavagan's Bar
By L. Sprague de Camp and
Fletcher Pratt

1. Elephas Frumenti

The thin, balding man in tweeds almost tipped over his glass as he set it down with a care that showed care had become necessary. "Think of dogs," he said. "Relly, my dear, there is no practical limit to what can be accomplished by selective breeding."

*only "Elephas Frumenti" is included here.

"Except that where I come from, we sometimes think of other things," said the brass-blonde, emphasizing the ancient *New Yorker* joke with a torso-wriggle that was pure *Police Gazette*.

Mr. Witherwax lifted his nose from the second Martini. "Do you know them, Mr. Co-han?" he asked.

Mr. Cohan turned in profile to swab a glass. "That would be Professor Thott, and a very educated gentleman, too. I don't rightly know the name of the lady, though I think he has been calling her Elly, or something like that. Would you like to be meeting them, now?"

"Sure. I was reading in a book about this selective breeding, but I don't understand it so good, and maybe he could tell me something about it."

Mr. Cohan made his way to the end of the bar and led ponderously toward the table. "Pleased to meet you, Professor Thott," said Witherwax.

"Sir, the pleasure is all mine, all mine. Mrs. Jonas, may I present an old friend of mine, yclept Witherwax? Old in the sense that he is aged in the admirable liquids produced by Gavagan's, while the liquids themselves are aged in wood, ha—ha—a third-premise aging. Sit down, Mr. Witherwax. I call your attention to the remarkable qualities of alcohol, among which *peripateia* is not the least."

"Yeah, that's right," said Mr. Witherwax, his expression taking on a resemblance to that of the stuffed owl over the bar. "What I was going to ask—"

"Sir, I perceive that I have employed a pedantry more suitable to the classroom, with the result that communication has not been established. *Peripateia* is the reversal of roles. While in a state of saintly sobriety, I pursue Mrs. Jonas; I entice her to alcoholic diversions. But after the third Presidente, she pursues me, in accordance with the ancient biological rule that alcohol increases feminine desire while decreasing masculine potency."

Mr. Cohan from the bar appeared to have caught only a part of this speech. "Rolls we ain't got," he said, "but you can have some pretzel sticks." He reached under the bar for the bowl. "All gone; and I just laid out a new box this morning. That's where Gavagan's profits go."

"What I was going to ask—" said Witherwax.

Professor Thott stood up and bowed, a bow which ended in his sitting down again rather suddenly. "Ah, the mystery of the universe and music of the spheres, as Prospero might have phrased it! Who pursues? Who flies? The wicked. One preserves philosophy by remaining at the Platonian mean, the knife-edge between pursuit and flight, wickedness and virtue. Mr. Cohan, a round of Presidentes please, including one for my aged friend."

"Let me buy this one," said Witherwax firmly. "What I was going to ask was about this selective breeding."

The professor shook himself, blinked twice, leaned back in his chair and placed one hand on the table. "You wish me to be academic? Very well; but I have witnesses that it was at your own request."

Mrs. Jonas said: "Now look what you've done. You've got him started and he won't run down until he falls asleep."

"What I want to know—". began Witherwax, but Thott beamingly cut across: "I shall present only the briefest and most nontechnical of outlines," he said. "Let us suppose that of sixteen mice you took the two largest and bred them together. Their children would in turn be mated with those of the largest pair from another group of sixteen. And so one. Given time and material enough, and making it advantageous to the species to produce larger members, it would be easy to produce mice the size of lions."

"Ugh!" said Mrs. Jonas. "You ought to give up drinking. Your imagination gets gruesome."

"I see," said Witherwax, "like in a book I read once where they had rats so big they ate horses and wasps the size of dogs."

"I recall the volume," said Thott, sipping his Presidente. "It was *The Food of the Gods,* by H. G. Wells. I fear, however, that the method he describes was not that of genetics, and therefore had no scientific validity."

"But could you make things like that by selective breeding?" asked Witherwax.

"Certainly. You could produce house-flies the size of tigers."

Mrs. Jonas raised a hand. "Alvin, what an awful thought. I hope you don't ever try it."

"There need be no cause for apprehension, my dear. The square-cube law will forever protect us from such a visitation."

"Huh?" said Witherwax.

"The square-cube law. If you double the dimensions, you quadruple the area and octuple the masses. The result is—well, in a practical nontechnical sense, a tiger-sized house-fly would have legs too thin and wings too small to support his weight."

Mrs. Jonas said: "Alvin, that's impractical. How could it move?"

The Professor essayed another bow, which was even less successful than the first, since it was made from a sitting position. "Madame, the purpose of such an experiment would not be practical but demonstrative. A tiger-sized fly would be a mass of jelly that would have to be fed from a spoon." He raised a hand. "There is no reason why anyone should produce such a monster, and since nature has no advantages to offer insects of large size, it will decline to produce them. I agree that the thought is repulsive; myself, I would prefer the alternative project of producing elephants the size of flies."

Witherwax beckoned to Mr. Cohan. "These are good. Do it again. But wouldn't your square-cube law get you in Dutch there, too?"

"By no means, sir. In the case of size-reduction, it works in your favor. The mass is divided by eight, but the muscles remain proportionately the same, capable of supporting a vastly greater weight. The legs and wings of a tiny elephant would not only support him, but give him the agility of a humming-bird. Consider the dwarf elephants of Sicily during the Plish—"

"Alvin," said Mrs. Jonas, "you're drunk. Otherwise you'd remember how to pronounce Pleistocene, and you wouldn't be talking about elephants' wings."

"Not at all, my dear. I should confidently expect such a species to develop flight by means of enlarged ears, like the Dumbo of the movies."

Mrs. Jonas giggled. "Still, I wouldn't want one the size of a house fly. It would be too small for a pet and would get into things. Let's make it the size of a kitten, like this." She held out her index fingers about five inches apart.

"Very well, my dear," said the Professor. "As soon as I can obtain a grant from the Carnegie Foundation the project will be under taken."

"Yes, but," said Witherwax, "how would you feed an elephant like that? And could they be house-broken?"

"If you can house-break a man, an elephant ought to be easy," said Mrs. Jonas. "And you could feed them oats or hay. Much cleaner than keeping cans of dog-food around."

The Professor rubbed his chin. "Hmmm," he said. "The rate of absorption of nourishment would vary directly as the intestinal area—which would vary as the square of the dimensions—I'm not sure of the results, but I'm afraid we'd have to provide more concentrated and less conventional food. I presume that we could feed our *Elephas pollostei*, as I propose to call him, on lump sugar. No, not *Elephas pollostei, Elephas pollostratos,* the 'utmost littlest, tiniest elephant.' "

Mr. Cohan who had been neglecting his only other customer to lean on the bar in their direction, spoke up: "Mr. Considine, that's the salesman, was telling me that the most concentrated food you can get is good malt whiskey."

"That's it!" The Professor slapped the table. "Not *Elephas pollostratos* but *Elephas frumenti,* the whiskey elephant, from what he lives on. We'll breed them for a diet of alcohol. High energy content."

"Oh, but that won't do," protested Mrs. Jonas. "Nobody would want a house pet that had to be fed on whiskey all the time. Especially with children around."

Said Witherwax: "Look, if you really want these animals, why don't you keep them some place where children aren't around and whiskey is—bars, for instance."

"Profound observation," said Professor Thott. "And speaking of rounds, Mr. Cohan, let us have another. We have horses as outdoor pets, cats as house pets, canaries as cage pets. Why not an animal especially designed and developed to be a bar pet. Speaking of which—that stuffed owl you keep for a pet, Mr. Cohan, is getting decidedly mangy."

"They would steal things like that," said Mrs. Jonas dreamily. "They would take things like owls' feathers and pretzel sticks and beer mats to build their nests with, up in the dark corners somewhere near the ceiling."

The Professor bent a benignant gaze on her as Mr. Cohan set out the drinks. "My dear," he said, "either this discussion of the future *Elephas frumenti* or the actual *spiritus frumenti* is going to your head. When you become poetical—"

The brass-blonde had leaned back and was looking upward. "I'm not poetical. That thing right up there on top of the pillar is the nest of one of your bar-elephants."

"What thing up where?" said Thott.

"That thing up there, where it's so dark."

"I don't see nothing," said Mr. Cohan, "and if you don't mind saying so, this is a clean bar, not a rat in the place."

"They wouldn't be quite tame, ever," said Mrs. Jonas, still looking upward, "and if they didn't feel they were fed enough, they'd come and take for themselves when the bartender wasn't looking.''

"That does look funny," said Thott, pushing his chair back and beginning to climb on it.

"Don't Alvin," said Mrs. Jonas. "You'll break your neck."

"Stand by me, then, and let me put my hand on your shoulder."

"Hi!" said Witherwax, suddenly. "Who drank my drink?"

Mrs. Jonas lowered her eyes. "Didn't you?"

"I didn't even touch it. Mr. Cohan just put it down, didn't you?"

"I did that. But that would be a couple of minutes back, and maybe you could—"

"I could not. I definitely, positively did not drink—hey, you people, look at the table!"

"If I had my other glasses . . ." said Thott, swaying somewhat uncertainly as he peered upward into the shadows.

"Look at the table," repeated Witherwax, pointing.

The glass that had held his drink was empty. Thott's still held about half a cocktail. Mrs. Jonas' glass lay on its side, and from its lip about a thimbleful of Presidente cocktail had flowed pinkly into an irregular patch the size of a child's hand.

As the other two followed Witherwax's finger, they saw that from this patch a line of little liquid footprints led across the table to the far edge, where they ceased suddenly. They were circular, each about the size of a dime, with a small scalloped front edge, as if made by . . .

Henderson-Editors Correspondence

3 December 1950

Dear Miss Henderson:

We were deeply impressed with your story, COME ON WAGON! It's fine fantasy, written in a neat terse style that we like a lot.

However, we don't think you have fully developed your situation. We'd like to offer the following suggestions for revision, with the hope you'll see fit to work on them and let us see what happens. If you can do a satisfactory rewrite, we'll want the story.

There should be one more episode illustrating Thaddeus' curious powers. It would be effective, I think, if this were written to the narrator, while he's in the hospital, by his Dad. It should be written so that Dad is not fully aware of just what Thaddeus can do, or just how strange is the happening he relates, but the narrator *is*.

Then, leave the story as is until the tractor accident occurs, right up to the advent of Thaddeus. *But,* in your rewrite, have Thad refuse to help.

That makes for a stronger situation, stresses the gulf between children and adults, ends your story on a horrible question. Make sure that the reader understands that Thaddeus won't help because he can't.

Hoping to see a rewrite on this.

Sincerely,

J. Francis McComas

9 February 1951

Dear Mrs. Henderson:

Please forgive the extremely long silence on COME ON, WAGON—a complex matter of editorial illnesses and absences.

The rewrite's a very attractive job, which we certainly want to use.

Has good luck been befalling you in the meanwhile, or is this your first sale? Purely selfishly, we hope that all your other stories have not sold (but will immediately *after* this); we like the smug satisfaction of being able to claim, years later, "Look, we discovered her."

Cordially,

Anthony Boucher

6 October 1952

Dear Miss Henderson:

And still the raves on ARARAT keep rolling in!

I'd like very much to felicitate you on making Martha Foley's Role of Honor with COME ON, WAGON! While Foley stresses snob appeal, yet it is obvious that she knows a good story when she sees one.

Sincerely,

J. Francis McComas

Zenna Henderson teaches the first grade in Phoenix, and has been writing ever since she herself was in the third grade. She has published occasional poetry and one juvenile book, but no previous adult fiction (though she started her first novel in the seventh grade). We're very happy to present her first published short story here and to assure you that there'll be more in later issues of F&SF. (It's gratifying to see how many of our "first" writers repeat, and admirably.) As fathers ourselves, we have never been quite sure how primary grade teachers maintain their sanity; but Mrs. Henderson has found one way of survival: to use her intimate knowledge of children in fictional studies of the terrible gap between child and man.

Anthony Boucher
J. F. McComas

Come On, Wagon!
By Zenna Henderson

I don't like kids—never have. They're too uncanny. For one thing, there's no bottom to their eyes. They haven't learned to pull down their mental curtains the way adults have. For another thing, there's so much they don't know. And not knowing things makes them know lots of other things grown-ups can't know. That sounds confusing and it is. But look at it this way. Every time you teach a kid something, you teach him a hundred things that are impossible because that one thing is so. By the time we grow up, our world is so hedged around by impossibilities that it's a wonder we ever try anything new.

Anyway, I don't like kids, so I guess it's just as well that I've stayed a bachelor.

Now take Thaddeus. I don't like Thaddeus. Oh, he's a fine kid, smarter than most—he's my nephew—but he's too young. I'll start liking him one of these days when he's ten or eleven.

No, that's still too young. I guess when his voice starts cracking and he begins to slick his hair down, I'll get to liking him fine. Adolescence ends lots more than it begins.

The first time I ever really got acquainted with Thaddeus was the Christmas he was three. He was a solemn little fellow, hardly a smile out of him all day, even with the avalanche of everything to thrill a kid. Starting first thing Christmas Day, he made me feel uneasy. He stood still in the middle of the excited squealing bunch of kids that crowded around the Christmas tree in the front room at the folks' place. He was holding a big rubber ball with both hands and looking at the tree with his eyes wide with wonder. I was sitting right by him in the big chair and I said, "How do you like it, Thaddeus?"

He turned his big solemn eyes to me and, for a long time, all I could see was the deep, deep reflections in his eyes of the glitter and glory of the tree and a special shiningness that originated far back in his own eyes. Then he blinked slowly and said solemnly, "Fine."

Then the mob of kids swept him away as they all charged forward to claim their Grampa-gift from under the tree. When the crowd finally dissolved and scattered all over the place with their play-toys, there was Thaddeus squatting solemnly by the little red wagon that had fallen to him. He was examining it intently, inch by inch, but only with his eyes. His hands were pressed between his knees and his chest as he squatted.

"Well, Thaddeus," his mother's voice was a little provoked. "Go play with your wagon. Don't you like it?"

Thaddeus turned his face up to her in that blind, unseeing way little children have.

"Sure," he said and, standing up, tried to take the wagon in his arms.

"Oh for pity sakes," his mother laughed. "You don't carry a wagon, Thaddeus." And aside to us, "Sometimes I wonder. Do you suppose he's got all his buttons?"

"Now, Jean," our brother Clyde leaned back in his chair. "Don't heckle the kid. Go on, Thaddeus. Take the wagon outside."

So what does Thaddeus do but start for the door, saying over his shoulder, "Come on, Wagon."

Clyde laughed. "It's not that easy, Punkin-Yaller, you've gotta have pull to get along in this world."

So Jean showed Thaddeus how and he pulled the wagon

outdoors, looking down at the handle in a puzzled way, absorbing this latest rule for acting like a big boy.

"Honest. You'd think he never saw a wagon before."

"He never did," I said idly. "Not his own, anyway." And had the feeling that I had said something profound, but wasn't quite sure what.

The whole deal would have gone completely out of my mind if it hadn't been for one more little incident. I was out by the barn waiting for Dad. Mom was making him change his pants before he demonstrated his new tractor for me. I saw Thaddeus loading rocks into his little red wagon. Beyond the rock pile, I could see that he had started a play house or ranch of some kind, laying the rocks out to make rooms or corrals or whatever. He finished loading the wagon and picked up another rock that took both arms to carry, then he looked down at the wagon.

"Come on, Wagon." And he walked over to his play-place.

And the wagon went with him, trundling along over the uneven ground, following at his heels like a puppy.

I blinked and inventoried rapidly the Christmas Cheer I had imbibed. It wasn't enough for an explanation. I felt a kind of cold grue creep over me.

Then Thaddeus emptied the wagon and the two of them went back for more rocks. He was just going to pull the same thing again when a big boy-cousin came by and laughed at him.

"Hey, Thaddeus, how you going to pull your wagon with both hands full? It won't go unless you pull it."

"Oh," said Thaddeus and looked off after the cousin who was headed for the back porch and some pie.

So Thaddeus dropped the big rock he had in his arms and looked at the wagon. After struggling with some profound thinking, he picked the rock up again and hooked a little finger over the handle of the wagon.

"Come on, Wagon," he said, and they trundled off together, the handle of the wagon still slanting back over the load while Thaddeus grunted along by it with his heavy arm-load.

I was glad Dad came just then, hooking the last strap of his striped overalls. We started into the barn together. I looked back at Thaddeus. He apparently figured he'd need his little finger on the next load, so he was squatting by the wagon, absorbed with a piece of flimsy red Christmas string. He had twisted one end around his wrist and was intent on tying the other to the handle of the little red wagon.

It wasn't so much that I avoided Thaddeus after that. It isn't hard for grown-ups to keep from mingling with kids. After all, they do live in two different worlds. Anyway, I didn't have much to do with Thaddeus for several years after that Christmas. There was the matter of a side trip to the South Pacific where even I learned that there are some grown-up impossibilities that are not always absolute. Then there was a hitch in the hospital where I waited for my legs to put themselves together again. I was luckier than most of the guys. The folks wrote often and regularly and kept me posted on all the home talk. Nothing spectacular, nothing special, just the old familiar stuff that makes home, home and folks, folks.

I hadn't thought of Thaddeus in a long time. I hadn't been around kids much and unless you deal with them, you soon forget them. But I remembered him plenty when I got the letter from Dad about Jean's new baby. The kid was a couple of weeks overdue and when it did come—a girl—Jean's husband, Bert, was out at the farm checking with Dad on a land deal he had cooking. The baby came so quickly that Jean couldn't even make it to the hospital and when Mom called Bert, he and Dad headed for town together, but fast.

"Derned if I didn't have to hold me hair on," wrote Dad, "I don't think we hit the ground but twice all the way to town. Dern near over-shot the gate when we finally tore up the hill to their house. Thaddeus was playing out front and we dang near ran him down. Smashed his trike to flinders. I saw the handle bars sticking out from under the front wheel when I followed Bert in. Then I got to thinking that he'd get a flat parking on all that metal so I went out to move the car. Lucky I did. Bert musta forgot to set the brakes. Derned if that car wasn't headed straight for Thaddeus. He was walking right in front of it. Even had his hand on the bumper and the dern thing rolling right after him. I yelled and hit out for the car. But by the time I got there, it had stopped and Thaddeus was squatting by his wrecked trike. What do you suppose the little cuss said? 'Old car broke my trike. I made him get off.'

"Can you beat it? Kids get the dernedest ideas. Lucky it wasn't much downhill, though. He'd have been hurt sure."

I lay with the letter on my chest and felt cold. Dad had forgotten that they "tore up the hill" and that the car must have rolled up the slope to get off Thaddeus' trike.

That night I woke up the ward yelling, "Come on, Wagon!"

*   *   *

It was some months later when I saw Thaddeus again. He and a half a dozen other nephews—and the one persistent niece—were in a tearing hurry to be somewhere else and nearly mobbed Dad and me on the front porch as they boiled out of the house with mouths and hands full of cookies. They all stopped long enough to give me the once-over and fire a machine gun volley with my crutches, then they disappeared down the lane on their bikes, heads low, rear-ends high, and every one of them being bombers at the tops of their voices.

I just had time enough to notice that Thaddeus had lanked out and was just one of the kids as he grinned engagingly at me with the two-tooth gap in his front teeth.

"Did you ever notice anything odd about Thaddeus?" I pulled out the makin's.

"Thaddeus?" Dad glanced up at me from firing up his battered old corn-cob pipe. "Not particularly. Why?"

"Oh, nothing." I ran my tongue along the paper and rolled the cigarette shut. "He just always seemed kinda different."

"Well, he's always been kinda slow about some things. Not that he's dumb. Once he catches on, he's as smart as anyone, but he's sure pulled some funny ones."

"Give me a fer-instance," I said, wondering if he'd remember the trike deal.

"Well, coupla years ago at a wienie roast he was toting something around wrapped in a paper napkin. Jean saw him put it in his pocket and she thought it was probably a dead frog or a beetle or something like that, so she made him fork it over. She unfolded the napkin and derned if there wasn't a big live coal in it. Dern thing flamed right up in her hand. Thaddeus bellered like a bull calf. Said he wanted to take it home cause it was pretty. How he ever carried it around that long without setting himself afire is what got me."

"That's Thaddeus," I said: "odd."

"Yeah." Dad was firing his pipe again, flicking the burned match down, to join the dozen or so others by the porch railing. "I guess you might call him odd. But he'll outgrow it. He hasn't pulled anything like that in a long time."

"They do outgrow it," I said. "Thank God." And I think it was a real prayer. I *don't* like kids. "By the way, where's Clyde?"

"Down in the East Pasture, plowing. Say, that tractor I got

that last Christmas you were here is a bear-cat. It's lasted me all this time and I've never had to do a lick of work on it. Clyde's using it today.''

"When you get a good tractor you got a good one," I said. "Guess I'll go down and see the old son-of-a-gun—Clyde, I mean. Haven't seen him in a coon's age." I gathered up my crutches.

Dad scrambled to his feet. "Better let me run you down in the pick-up. I've gotta go over to Jesperson's anyway."

"O.K.," I said. "Won't be long till I can throw these things away." So we piled in the pick-up and headed for the East Pasture.

We were ambushed at the pump corner by the kids and were killed variously by P-38's, atomic bombs, ack-ack and the Lone Ranger's six-guns. Then we lowered our hands which had been raised all this time and Dad reached out and collared the nearest nephew.

"Come along, Punkin-Yaller. That blasted Holstein has busted out again. You get her out of the alfalfa and see if you can find where she got through this time."

"Aw, gee whiz!" The kid—and of course it was Thaddeus—climbed into the back of the pick-up. "That dern cow."

We started up with a jerk and I turned half around in the seat to look back at Thaddeus.

"Remember your little red wagon?" I yelled over the clatter.

"Red wagon?" Thaddeus yelled back. His face lighted. "Red wagon?"

I could tell he had remembered and then, as plainly as the drawing of a shade, his eyes went shadowy and he yelled, "Yeah, kinda." And turned around to wave violently at the unnoticing kids behind us.

So, I thought, he is outgrowing it. Then spent the rest of the short drive trying to figure just what it was he was outgrowing.

Dad dumped Thaddeus out at the alfalfa field and took me on across the canal and let me out by the pasture gate.

"I'll be back in about an hour if you want to wait. Might as well ride home."

"I might start back afoot," I said. "It'd feel good to stretch my legs again."

"I'll keep a look out for you on my way back." And he rattled away in the ever-present cloud of dust.

I had trouble managing the gate. It's one of those wire affairs that open by slipping a loop off the end post and lifting the bottom of it out of another loop. This one was taut and hard to handle. I just got it opened when Clyde turned the far corner and started back toward me, the plow behind the tractor curling up red-brown ribbons in its wake. It was the last go-round to complete the field.

I yelled "Hi!" and waved a crutch at him.

He yelled "Hi!" back at me. What came next was too fast and too far away for me to be sure what actually happened. All I remember was a snort and roar and the tractor bucked and bowed. There was a short yell from Clyde and the shriek of wires pulling loose from a fence post followed by a choking smothering silence.

Next thing I knew, I was panting half-way to the tractor, my crutches sinking exasperatingly into the soft ploughed earth. A nightmare year later I knelt by the stalled tractor and called, "Hey, Clyde!"

Clyde looked up at me, a half grin, half grimace on his muddy face.

"Hi. Get this thing off me, will you. I need that leg." Then his eyes turned up white and he passed out.

The tractor had toppled him from the seat and then run over top of him, turning into the fence and coming to rest with one huge wheel half burying his leg in the soft dirt and pinning him against a fence post. The far wheel was on the edge of the irrigation ditch that bordered the field just beyond the fence. The huge bulk of the machine was balanced on the raw edge of nothing and it looked like a breath would send it over—then God have mercy on Clyde. It didn't help much to notice that the red-brown dirt was steadily becoming redder around the imprisoned leg.

I knelt there, paralyzed with panic. There was nothing I could do. I didn't dare try to start the tractor. If I touched it, it might go over. Dad was gone for an hour. I couldn't make it by foot to the house in time.

Then all at once out of nowhere I heart a startled "Gee whiz!" and there was Thaddeus standing goggle-eyed on the ditch bank.

Something exploded with a flash of light inside my head and I whispered to myself, *Now take it easy. Don't scare the kid, don't startle him.*

"Gee whiz!" said Thaddeus again. "What happened?"

I took a deep breath. "Old Tractor ran over Uncle Clyde. Make it get off."

Thaddeus didn't seem to hear me. He was intent on taking in the whole shebang.

"Thaddeus," I said, "make Tractor get off."

Thaddeus looked at me with that blind, unseeing stare he used to have. I prayed silently, *Don't let him be too old. Oh God, don't let him be too old.* And Thaddeus jumped across the ditch. He climbed gingerly through the barbwire fence and squatted down by the tractor, his hands caught between his chest and knees. He bent his head forward and I stared urgently at the soft vulnerable nap of his neck. Then he turned his blind eyes to me again.

"Tractor doesn't want to."

I felt a yell ball up in my throat, but I caught it in time. *Don't scare the kid,* I thought. *Don't scare him.*

"Make Tractor get off anyway," I said as matter-of-factly as I could manage. "He's hurting Uncle Clyde."

Thaddeus turned and looked at Clyde.

"He isn't hollering."

"He can't. He's unconscious." Sweat was making my palms slippery.

"Oh." Thaddeus examined Clyde's quiet face curiously. "I never saw anybody unconscious before."

"Thaddeus." My voice was sharp. "Make—Tractor—get—off."

Maybe I talked too loud. Maybe I used the wrong words, but Thaddeus looked up at me and I saw the shutters close in his eyes. They looked up at me, blue and shallow and bright.

"You mean start the tractor?" His voice was brisk as he stood up. "Gee whiz! Grampa told us kids to leave the tractor alone. It's dangerous for kids. I don't know whether I know how—"

"That's not what I meant," I snapped, my voice whetted on the edge of my despair. "Make it get off Uncle Clyde. He's dying."

"But I can't! You can't just make a tractor do something. You gotta run it." His face was twisting with approaching tears.

"You could if you wanted to," I argued, knowing how useless it was. "Uncle Clyde will die if you don't."

"But I can't! I don't know how! Honest I don't." Thaddeus scrubbed one bare foot in the ploughed dirt, sniffing miserably.

I knelt beside Clyde and slipped my hand inside his dirt-smeared shirt. I pulled my hand out and rubbed the stained palm against my thigh. "Never mind," I said bluntly, "it doesn't matter now. He's dead."

Thaddeus started to bawl, not from grief but bewilderment. He knew I was put out with him and he didn't know why. He crooked his arm over his eyes and leaned against a fence post, sobbing noisily. I shifted myself over in the dark furrow until my shadow sheltered Clyde's quiet face from the hot afternoon sun. I clasped my hands palm to palm between my knees and waited for Dad.

I knew as well as anything that that *once* Thaddeus could have helped. Why couldn't he then, when the need was so urgent? Well, maybe he really *had* outgrown his strangeness. Or it might be that he actually couldn't do anything just because Clyde and I were grown-ups. Maybe if it had been another kid—

Sometimes my mind gets cold trying to figure it out. Especially when I get the answer that kids and grown-ups live in two worlds so alien and separate that the gap can't be bridged even to save a life. Whatever the answer is—I still don't like kids.

Bester-Editors Correspondence

22 March 1950

Dear Boucher:

I haven't bothered to enclose a return envelope because I slanted this one* for "Fantasy and SF" specifically and if you guys don't like it, to hell with it. Just toss it in the nearest waste-basket.

> Best of luck with your swell magazine
>
> *Alfred Bester*

12 April 1950

Dear Mr. Bester:

One of the nicer things about grinding out this magazine is that I occasionally meet, if only by correspondence, some of my pet authors from ADVENTURES IN TIME & SPACE. Needless to say, both Boucher and I were delighted to hear from you.

The story's coming back with the hope that you'll do some suggested revision. While we can't give you a definite promise until we see the rewrite, we aren't worried about your ability to do the job.

We think you've missed your real point (a fine one, by the way) in not differentiating between tomorrow's (or 1990's) newspaper—which is the routine gimmick—and 1990's *almanac*. Show how *broad* knowledge from an almanac would be. Boyne's argument would be, of course, that gaining the wealth possible would eventually lose all zest from the foreknowledge.

*"Of Time and Third Avenue" originally titled "Don't Look Now"

The foregoing should indicate how much broader in scope are the potentialities of a future almanac.

Think you have reversed the comprehension ability of your characters. Boyne should *always* know what Knight and Clinton are saying; *they* shouldn't always understand *him*. If you or I went back to 1910, we'd understand them completely, but a considerable part of our vocabulary would be so much gibberish to them. I'd suggest that his talk be quite 1950 until he loses himself in the passion of his arguments; then he may at times be incomprehensible—but quickly recovers.

The end is a little incongruous. Don't believe Boyne would have made the trip from 1950 without proper money.

I hope all this makes sense to you and that we'll see the story soon.

Kindest regards,

J. Francis McComas
Co-editor

18 April 1950

Dear Mr. McComas:

Perhaps the only nice thing about being a writer is the occasional word of praise you get from a fellow pro. Thank you. Thank you. Thank you.

Re: Your suggestions on "Don't Look Now"* I agree with them and I'll do them. However I do think that the point of the story is not so much the broader applications of an almanac, as opposed to a newspaper which, after all, is only a difference of degree . . . as it is the fact that it's no fun winning at solitaire if you cheat. But I'll plug your point as well, and if the rewrite is satisfactory we'll see which of the two strikes home with the readers.

Sincerely

Alfred Bester

I don't know the occasion or exact date. I like the anecdote.

*Later titled "Of Time and Third Avenue"

Dear Mick:

It was nice meeting Mr. B.* at last, but we didn't get much chance to talk. That is, Tony didn't. I quonked to the assembled multitude, frequently turning to Tony for a reply. No reply. Finally I gave him a long pause. He opened his mouth. I hung breathless. He said: "There is no doubt that you are the loudest talker I've ever met."

In consequence I am marking his vote as doubtful.

Yours for the Vegetarian Party

Alfie

*Tony Boucher

6 April 1950

Dear Alford:

That bulwark of American letters, Shasta Pubs, sent me a copy of THE DEMOLISHED MAN (To the wrong address, of course!) I was deeply flattered at the author's inscription; if I may coin one of my more brilliant phrases, that is one volume I shall *cherish*! Thank you!

Since I am at p. 109 I won't pass along any comment yet—save to say I wistfully hope the *Times* sends it to me for review. It has been so long since I've done an unqualified rave for them.

Yrs. etc.

Mick

Alfred Bester has written regrettably little science fiction in recent years; radio is (one of your editors speaks from the heart) as much more profitable as it is less enjoyable. But those who remember such Bester classics as Adam and No Eve *(possibly the most ingenuous solution ever offered to the last-man-on-earth gambit) will be happy to learn that he still retains his skill at giving a fresh twist to familiar problems. Here he treats the always fascinating paradox of the power bestowed by possession of, in the simplest form, tomorrow's newspaper. A World Almanac for 1990 is an even more provocative object; and in the course of unraveling its implications, Bester shows that there are facets of Third Avenue which even John McNulty doesn't know.*

Anthony Boucher
J. F. McComas

Of Time and Third Avenue
By Alfred Bester

What Macy hated about the man was the fact that he squeaked. Macy didn't know if it was the shoes, but he suspected the clothes. In the backroom of his Tavern, under the poster that asked: WHO FEARS MENTION THE BATTLE OF THE BOYNE? Macy inspected the stranger. He was tall, slender, and very dainty. Although he was young, he was almost bald. There was fuzz on top of his head and over his eyebrows. When he reached into his jacket for a wallet, Macy made up his mind. It was the clothes that squeaked.

"MQ, Mr. Macy," the stranger said in a staccato voice. "Very good. For rental of this backroom including exclusive utility for one chronos—"

"One whatos?" Macy asked nervously.

"Chronos. The incorrect word? Oh yes. Excuse me. One hour."

"You're a foreigner," Macy said. "What's your name? I bet it's Russian."

"No. Not foreign," the stranger answered. His frightening eyes whipped around the backroom. "Identify me as Boyne."

"Boyne!" Macy echoed incredulously.

"MQ Boyne." Mr. Boyne opened a wallet like an accordion, ran his fingers through various colored papers and coins, then withdrew a hundred-dollar bill. He jabbed it at Macy and said: "Rental fee for one hour. As agreed. One hundred dollars. Take it and go."

Impelled by the thrust of Boyne's eyes, Macy took the bill and staggered out to the bar. Over his shoulder he quavered: "What'll you drink?"

"Drink? Alcohol? Never!" Boyne answered.

He turned and darted to the telephone booth, reached under the pay-phone and located the lead-in wire. From a side pocket he withdrew a small glittering box and clipped it to the wire. He tucked it out of sight, then lifted the receiver.

"Co-ordinates West 73–58–15," he said rapidly, "North 40–45–20. Disband sigma. You're ghosting . . ." After a pause he continued: "Stet. Stet! Transmission clear. I want a fix on Knight. Oliver Wilson Knight. Probability to four significant figures. You have the co-ordinates. . . . 99.9807? MQ. Stand by. . . ."

Boyne poked his head out of the booth and peered toward the Tavern door. He waited with steely concentration until a young man and a pretty girl entered. Then he ducked back to the phone. "Probability fulfilled. Oliver Wilson Knight in contact. MQ. Luck my Para." He hung up and was sitting under the poster as the couple wandered toward the backroom.

The young man was about twenty-six, of medium height and inclined to be stocky. His suit was rumpled, his seal-brown hair was rumpled, and his friendly face was crinkled by good-natured creases. The girl had black hair, soft blue eyes, and a small private smile. They walked arm in arm and liked to collide gently when they thought no one was looking. At this moment they collided with Mr. Macy.

"I'm sorry, Mr. Knight," Macy said. "You and the young lady can't sit back there this afternoon. The premises have been rented."

Their faces fell. Boyne called: "Quite all right, Mr. Macy. All correct. Happy to entertain Mr. Knight and friend as guests."

Knight and the girl turned to Boyne uncertainly. Boyne smiled and patted the chair alongside him. "Sit down," he said. "Charmed, I assure you."

The girl said: "We hate to intrude, but this is the only place in town where you can get genuine stone gingerbeer."

"Already aware of the fact, Miss Clinton." To Macy he said: "Bring gingerbeer and go. No other guests. These are all I'm expecting."

Knight and the girl stared at Boyne in astonishment as they sat down slowly. Knight placed a wrapped parcel of books on the table. The girl took a breath and said: "You know me . . . Mr. . . . ?"

"Boyne. As in Boyne, Battle of. Yes, of course. You are Miss Jane Clinton. This is Mr. Oliver Wilson Knight. I rented premises particularly to meet you this afternoon."

"This supposed to be a gag?" Knight asked, a dull flush appearing on his cheeks.

"Gingerbeer," answered Boyne gallantly as Macy arrived, deposited bottles and glasses, and departed in haste.

"You couldn't know we were coming here," Jane said. "We didn't know ourselves . . . until a few minutes ago."

"Sorry to contradict, Miss Clinton," Boyne smiled. "The probability of your arrival at Longitude 73–58–15 Latitude 40–45–20 was 99.9807 percent. No one can escape four significant figures."

"Listen," Knight began angrily, "if this is your idea of—"

"Kindly drink gingerbeer and listen to my idea, Mr. Knight." Boyne leaned across the table with galvanic intensity. "This hour has been arranged with difficulty and much cost. To whom? No matter. You have placed us in an extremely dangerous position. I have been sent to find a solution."

"Solution for what?" Knight asked.

Jane tried to rise. "I . . . I think we'd b-better be go—"

Boyne waved her back, and she sat down like a child. To Knight he said: "This noon you entered premises of J. D. Craig & Co., dealer in printed books. You purchased, through transfer of money, four books. Three do not matter, but the fourth . . ." He tapped the wrapped parcel emphatically. "That is the crux of this encounter."

"What the hell are you talking about?" Knight exclaimed.

"One bound volume consisting of collected facts and statistics."

"The Almanac?"

"The Almanac."

"What about it?"

"You intended to purchase a 1950 Almanac."

"I bought the '50 Almanac."

"You did not!" Boyne blazed. "You bought the Almanac for 1990."

"What?"

"The World Almanac for 1990," Boyne said clearly, "is in this package. Do not ask how. There was a mistake that has already been disciplined. Now the error must be adjusted. That is why I am here. It is why this meeting was arranged. You cognate?"

Knight burst into laughter and reached for the parcel. Boyne leaned across the table and grasped his wrist. "You must not open it, Mr. Knight."

"All right." Knight leaned back in his chair. He grinned at Jane and sipped gingerbeer. "What's the pay-off on the gag?"

"I must have the book, Mr. Knight. I would like to walk out of this Tavern with the Almanac under my arm."

"You would, eh?"

"I would."

"The 1990 Almanac?"

"Yes."

"If," said Knight, "there was such a thing as a 1990 Almanac, and if it was in that package, wild horses couldn't get it away from me."

"Why, Mr. Knight?"

"Don't be an idiot. A look into the future? Stock market reports . . . Horse races . . . Politics. It'd be money from home. I'd be rich."

"Indeed yes." Boyne nodded sharply. "More than rich. Omnipotent. The small mind would use the Almanac from the future for small things only. Wagers on the outcome of games and elections. And so on. But the intellect of dimensions . . . *your* intellect . . . would not stop there."

"You tell me," Knight grinned.

"Deduction. Induction. Inference." Boyne ticked the points off on his fingers. "Each fact would tell you an entire history. Real estate investment, for example. What lands to buy and sell. Population shifts and census reports would tell you. Transportation. Lists of marine disasters and railroad wrecks would tell you whether rocket travel has replaced the train and ship."

"Has it?" Knight chuckled.

"Flight records would tell you which company's stock should be bought. Lists of postal receipts would tell you which are the cities of the future. The Nobel Prize winners would tell you which factories and industries to control. Cost of living reports would tell you how best to protect your wealth against inflation or deflation. Foreign exchange rates, stock exchange reports, bank suspensions and life insurance indexes would provide the clues to protect you against any and all disasters."

"That's the idea," Knight said. "That's for me."

"You really think so?"

"I know so. Money in my pocket. The world in my pocket."

"Excuse me," Boyne said keenly, "but you are only repeating the dreams of childhood. You want wealth. Yes. But only won through endeavor . . . your own endeavor. There is no joy in success as an unearned gift. There is nothing but guilt and unhappiness. You are aware of this already."

"I disagree," Knight said.

"Do you? Then why do you work? Why not steal? Rob? Burgle? Cheat others of their money to fill your own pockets?"

"But I—" Knight began, and then stopped.

"The point is well taken, eh?" Boyne waved his hand impatiently. "No, Mr. Knight. Seek a mature argument. You are too ambitious and healthy to wish to steal success."

"Then I'd just want to know if I would be successful."

"Ah? Stet. You wish to thumb through the pages looking for your name. You want reassurance. Why? Have you no confidence in yourself? You are a promising young attorney. Yes. I know that. It is part of my data. Has not Miss Clinton confidence in you?"

"Yes," Jane said in a loud voice. "He doesn't need reassurance from a book."

"What else, Mr. Knight?"

Knight hesitated, sobering in the face of Boyne's overwhelming intensity. Then he said: "Security."

"There is no such thing. Life is insecurity. You can only find safety in death."

"You know what I mean," Knight muttered. "The knowledge that life is worth planning. There's the H-Bomb."

Boyne nodded quickly. "True. It is a crisis. But then, I'm here. The world will continue. I am proof."

"If I believe you."

"And if you do not?" Boyne blazed. "You do not want security. You want courage." He nailed the couple with a contemptuous glare. "There is in this country a legend of pioneer forefathers from whom you are supposed to inherit courage in the face of odds. D. Boone, E. Allen, S. Houston, A. Lincoln, G. Washington and others. Fact?"

"I suppose so," Knight muttered. "That's what we keep telling ourselves."

"And where is the courage in you? Pfui! It is only talk. The unknown terrifies you. Danger does not inspire you to fight, as it did D. Crockett; it makes you whine and reach for the reassurance in this book. Fact?"

"But the H-Bomb . . ."

"It is a danger. Yes. One of many. What of that? Do you cheat at Solhand?"

"Solhand?"

"Your pardon." Boyne reconsidered, impatiently snapping his fingers at the interruption to the white heat of his argument. "It is a game played singly against chance relationships in an arrangement of cards. I forget your noun. . . ."

"Oh!" Jane's face brightened. "Solitaire."

"Quite right. Solitaire. Thank you, Miss Clinton." Boyne turned his frightening eyes on Knight. "Do you cheat at Solitaire?"

"Occasionally."

"Do you enjoy games won by cheating?"

"Not as a rule."

"They are thisney, yes? Boring. They are tiresome. Pointless. Null-Co-ordinated. You wish you had won honestly."

"I suppose so."

"And you will suppose so after you have looked at this bound book. Through all your pointless life you will wish you had played honestly the games of life. You will verdash that look. You will regret. You will totally recall the pronouncement of our great poet-philosopher Trynbyll who summed it up in one lightning, skazon line. 'The Future is Tekon,' said Trynbyll. Mr. Knight, do not cheat. Let me implore you to give me the Almanac."

"Why don't you take it away from me?"

"It must be a gift. We can rob you of nothing. We can give you nothing."

"That's a lie. You paid Macy to rent this backroom."

"Macy was paid, but I gave him nothing. He will think he

was cheated, but you will see to it that he is not. All will be adjusted without dislocation.''

"Wait a minute. . . ."

"It has all been carefully planned. I have gambled on you, Mr. Knight. I am depending on your good sense. Let me have the Almanac. I will disband . . . re-orient . . . and you will never see me again. Vorloss verdash! It will be a bar adventure to narrate for friends. Give me the Almanac!''

"Hold the phone," Knight said. "This is a gag. Remember? I—''

"Is it?" Boyne interrupted. "Is it? Look at me."

For almost a minute the young couple stared at the bleached white face with its deadly eyes. The half smile left Knight's lips, and Jane shuddered involuntarily. There was chill and dismay in the backroom.

"My God!" Knight glanced helplessly at Jane. "This can't be happening. He's got me believing. You?''

Jane nodded jerkily.

"What should we do? If everything he says is true we can refuse and live happily ever after.''

"No," Jane said in a choked voice. "There may be money and success in that book, but there's divorce and death too. Give him the book.''

"Take it," Knight said faintly.

Boyne rose instantly. He picked up the parcel and went into the phone booth. When he came out he had three books in one hand and a smaller parcel made up of the original wrapping in the other. He placed the books on the table and stood for a moment, smiling down.

"My gratitude," he said. "You have eased a precarious situation. It is only fair you should receive something in return. We are forbidden to transfer anything that might divert existing phenomena streams, but at least I can give you one token of the future.''

He backed away, bowed curiously, and said: "My service to you both." Then he turned and started out of the Tavern.

"Hey!" Knight called. "The token?''

"Mr. Macy has it," Boyne answered and was gone.

The couple sat at the table for a few blank moments like sleepers slowly awakening. Then, as reality began to return, they stared at each other and burst into laughter.

"He really had me scared," Jane said.

"Talk about Third Avenue characters. What an act. What'd he get out of it?"

"Well . . . he got your Almanac."

"But it doesn't make sense." Knight began to laugh again. "All that business about paying Macy but not giving him anything. And I'm supposed to see that he isn't cheated. And the mystery token of the future . . ."

The Tavern door burst open and Macy shot through the saloon into the backroom. "Where is he?" Macy shouted. "Where's the thief? Boyne, he calls himself. More likely his name is Dillinger."

"Why, Mr. Macy!" Jane exclaimed. "What's the matter?"

"Where is he?" Macy pounded on the door of the Men's Room. "Come out, ye blaggard!"

"He's gone," Knight said. "He left just before you got back."

"And you, Mr. Knight!" Macy pointed a trembling finger at the young lawyer. "You, to be party to thievery and racketeers. Shame on you!"

"What's wrong?" Knight asked.

"He paid me one hundred dollars to rent this backroom," Macy cried in anguish. "One hundred dollars. I took the bill over to Bernie the pawnbroker, being cautious-like, and he found out it's a forgery. It's a counterfeit."

"Oh no," Jane laughed. "That's too much. Counterfeit?"

"Look at this," Mr. Macy shouted, slamming the bill down on the table.

Knight inspected it closely. Suddenly he turned pale and the laughter drained out of his face. He reached into his inside pocket, withdrew a checkbook and began to write with trembling fingers.

"What on earth are you doing?" Jane asked.

"Making sure that Macy isn't cheated," Knight said. "You'll get your hundred dollars, Mr. Macy."

"Oliver! Are you insane? Throwing away a hundred dollars . . ."

"And I won't be losing anything either," Knight answered. "All will be adjusted without dislocation! They're diabolical. Diabolical!"

"I don't understand."

"Look at the bill," Knight said in a shaky voice. "Look closely."

It was beautifully engraved and genuine in appearance. Benjamin Franklin's benign features gazed up at them mildly and authentically; but in the lower right-hand corner was printed: Series 1980 D. And underneath that was signed: Oliver Wilson Knight, Secretary of the Treasury.

Matheson-Editors Correspondence

7 December 1949

Dear Mr. Matheson:

My coeditor McComas and I both feel that BORN OF MAN is an extraordinarily powerful and effective piece of writing, and we'd like very much to use it, possibly for our 3d issue.

The situation is awkward. We're still on an experimental issue-to-issue basis. #2 will hit the stands in early Jan; we won't know until some time in Feb whether there'll be a 3d (though from reactions on the 1st, we don't have much real doubt).

We do hope that you will let us hold BORN—and that it will be far from the last Matheson story we'll publish.

Sincerely yours,

Anthony Boucher

10 December 1949

Dear Mr. Boucher,

I hope it won't shock you to learn it is the first story I ever sold in my life. I have written for years, of course. I can only suggest that my lack of success, until now, has been due to a very limited effort at marketing my work.

I'm 23. I graduated from the University of Missouri Journalism School in June. Since then I have spent my days writing, working at night for sustenance.

Sincerely yours,

Richard Matheson

21 May 1950

Dear Richard Matheson:

First, without exception, BORN OF MAN AND WO-MAN has been singled out as the #1 story of our current issue. Boucher's and my heartiest congratulations! (You will forgive us for congratulating each other on being such clever editors!) What you can really be pleased about is that you were up against some awfully stiff competition in that issue.

With kindest regards.
Sincerely,

J. Francis McComas

29 January 1951

Dear Tony:

As you suggest, I'll assume momma to be some type of were-creature who does not necessarily change on the outside. I'll work in that ring finger idea. (I never knew of that before.) [in story DRESS OF WHITE SILK]*

As to the dress I'll try and make it clearer what I mean. I had visualized that what was left of momma's powers were in the dress she had once worn during those times she traipsed around digesting the good citizens of the town. The leaves and smell bags were meant to be some sort of abortive power like garlic with the vampire. I'll see if I can bring it out better.

Best,

Dick Matheson

P.S. Just looked at my own hand. Ye gads!

*I suppose it is common knowledge that one identification of a werewolf can be made by establishing that the ring finger is longer than the middle finger of the hand. Personally, I had to check it out with better-versed supernaturalists.

BORN OF MAN AND WOMAN has been anthologized so many times, that it seemed refreshing to use another splendid story by Mr. Matheson this time.

Richard Matheson's first published story, Born of Man and Woman, *is probably, to judge from your letters, the most popular single story we've printed to date—an astonishing record for a short-short by a beginner. Since that classic (about to be reprinted in the Bleiler-Dikty* BEST SCIENCE FICTION STORIES 1951), *Matheson has published many stories here and elsewhere, admirable tales but never quite equaling the sheer originality and shock-impact of his first. Now at last, in* Dress of White Silk, *we think that Dick Matheson has done it again. That's introduction enough.*

Anthony Boucher
J. F. McComas

Dress of White Silk
By Richard Matheson

Quiet is here and all in me.

Granma locked me in my room and wont let me out. Because its happened she says. I guess I was bad. Only it was the dress. Mommas dress I mean. She is gone away forever. Granma says your momma is in heaven. I dont know how. Can she go in heaven if shes dead?

Now I hear granma. She is in mommas room. She is putting mommas dress down the box. Why does she always? And locks it too. I wish she didnt. Its a pretty dress and smells sweet so. And warm. I love to touch it against my cheek. But I cant never again. I guess that is why granma is mad at me.

But I amnt sure. All day it was only like everyday. Mary Jane came over to my house. She lives across the street. Everyday she comes to my house and play. Today she was.

I have seven dolls and a fire truck. Today granma said play with your dolls and it. Dont you go inside your mommas room now she said. She always says it. She just means not mess up I

116

think. Because she says it all the time. Dont go in your mommas room. Like that.

But its nice in mommas room. When it rains I go there. Or when granma is doing her nap I do. I dont make noise. I just sit on the bed and touch the white cover. Like when I was only small. The room smells like sweet.

I make believe momma is dressing and I am allowed in. I smell her white silk dress. Her going out for night dress. She called it that I dont remember when.

I hear it moving if I listen hard. I make believe to see her sitting at the dressing table. Like touching on perfume or something I mean. And see her dark eyes. I can remember.

Its so nice if it rains and I see eyes on the window. The rain sounds like a big giant outside. He says shushshush so every one will be quiet. I like to make believe that in mommas room.

What I like almost best is sit at mommas dressing table. It is like pink and big and smells sweet too. The seat in front has pillow sewed in it. There are bottles and bottles with bumps and have colored perfume in them. And you can see almost your whole self in the mirror.

When I sit there I make believe to be momma. I say be quiet mother I am going out and you can not stop me. It is something I say I dont know why like hear it in me. And oh stop your sobbing mother they will not catch me I have my magic dress.

When I pretend I brush my hair long. But I only use my own brush from my room. I didnt never use mommas brush. I dont think granma is mad at me for that because I never use mommas brush. I wouldnt never.

Sometimes I did open the box up. Because I know where granma puts the key. I saw her once when she wouldn't know I saw her. She puts the key on the hook in mommas closet. Behind the door I mean.

I could open the box lots of times. Thats because I like to look at mommas dress. I like best to look at it. It is so pretty and feels soft and like silky. I could touch it for a million years.

I kneel on the rug with roses on it. I hold the dress in my arms and like breathe from it. I touch it against my cheek. I wish I could take it to sleep with me and hold it. I like to. Now I cant. Because granma says. And she says I should burn it up but I loved her so. And she cries about the dress.

I wasnt never bad with it. I put it back neat like it was never touched. Granma never knew. I laughed that she never knew before. But she knows now I did it I guess. And shell punish me. What did it hurt her? Wasnt it my mommas dress?

What I like the real best in mommas room is look at the picture of momma. It has a gold thing around it. Frame is what granma says. It is on the wall on top the bureau.

Momma is pretty. Your momma was pretty granma says. Why does she? I see momma there smiling on me and she *is* pretty. For always.

Her hair is black. Like mine. Her eyes are even pretty like black. Her mouth is red so red. I like the dress and its the white one. It is all down on her shoulders. Her skin is white almost white like the dress. And so too are her hands. She is so pretty. I love her even if she is gone away forever I love her so much.

I guess I think thats what made me bad. I mean to Mary Jane.

Mary Jane came from lunch like she does. Granma went to do her nap. She said dont forget now no going in your mommas room. I told her no granma. And I was saying the truth but then Mary Jane and I was playing fire truck. Mary Jane said I bet you havent no mother I bet you made up it all she said.

I got mad at her. I have a momma I know. She made me mad at her to say I made up it all. She said Im a liar. I mean about the bed and the dressing table and the picture and the dress even and every thing.

I said well Ill show you smarty.

I looked into granmas room. She was doing her nap still. I went down and said Mary Jane to come on because granma wont know.

She wasnt so smart after then. She giggled like she does. Even she made a scaredy noise when she hit into the table in the hall upstairs. I said youre a scaredy cat to her. She said back well *my* house isnt so dark like this. Like that was so much.

We went in mommas room. It was more dark than you could see. So I took back the curtains. Just a little so Mary Jane could see. I said this is my mommas room I suppose I made up it all.

She was by the door and she wasnt smart then either. She didnt say any word. She looked around the room. She jumped when I got her arm. Well come on I said.

I sat on the bed and said this is my mommas bed see how soft it is. She didnt say nothing. Scaredy cat I said. Am not she said like she does.

I said to sit down how can you tell if its soft if you dont sit down. She sat down by me. I said feel how soft it is. Smell how like sweet it is.

I closed my eyes but funny it wasnt like always. Because Mary Jane was there. I told her to stop feeling the cover. You said to she said. Well stop it I said.

See I said and I pulled her up. Thats the dressing table. I took her and brought her there. She said let go. It was so quiet and like always. I started to feel bad. Because Mary Jane was there. Because it was in my mommas room and momma wouldnt like Mary Jane there.

But I had to show her the things because. I showed her the mirror. We looked at each other in it. She looked white. Mary Jane is a scaredy cat I said. Am not she said anyway nobodys house is so quiet and dark inside. Anyway she said it smells.

I got mad at her. No it doesnt smell I said. Does so she said you said it did. I got madder too. It smells like sugar she said. It smells like sick people in your mommas room.

Dont say my mommas room is like sick people I said to her.

Well you didnt show me no dress and youre lying she said there isnt no dress. I felt all warm inside so I pulled her hair. Ill show you I said and dont never say Im a liar again.

She said Im going home and tell my mother on you. You are not I said youre going to see my mommas dress and youll better not call me a liar.

I made her stand still and I got the key off the hook. I kneeled down. I opened the box with the key.

Mary Jane said pew that smells like garbage.

I put my nails in her and she pulled away and got mad. Dont you pinch me she said and she was all red. Im telling my mother on you she said. And anyway its not a white dress its dirty and ugly she said.

Its not dirty I said. I said it so loud I wonder why granma didnt hear. I pulled out the dress from the box. I held it up to show her how its white. It fell open like the rain whispering and the bottom touched on the rug.

It is too white I said all white and clean and silky.

No she said she was so mad and red it has a hole in it. I got more madder. If my momma was here shed show you I said. You got no momma she said all ugly. I hate her.

I *have*. I said it way loud. I pointed my finger to mommas picture. Well who can see in this stupid dark room she said. I pushed her hard and she hit against the bureau. See then I said mean look at the picture. Thats my momma and shes the most beautiful lady in the whole world.

Shes ugly she has funny hands Mary Jane said. She hasnt I said shes the most beautiful lady in the world!

Not not she said *she has buck teeth*.

I dont remember then. I think like the dress moved in my arms. Mary Jane screamed. I dont remember what. It got dark and the curtains were closed I think. I couldn't see anyway. I couldnt hear nothing except buck teeth funny hands buck teeth funny hands even when no one was saying it.

There was something else because I think I heard some one call *dont let her say that!* I couldnt hold to the dress. And I had it on me I cant remember. Because I was like grown up strong. But I was a little girl still I think. I mean outside.

I think I was terrible bad then.

Granma took me away from there I guess. I dont know. She was screaming god help us its happened its happened. Over and over. I dont know why. She pulled me all the way here to my room and locked me in. She wont let me out. Well Im not so scared. Who cares if she locks me in a million billion years? She doesnt have to even give me supper. Im not hungry anyway.

Im full.

Epitaph Near Moonport

He got off in mid-passage, did Sandy MacPhee.
He'd be damned if he'd pay for a fall that was free.

SHERWOOD SPRINGER

The Trade—
The Tricks of
and the Art of

The fall of 1952 found the editors firmly established with a "monthly." L. Sprague de Camp, writing a book on science fiction writing, and William Nolan, compiling a pamphlet, both submitted questions to the editors. The answers provide an interesting overview of the growth of editorial acumen and the policies and handling of the magazine material.

Our biggest headache has been, simply, learning to be editors. When we started it, we thought all we had to do was pick good stories and put them in a mag. The infinite amount of mechanics we've had to learn since then . . . copy-reading, styling, word-count (at which I* have developed a miraculous efficiency comparable only to a good cybernetic machine), page-count, issue-balancing . . . to say nothing of the delicate art of Care and Feeding of Authors.

A.B. to W. Nolan

Collaboration is an impossible process to describe. Very often, a year later Mick and I couldn't tell you who wrote what. Editorial letters of any importance are discussed by both, then written by one. Introductions & Recommended Reading are divided up; one writes, the other revises, the final product is an amalgam.

Violent editorial agreements have happened. Sometimes the Pro party converts the Con; sometimes we compromise on a suggested rewrite; sometimes we both remain stubborn—in which case Con wins. Rule is: Either of us can reject; only both of us can accept.

A.B. to W.N.

12 November 1952

Dear Sprague [de Camp]:

What you suggest in your card of Nov 8 as to F&SF's policy seems accurate, provided it's not intended as all-inclusive. Certainly the "sophisticated humorous" piece isn't all we use.

I wouldn't say we're against "densely scientific ideas." Matter of fact, we're all for them (provided they're properly integrated into fiction); haven't published any only because nobody sends them to us (or, so far as I can judge, to any market at present).

We should like very much to publish (matter of fact, as reviewers, we'd simply like to read) some honesttogod science fiction, with both words equally stressed, such as JWC* developed in his Golden Age.

A.B.

*John W. Campbell

20 October 1952

Dear Sprague:

I would guess that we buy anywhere from ten to thirty percent of all the fiction that comes into the office. Sometimes weeks will go by without us finding anything that makes the grade, sometimes we'll have a very very fruitful seven days. Average it out about twenty percent and I think you've got it. We average about 240 manuscripts a month, as we consider the past 12 months. Here are the leading causes of rejection:

A. Overfamiliar, trite, stale ideas. (This is especially true of authors, well established in other fields, writing their first fantasy.)

B. Weak characterization, poor plot development. All too many stories come in with a fine idea that is poorly treated; either the author cannot write character or he cannot develop a suitable plot for his basically sound idea.

C. Dullness, ponderousness, heavy-handedness of treatment.

We get an awful lot of stories with flatly incredible situations from a scientific viewpoint, we get many stories— much too many—that do not proceed logically from their fantasy premise, nor do they give a good fantasy "why." We also note that many, many stories are much too long for themselves; I cannot remember the number of times that we have sent stories back for compression and tightening up. Invariably this process has resulted in changing a dull long short story or a novelette into a bright brief piece that has made an enormous hit with our readers.

J.F. McC

The average number of manuscripts received in the past twelve months (October 1951–October 1952) is approximately 240 per month.

A.B. to W.N.

Returned for rewrites . . . don't have any exact figures. Might run as high as 50%, if you include small changes. Occasionally we do rewrite ourselves . . . *with* the permission of the author or agent, but only as a last resort. We much prefer to persuade the author to do his own rewriting. We may, in preparing copy for printer, discover that some grammatical and stylistic revision is necessary; but we would never dream of doing the unauthorized changes in story of which some editors are guilty.

A.B. to W.N.

In our 1st year we had a rash of plagiarisms—Shirley Jackson's THE LOTTERY (from a quite well-known semi-pro!), Chambers' KING IS YELLOW and several others. Lately they've been infrequent. An awful lot of resemblances and derivativeness, but no out and out plagiarisms.

A.B. to W.N.

Then Nolan wanted to know how many issues ahead the editors were at any given month.

3) Let's see if I can make this clear. It isn't always too clear to me. An example should do it:

Our #21 (Feb 53) will be on the stands Jan 2 (sub copies out a little earlier). At that date #22 (Mar) will be completely printed and the factory is starting binding. #23 (Apr) will be completely edited and in the hands of our Eastern office. And we will be beginning to work on #24 (May). So we're approx 1 issue farther ahead of ourselves than you thought.

These few honest answers certainly should cue in the readers of this book as to the complexity of the operation. It is certain that the editors really worked at both the art of—and the tricks of the trade.

A question posed by C. Daly King elicited a thought-provoking breakdown on how the editors judged reader reaction.

23 August 1950

Judging reader-reaction is, we'll admit, just about impossible on any magazine. (I remember when a very good editor some years ago asked me to stop a series I was writing because reaction was bad—now years later everybody remembers the series, keeps asking me to resume them—they are, in fact, the most popular science fiction I ever wrote, and the editor obviously got a very inaccurate representation by mail.)

We use several sources:

A) Letters from unknown readers;

B) Comments in the various amateur publications devoted to fantasy literature;

C) Letters from our writers (such as yours on HUGE BEAST—and we'd welcome any further comments from you, favorable or adverse) and from various scholars, collectors, etc.;

D) Word of mouth in the local groups of enthusiasts and loyal readers;

E) Personal reactions of various friends (to say nothing of wives and such) who seem to us to typify certain groups of readers;

F) (which comes up surprisingly often) requests for permission to reprint and anthologize stories.

When all of these agree in praise, we can be fairly certain we've picked a honey; when they all agree in dislike, we can be reasonably sure we've made a mistake. In between we try to figure a balance—not uninfluenced by our own personal fondness for the story in question.

Why, query the readers, doesn't every issue of the magazine feature the "giants" of the field?

23 August 1953

Dear Mr. Thompson:

We have had so many requests for the work of such as Heinlein, Bradbury, Kuttner et al. that we are making a policy of explaining their absence and/or presence. Bob Heinlein has written one short story in the past three years. For reasons unknown to us, his agent did not send it to us. Editors can only make their wants and terms known to agents . . . from then on it's up to the latter to do as they wish. Bradbury's stuff generally goes to the slicks with whose rates we cannot compete. You'll note our published Bradbury stories were reprints—not always easy to get because of rights, etc. We have a Sturgeon story coming up in an early issue. Van Vogt has been so pre-occupied with dianetics and other universal panaceas that he hasn't written a new word for some nine years. Hank Kuttner has promised us that we'll get first look when he starts shorts again. Due to other obligations, he hasn't produced any *new* ones for nearly two years.

I hope this has been of some interest to you and will indicate some of the difficulties attending the editorial job. It would be so easy if Bob Heinlein, Bradbury and others would just form a line outside our door, their hot little hands full of new mss.

J.F. McC

These last bits speak for themselves as to editor-type headaches.

8 September 1950

This was incredible! A novel of at least 60,000 words translated *from the Esperanto*! And accompanied by 4 single-spaced pp of translations of Esperanto reviews which made it sound like an incredibly bad quasi-mystic Atomigeddon interplanetary—not for us if it had been only 3500! You won't blame me for, for once, charging an agent for its return?

[Ed. Note AB to JF McC]

25 January 1950

Mr. Bennett Cerf
Saturday Review of Literature
25 W 45 St
New York 19, NY

Dear Bennett:

My thanks for your plug on the magazine. Mick sent you one of the gems from our unsolicited MSS; another turned up recently when a man being abducted I believe by Martians turned and caught one last *glimace* of earth—a word that has now permanently entered our vocabularies.

We keep announcing that we publish fantasy fiction; so of course people keep sending us detective stories, fact articles, and epic poems. The highpoint was reached when a woman sent us a 250-word piece on What To Do With Leftovers—the element of fantasy lying, I imagine, in the notion that anyone would eat food prepared according to her recipes.

Congratulations on signing up Anthony Gilbert.

Sincerely,

Anthony Boucher

Oliver-Editors
Correspondence

Dear Mr. [Chad] Oliver:

My coeditor McComas and I are both completely delighted with THE BOY NEXT DOOR—you've taken an almost hackneyed theme and made something new and wonderful out of it by pure damned good fresh writing.

Sincerely,

Anthony Boucher, coeditor

18 February 1950

Dear Mr. Boucher:

First, an explanation for my delay in answering your letter. I am a senior at the University of Texas, in Austin, and your letter was not forwarded to me from my home in Kerrville.

I was never much of a hand at evasive diplomacy, so I'll tell you frankly that I would consider it an honor to have THE BOY NEXT DOOR published in *The Magazine of Fantasy and Science Fiction,* even if I *never* got paid a cent for it. I hope the fact that I am quite delerious with delight is not too painfully evident. You most certainly have my permission to hold the story.

About myself? Well, I'm 22 years old and a senior English major at the University of Texas.

THE BOY NEXT DOOR was written partly as an exasperated protest against two radio stereotypes—the kiddie's hour and the ha-ha announcer, who is currently to be found chuckling away on assorted all-night record programs.

That was not all, however. I was trying to give expression to some of my pet ideas. For one, it has always seemed to me that one of fantasy's most attractive (and effective) aspects is that it can create a situation in which various secret desires can actually come true, regardless of the material world. (That is a rotten way of putting it, but I know that you realize what I'm trying to say—I can remember your lovely MR LUPESCU without any trouble.) Whenever someone is absolutely cock-sure about something, I always find myself wishing that he would be rudely disillusioned. It's like hoping fervently that the smug chemistry professor will inadvertently blow the lab up.

May I thank you, Mr. Boucher, for your letter—if I get nothing else from THE BOY NEXT DOOR I will always be grateful.

Most sincerely,

Chad Oliver

We pride ourselves, as you know, on bringing you fresh new talents by buying the first stories of unpublished writers; and more than one of our discoveries (such as Betsy Curtis or Richard Matheson) have already become well established as writers in the field of fantasy and science fiction. But publishing schedules are capricious things; and occasionally a discovery double-crosses us by selling and having published a half dozen stories before we've managed to bring you his "first." You've already seen some bright items elsewhere from Chad Oliver, a Texas college student who recently graduated from science fiction fan to professional writer; now, with our patented and exclusive editorial time machine, we take you back to Mr. Oliver's debut in the first story he ever sold—a highly satisfactory blend of comedy and chills, of the absurdities of mid-twentieth century progress and the grimness of an undatable horror.

Anthony Boucher
J. F. McComas

The Boy Next Door
By Chad Oliver

It was five o'clock by the clock on the studio wall. Behind his glass partition, the balding engineer waved his right hand at Harry Royal.

"Hello again, kids!" Harry said in a hearty voice.

The youthful studio audience squealed with delight. A little girl in a pink dress smacked her hands together enthusiastically. Harry moaned to himself. What a way to make a living!

"Yes, sir," he said, careful to keep a big, cheery smile on his face. "Five o'clock again, boys and girls, and you all know what *that* means!" He winked at the adults in his audience— must be parents, he thought. Why else should they torture themselves? He said: "Ha, ha. Station ZNOX, right here in the good old Hotel Murphy, again brings you *The Boy Next Door*, the program where you get to hear your very own friends speak to you over the radio. This is your old Uncle Harry Royal, getting the old program under way again. How are you all this evening, hmmm?''

The kids in the audience assured him that they were fine. They always were, thought Harry grimly. They would be. He smiled wanly and tried to look like a good scout.

"Well sir," he continued, "as you all know, old Uncle Harry picks one of your names out of the little old red box every day, Monday through Friday, and invites the lucky winner down here to the good old Hotel Murphy to talk over the radio." His smile felt a trifle limp and he engineered a fresh one. "This afternoon, our guest is young Jimmy Walls, from away out in Terrace Heights.''

Applause. Harry wondered why. What had Jimmy Walls ever done? Set fire to the school?

Jimmy Walls eyed Harry gravely. He was an eager looking boy in what was obviously a brand new suit. His straw-colored hair was slicked back precariously. He had bright blue eyes and his tie was crooked.

"Don't be afraid now, Jimmy," said Harry Royal.

"I'm not afraid," Jimmy Walls assured him.

"Well, well—that's fine, Jimmy, fine. There—stand a little closer to the microphone. Fine. Dandy. How old are you, Jimmy?''

"I'm eight years old, going on nine.''

The same questions. The same answers. Harry Royal decided, not for the first time, that he hated kids. All of them.

"Mighty fine, Jimmy," he said. "Mighty fine. Yes sir, that's fine. Where do you go to school, Jimmy?''

"I go to Terrace Heights School," answered Jimmy. He added: "When I go.''

"When you go? Ha, ha. You don't mean to tell your old Uncle Harry that you skip school sometimes?''

"Sometimes," Jimmy admitted.

Harry worked on his smile again. Didn't they ever say anything new or interesting?

"You're not very bright, are you?" he wanted to say.

"What programs on good old ZNOX do you like best?" he said.

Jimmy Walls thought about it briefly. Then his blue eyes

glistened. "Golly," he exclaimed, "I like *The Hag's Hut* best. I like *Terror in the Night,* too!"

Well, thought Harry. Just a nice, healthy, American boy. Nothing like horror programs for the little, growing minds.

"Ha, ha," Harry Royal chuckled dutifully. "Don't those programs scare you, Jimmy?"

"They don't scare *me,*" Jimmy retorted indignantly.

"Ha, ha. I see. Yes, I see." Harry Royal fumbled around for something to say and came up with: "Why do you like those programs best, Jimmy?"

"I like the way they kill people," Jimmy replied instantly. "They sure are smart!" His blue eyes were bright with admiration.

That one stopped Harry Royal for a second, but he bounced back in a hurry. Nothing ever stopped Harry Royal for long, no sir! "But they always get caught, don't they, Jimmy?" he suggested. "Crime doesn't pay, you know."

He winked broadly at the adults in the studio.

"Maybe," hedged Jimmy Walls reluctantly.

"Hmmmm. Well, well. I see. Yes, sir." Better change the subject, Harry decided. Definitely. You never could tell about parents, studio brass, and the FCC. He chose a safe topic: "What have you been doing all week, old man?"

"Killing people," Jimmy Walls announced proudly.

Pause. Harry began to feel uncomfortable. "Ha, ha," he said, without humor. "Come now, Jimmy. Ha, ha. Come now—honesty is the best policy."

"I *am* honest," muttered Jimmy Walls insistently. He shuffled his feet, smearing the fresh polish on his shiny brown shoes. "Nobody ever believes me."

"Oh, I believe you, all right. If you say so, Jimmy. Ha, ha—just a regular cut-up, I guess! Do you use a knife, Jimmy? Ha, ha."

"No," Jimmy Walls stated flatly.

"Well, well. Yes, sir! This younger generation!" Harry winked hugely at the studio audience. Several of the adults smiled weakly, but the children sat very still, listening to Jimmy Walls raptly.

"You don't believe me, honest," accused Jimmy. "You're just saying that. You'll see."

Harry felt peculiar. Not worried, or afraid, or anything like that, he assured himself. Of course not. Just—well, *funny.*

"Well, Jimmy," he said, feeling quite clever, "if you kill

people, why don't you get caught, eh? Crime doesn't pay, you know! Ha, ha. No, sir. Honesty is the best policy. I guess you listen to old ZNOX and try out everything you hear, hmmm?''

"*That's* not the way." Jimmy Walls looked disgusted.

"How do you do it then?" Harry was getting desperate. "You must be awfully smart."

"I'm not so smart."

Harry Royal worked up a new smile. He glanced at the clock on the wall. Seven minutes to go. He decided to try another angle.

"Then you were just kidding your old Uncle Harry, huh, Jimmy? Ha, ha. You have a lively sense of humor, all right."

"Golly, no." Jimmy Walls tugged nervously at his tight collar. "You don't understand. I've killed *lots* of people."

Harry Royal frowned. Then, remembering himself, he turned it into what would have to pass for a smile. Until the real thing came along, he thought to himself. He felt a little better. Time for the man-to-man angle, he decided.

"Well sir, Jimmy," he said heartily, "you want to be careful with that kind of talk. Yes, sir. Now, *I* understand, of course— old Uncle Harry understands kids pretty well, you bet. But other people might get the wrong idea. Then what will you do?"

"Uncle George will fix it," Jimmy said, after a short pause.

"Uncle George?"

"Uncle George."

Harry Royal felt an unaccustomed chill race down his spine. It felt like a cold centipede with little crystals of ice on its legs. Harry didn't like it. Something was wrong here. He knew it. Maybe Jimmy was just kidding him along—of course he was! Of course. But amateurs—kids at that—seldom carried out a gag over the air, even if they had one planned. There was something about a microphone—

"Uncle George must be quite a man," he heard himself saying.

"Oh gosh no!" Jimmy protested.

"You mean he isn't remarkable, then?"

"I mean he isn't a *man,* Uncle George isn't."

Harry determined to keep talking. "I see, I see," he said, not seeing in the least. "A blue midget with twelve legs, maybe? Ha, ha." Harry managed a wink for the audience, but he had given up his smile. He noticed that several of the adults were looking startled, and one old lady was frowning her disapproval.

That was bad. The children looked awed and envious—a composite picture of shining eyes and open mouths. Fiends, thought Harry.

"He is not a midget with twelve legs, Uncle George isn't," Jimmy Walls declared. "I'd be scared. Uncle Geroge *looks* like a man."

"But he—isn't?" asked Harry, knowing the answer in advance.

"No."

"How do you know?"

"You can tell."

It was a mad conversation—mad for anywhere, but unthinkable for radio. Harry Royal was worried; he'd hear about this. He tried to smooth it over. "Well," he said jovially, "you out there in the radio audience must be having quite a time, ha, ha. Yes, sir. It isn't often that we get a real killer here on *The Boy Next Door*, ha ha. But I'm sure that you all remember little Bobby Boyle, who said he was a werewolf. There just isn't any limit to young imaginations, no, sir. Quite a healthy sign, too—take it from old Harry Royal."

He turned back to Jimmy, who had remained perfectly impassive during Harry's speech to the radio audience. "What do you want to be when you grow up, Jimmy?" he asked, searching for a safe subject. "A fireman? A G-man?"

Jimmy Walls looked thoughtful. Then: "No," he said suddenly. His blue eyes glistened. "I want to be a—"

A horrible thought crossed Harry Royal's mind and he cut Jimmy short. "Let's talk about baseball," he boomed heartily. "Grand old game, baseball. I'll bet you like baseball, eh, Jimmy?" He wouldn't have bet much, he assured himself.

"It's all right, I guess." Jimmy wasn't very enthused.

"I'll bet you get real excited when you listen to a game, don't you?" continued Harry doggedly.

"No," said Jimmy. "It's not near as much fun as—"

"Football," supplied Harry Royal. "Football. Grand old game." He looked grimly at the studio clock. Two minutes to go.

"I didn't mean—" Jimmy began patiently.

"Ha, ha. Of course you didn't mean all that about killing people, Jimmy. Boys will be boys, yes, sir! Old Uncle Harry understands. You don't have to explain to him, no, sir."

For once in his life, Harry Royal didn't know what to say. He winked again at the studio audience and decided to end it before Jimmy started off on another grisly tangent. "Well, Jimmy," he said cheerfully, "I've sure enjoyed having you up here on *The Boy Next Door,* and I'm sure that all your little friends have enjoyed listening to you, too. I'm sorry that the little old clock tells me that our time is up. Good-by, Jimmy Walls! We hope that you'll be back with us again real soon." Over my dead body, thought Harry.

"Good-by, Mr. Royal," said Jimmy politely.

"Yes, sir," Harry continued. "Ha, ha. We had quite a time this evening here on *The Boy Next Door,* and I hope that all of you enjoyed Jimmy Walls as much as your Uncle Harry did. Yes, sir. You all want to be on hand again tomorrow, same time, same station, when old ZNOX, here in the Hotel Murphy, will again present your favorite program and mine, *The Boy Next Door.* Until then, this is your old friend, Harry Royal, wishing each and every one of you a very pleasant good evening."

Harry signaled the engineer and cut off the microphone. He sighed shortly. What a mess! How could he ever explain it? Of course, it wasn't his fault; he had done all he could. But try to tell that to the brass in the office! He wasn't looking forward to the occasion.

The studio was almost empty now. The silence began to hang heavily over the sound-proofed room, with the only sounds drifting in from the hall outside. As he watched, the last of the audience filed through the door, and the door closed behind him. Even the engineer had left. The silence was complete.

"Mr. Royal?" questioned a small voice.

Harry turned around slowly, hoping against hope that he hadn't identified that voice correctly. But he had. It was Jimmy Walls, sitting in one of the metal chairs on the stage. "What are you doing here?" demanded Harry. He felt distinctly uncomfortable. "Haven't you got a ride home?"

"Yes, sir."

"But it hasn't come yet, is that it?"

"Yes, sir."

"Well, it'll be along shortly," Harry Royal assured him. "It was nice knowing you." He started to leave.

"Mr. Royal?"

Harry stopped. "Yes?" he questioned sharply.

"Mr. Royal, will you wait here with me until my ride comes? I'd be scared in here." Jimmy Walls looked small and afraid in the bright studio lights.

Harry Royal hesitated. He didn't like studios, especially empty ones. They gave him the creeps; they were too quiet. But he was in enough hot water now—if he left the kid in there alone, and the bigwigs found out about it, it wouldn't help things any. After all, he told himself, it's just a little kid.

"*You* scared?" he laughed nervously. "That's a good one."

"I'd be scared all by myself, honest, Mr. Royal. Don't leave me here." Jimmy Walls looked up at him imploringly with big, blue eyes.

"Your parents coming here for you?" Harry asked, somewhat mollified.

"No, sir."

"I thought you said you had a ride home."

"I do, sir. Uncle George is coming."

That icy centipede tripped down Harry's spine again. He became acutely aware of the deserted studio, with its empty rows of staring seats. They were utterly alone. No one could hear through those sound-proofed walls. He looked narrowly at the small figure before him—young, blue-eyed.

He's just a kid. Relax!

"Uncle George," said Harry slowly. "That's the one who fixes things up for you?"

"Gosh, yes! He tells me just what to do. He sure is smart!"

"The one who looks like a man, but isn't?" Harry Royal wanted to hear his voice say that. It made him feel better; the whole thing was so ridiculous.

"Oh, you can *tell*."

"You certainly have some imagination, Jimmy." Harry hoped that it was imagination. It had better be imagination. He looked at Jimmy Walls speculatively. Jimmy Walls looked at him the same way.

"You'll be good," Jimmy said suddenly.

Harry felt the silence close in around him. He couldn't laugh, somehow. It wasn't funny any more. He decided that it was time for him to leave, ride or no ride.

Footsteps.

"Here comes Uncle George now," Jimmy said.

The steps paused outside the studio door. Uncle George walked in.

"See?" inquired Jimmy Walls proudly. "He *looks* human."

Harry Royal took a deep breath of relief. Uncle George *was* human. Of course he was! A nice little fat man with a red face who wheezed as he walked. Harry noted the conservative gray suit, the old hickory walking stick.

Jimmy Walls waved happily. "Hi, Uncle George!"

The cheery little fat man grinned at Harry Royal and patted Jimmy affectionately. "Hello, Jimmy my boy! Hello there!" He turned to Harry Royal and extended his hand.

"I'm George Johnson," he chuckled. He had a rich, mellow voice that bubbled with good nature. "I hope I haven't detained you? I heard the broadcast, but was unavoidably detained."

"Uncle George never goes out while the sun is up," Jimmy explained.

George Johnson laughed heartily, shaking Harry's hand. He had a firm, pleasant grip. "I hope Jimmy's talk hasn't upset you," he said solicitously.

"Not at all," lied Harry. "The boy has quite an imagination."

"Yes, yes! Jimmy's quite a talker, aren't you, Jimmy?"

Jimmy Walls squirmed nervously.

"Ha, ha," laughed Harry Royal. "Jimmy's been telling me that you help him kill people." He winked at George Johnson.

"He *does*," insisted Jimmy. "Don't you, Uncle George?"

"You bet I do," Uncle George assured him. "You bet I do, Jimmy." He winked broadly at the smiling Harry Royal.

George Johnson straightened Jimmy's tie for him and laughed jovially. "Now, Jimmy," he admonished. "You say good-by to Mr. Royal."

"Good-by, Mr. Royal," Jimmy said, a gleam of delight in his blue eyes.

"Good-by, Jimmy!" answered Harry Royal, unheeding. He felt fine now. "See you around, Mr. Johnson!"

"Quite possibly, quite possibly," bubbled Uncle George. He steered Jimmy Walls to the door and out of the studio. The happy little fat man turned back to Harry Royal, his red face beaming.

Harry Royal laughed and winked prodigiously.

Uncle George smiled and turned away again.

What is he doing? What is—

Harry Royal's heart pounded treacherously. His face paled suddenly and he clutched desperately at the dead microphone.

Uncle George was *backing* toward him from the studio door. That wasn't so bad. No. But in the exact center of the back of his balding head was a large, blue eye. And it *winked* at him with a hideous regularity, over and over again. Wink—step—wink—step—*wink*—

Harry Royal caught a fleeting glimpse of little Jimmy Walls. His small, eager face peered intently from the studio doorway, shining blue eyes wide in anticipation.

Knight-Editors Correspondence

22 September 1949

Dear Mr. [Damon] Knight:

We liked NOT WITH A BANG tremendously. However, this first issue of the magazine is strictly a one-shot proposition. We won't know until it has been on the stands a month or so, say the latter part of November, whether it will be a success or, God forbid! a flop. So, right now we are in no position to make formal acceptance of a story.

If your story is published by us we'd like to know something about you. As a matter of fact, we'd like to know anyway. . . . that's a lovely piece you've written.

Sincerely,

J. Francis McComas

24 September 1949

Dear Mr. McComas:

I'm delighted to hear that you and Mr. Boucher liked NOT WITH A BANG. I wrote the thing for fun and never really expected to sell it; as a matter of fact, I suppose I was letting off steam generated by working to pulp requirements.

What you want to know now, I imagine, is Who the hell is this guy? Well, I'm a 27-year-old character from Hood River, Oregon; read my first science-fiction magazine in 1933; published a short-lived but startling fan magazine in 1940; came to New York and abandoned my amateur status in 1941. Have done some pulp writing, also some pulp illustration; at present am associate editor of Super Science and three sports magazines at Popular Publications.

Yours truly,

Damon Knight

26 November 1949

Gentlemen:

I once wrote an autobiographical sketch for Planet Stories which began approximately like this: "I get all my best ideas at stool." The editor changed the phrase to "in an abandoned Turkish bath in Brooklyn," and I don't suppose you could print quite so unvarnished a truth either; but it is the truth. Perhaps you could mention that this story ran through my head during about two seconds in the can of a small Swedish restaurant called The Red Brick, while the door was closing behind me. On second thought, better not. There are some things Man wasn't meant to know.

With best wishes,

Damon Knight

The Last Man on Earth is one of the classic themes of science fiction, from Mary Wollstonecraft Shelley's THE LAST MAN *through M. P. Shiel's* THE PURPLE CLOUD *to the striking modern resolution of the situation in Alfred Bester's short story* Adam and No Eve. *The very grandeur of the theme has always evoked a certain solemnity of treatment; it took a fellow-editor, Damon Knight—weary perhaps of reading grandiose manuscripts— to see that the petty stupidity of man and his mores might mean that his world would end, in the words of T. S. Eliot, "not with a bang but a whimper." The result is a new kind of catastrophe— the cosmic cocktail mixed with a full jigger of wry.*

Anthony Boucher
J. F. McComas

Not With a Bang
By Damon Knight

Ten months after the last plane passed over, Rolf Smith knew beyond doubt that only one other human being had survived. Her name was Louise Oliver, and he was sitting opposite her in a department-store cafe in Salt Lake City. They were eating canned Vienna sausages and drinking coffee.

Sunlight struck through a broken pane, lying like a judgment on the cloudy air of the room. Inside and outside, there was no sound; only a stifling rumor of absence. The clatter of dishware in the kitchen, the heavy rumble of streetcars: never again. There was sunlight; and silence; and the watery, astonished eyes of Louise Oliver.

He leaned forward, trying to capture the attention of those fishlike eyes for a second. "Darling," he said, "I respect your views, naturally. But I've got to make you see that they're impractical."

She looked at him with faint surprise, then away again. Her head shook slightly: No. *No, Rolf. I will not live with you in sin.*

Smith thought of the women of France, of Russia, of Mexico, of the South Seas. He had spent three months in the ruined studios of a radio station in Rochester, listening to the voices until they stopped. There had been a large colony in Sweden, including an English cabinet minister. They reported that Europe was gone. Simply gone; there was not an acre that had not been swept clean by radioactive dust. They had two planes and enough fuel to take them anywhere on the Continent; but there was nowhere to go. Three of them had the plague; then eleven; then all.

There was a bomber pilot who had fallen near a government radio in Palestine. He did not last long, because he had broken some bones in the crash; but he had seen the vacant waters where the Pacific Islands should have been. It was his guess that the Arctic ice-fields had been bombed. He did not know whether that had been a mistake or not.

There were no reports from Washington, from New York, from London, Paris, Moscow, Chungking, Sydney. You could not tell who had been destroyed by disease, who by the dust, who by bombs.

Smith himself had been a laboratory assistant in a team that was trying to find an antibiotic for the plague. His superiors had found one that worked sometimes, but it was a little too late. When he left, Smith took along with him all there was of it—forty ampoules, enough to last him for years.

Louise had been a nurse in a genteel hospital near Denver. According to her, something rather odd had happened to the hospital as she was approaching it the morning of the attack. She was quite calm when she said this, but a vague look came into her eyes and her shattered expression seemed to slip a little more. Smith did not press her for an explanation.

Like himself, she had found a radio station which still functioned, and when Smith discovered that she had not contracted the plague, he agreed to meet her. She was, apparently, naturally immune. There must have been others, a few at least; but the bombs and the dust had not spared them.

It seemed very awkward to Louise that not one Protestant minister was left alive.

The trouble was, she really meant it. It had taken Smith a long time to believe it, but it was true. She would not sleep in the same hotel with him, either; she expected, and received, the utmost courtesy and decorum. Smith had learned his lesson. He walked on the outside of the rubble-heaped sidewalks; he opened doors for her, when there were still doors; he held her chair; he refrained from swearing. He courted her.

Louise was forty or thereabouts, at least five years older than Smith. He often wondered how old she thought she was. The shock of seeing whatever it was that had happened to the hospital, the patients she had cared for, had sent her mind scuttling back to her childhood. She tacitly admitted that everyone else in the world was dead, but she seemed to regard it as something one did not mention.

A hundred times in the last three weeks, Smith had felt an almost irresistible impulse to break her thin neck and go his own way. But there was no help for it; she was the only woman in the world, and he needed her. If she died, or left him, he died. *Old bitch!* he thought to himself furiously, and carefully kept the thought from showing on his face.

"Louise, honey," he told her gently, "I want to spare your feelings as much as I can. You know that."

"Yes, Rolf," she said, staring at him with the face of a hypnotized chicken.

Smith forced himself to go on. "We've got to face the facts, unpleasant as they may be. Honey, we're the only man and the only woman there are. We're like Adam and Eve in the Garden of Eden."

Louise's face took on a slightly disgusted expression. She was obviously thinking of fig-leaves.

"Think of the generations unborn," Smith told her, with a tremor in his voice. *Think about me for once. Maybe you're good for another ten years, maybe not.* Shuddering, he thought of the second stage of the disease—the helpless rigidity, striking without warning. He'd had one such attack already, and Louise had helped him out of it. Without her, he would have stayed like that till he died, the hypodermic that would save him within inches of his rigid hand. He thought desperately, *If I'm lucky, I'll get at least two kids out of you before you croak. Then I'll be safe.*

He went on, "God didn't mean for the human race to end like this. He spared us, you and me, to—" He paused; how could he say it without offending her? "Parents" wouldn't do—too suggestive. "—to carry on the torch of life," he ended. There. That was sticky enough.

Louise was staring vaguely over his shoulder. Her eyelids blinked regularly, and her mouth made little rabbit-like motions in the same rhythm.

Smith looked down at his wasted thighs under the tabletop. *I'm not strong enough to force her*, he thought. *Christ, if I were strong enough!*

He felt the futile rage again, and stifled it. He had to keep his head, because this might be his last chance. Louise had been talking lately, in the cloudy language she used about everything, of going up in the mountains to pray for guidance. She had not said, "alone," but it was easy enough to see that she pictured it that way. He had to argue her around before her resolve stiffened. He concentrated furiously, and tried once more.

The pattern of words went by like a distant rumbling. Louise heard a phrase here and there; each of them fathered chains of thought, binding her revery tighter. "Our duty to humanity . . ." Mama had often said—that was in the old house on Waterbury Street of course, before Mama had taken sick—she had said, "Child, your duty is to be clean, polite, and God-fearing. Pretty doesn't matter. There's a plenty of plain women that have got themselves good, Christian husbands."

Husbands . . . To have and to hold . . . Orange blossoms, and the bridesmaids; the organ music. Through the haze, she saw Rolf's lean, wolfish face. Of course, he was the only one she'd ever get; *she* knew that well enough. Gracious, when a girl was past twenty-five, she had to take what she could get.

But I sometimes wonder if he's really a nice man, she thought.

". . . in the eyes of God . . ." She remembered the stained-glass windows in the old First Episcopalian Church, and how she always thought God was looking down at her through that brilliant transparency. Perhaps He was still looking at her, though it seemed sometimes that He had forgotten. Well, of course she realized that marriage customs changed, and if you couldn't have a regular minister. . . . But it was really a shame, an outrage almost, that if she were actually going to marry this man, she couldn't have all those nice things . . . There wouldn't even be any wedding presents. Not even that. But of course Rolf would give her anything she wanted. She saw his face again, noticed the narrow black eyes staring at her with ferocious purpose, the thin mouth that jerked in a slow, regular tic, the hairy lobes of the ears below the tangle of black hair.

He oughtn't to let his hair grow so long, she thought, *it isn't quite decent.* Well, she could change all that. If she did marry him, she'd certainly make him change his ways. It was no more than her duty.

He was talking now about a farm he'd seen outside town—a good big house and a barn. There was no stock, he said, but they could get some later. And they'd plant things, and have their own food to eat, not go to restaurants all the time.

She felt a touch on her hand, lying pale before her on the table. Rolf's brown, stubby fingers, black-haired above and below the knuckles, were touching hers. He had stopped talking for a moment, but now he was speaking again, still more urgently. She drew her hand away.

He was saying, ". . . and you'll have the finest wedding dress you ever saw, with a bouquet. Everything you want, Louise, everything . . ."

A wedding dress! And flowers, even if there couldn't be any minister! Well, why hadn't the fool said so before?

Rolf stopped halfway through a sentence, aware that Louise had said quite clearly, "Yes, Rolf, I will marry you if you wish."

Stunned, he wanted her to repeat it, but dared not ask, "What did you say?" for fear of getting some fantastic answer, or none at all. He breathed deeply. He said, "Today, Louise?"

She said, "Well, *today* . . . I don't know quite . . . Of course, if you think you can make all the arrangements in time, but it does seem . . ."

Triumph surged through Smith's body. He had the advantage now, and he'd ride it. "Say you will, dear," he urged her; "say yes, and make me the happiest man . . ."

Even then, his tongue balked at the rest of it; but it didn't matter. She nodded submissively. "Whatever you think best, Rolf."

He rose, and she allowed him to kiss her pale, sapless cheek. "We'll leave right away," he said. "If you'll excuse me for just a minute, dear?"

He waited for her "Of course" and then left her, making footprints in the furred carpet of dust down toward the end of the room. Just a few more hours he'd have to speak to her like that, and then, in her eyes, she'd be committed to him forever. Afterwards, he could do with her as he liked—beat her when he pleased, submit her to any proof of his scorn and revulsion, use her. Then it would not be too bad, being the last man on Earth—not bad at all. She might even have a daughter . . .

He found the washroom door and entered. He took a step inside, and froze, balanced by a trick of motion, upright but helpless. Panic struck at his throat as he tried to turn his head and failed; tried to scream, and failed. Behind him, he was aware of a tiny click as the door, cushioned by the hydraulic check, shut forever. It was not locked; but its other side bore the warning: MEN.

Wellman-Editors Correspondence

Labor Day, 1949

Dear Antonio—

It is with considerable interest I read what Benet's *Phoenix Nest* says about you and your projected *Magazine of Fantasy*. More power to this effort to jack up the reputation and quality of the genre. My unsolicited opinion is that it will be tougher to do than Fred Dannay's similar detective-story labor, for there isn't quite the public for it, in spite of all the essays to that effect by Wolheim, Pratt, de Camp, et al.

Still, I'm somewhat of a laborer in the fantasy lodge myself. I'd rather write supernatural than science, and haven't done so because of the limited and underpaid market. Tell me, if you care to, what about *Magazine of Fantasy*? Preferred lengths, taboos, special needs? Also, in a sordid vein, what are you paying? I doubt if these frontier and rustic latitudes will have your publication on the stands—how about sending me a copy?

Let me say at once that I am not writing this letter with anything in the way of a rejected dud to send you. I have absolutely nothing on the stocks at present in the fantasy bracket. But, erroneously or not, I think that once and again I've thrown away some terribly effective writing on such pulps as WEIRD TALES, where nobody would know good writing from bad with a fifty-power microscope.

Best of luck with the magazine, from

Manly Wade Wellman

12 September 1950

Dear Manly:

Once again you have written on hell of a story! [O UGLY BIRD!]

Three small points:

A) Are silver strings practical and feasible on a guitar? If you're positive, we'll take your word; if you have any doubts, we'd like to consult Ted Sturgeon, who knows all about guitars.

B) We'd like to go back to the original ugly bird; the overlap between Jesse Stuart's public and ours is negligible.

C) (And the only really serious one) . . . the story bogs down pretty badly in a mess of explanations like a badly constructed whodunit. Can't you reconstruct—planting a little of this earlier, paring the rest down to a minimum— so that there's only a few hundred words between the destruction of Onselm and the curtain?

                                                              AB

19 September 1950

Dear Tony:

Your letter on how to do the yarn over arrived late Saturday, and I just bowed my neck and did the thing over. New title, as you see, O UGLY BIRD! I did it all except three of the early pages, and tried to fix those explanations at the end.

Answering your question about the silver strings, I went into that before ever I wrote. Silver strings were used before steel strings became good enough. Silver makes a good harmonious jangle, a la silver horns, etc. I checked again before I wrote, in Deems Taylor's MUSIC LOVER'S ENCYCLOPEDIA, which has this to say under "Stringed Instruments": Guitar strings today are sometimes silver wound on a steel or silk core. And under "Silver trumpet", it says that silver is used for strings on many instruments.

To switch things around and plant ahead, I took up slack here and there to allow new inserts; but the story comes out just about as long as it was when you saw it last.

Good luck to you, and I really want to hear that this magazine makes the grade. It's badly needed!

Best,

Manly

With this story we introduce a new character who's bound, we feel sure, to become a noted figure in the annals of American folk-fantasy: the wandering minstrel name of John, who strings his guitar with silver and who knows that evil and incomprehensible events_ can happen as well today as in the olden times whose ballads he knows by heart. John's creator, the unreconstructed and irregular Manly Wade Wellman, is a mean hand with a guitar ("nothing fancy or Segovian," he writes us, "just plain old country gut-fiddle stuff, like Purty Quadroon *and* I'm Just a Rebel Soldier"); *he knows the idiom and the folklore and the balladry of the South. And out of his knowledge he's fused a kind of fantasy story, a sort of prose ballad. You'll remember this first meeting with John—and be glad to learn that he'll appear in F&SF soon again.*

Anthony Boucher
J. F. McComas

O Ugly Bird!
By Manly Wade Wellman

I swear I'm licked before I start, trying to tell you all what Mr. Onselm looked like. Words give out—for instance, you're frozen to death for fit words to tell the favor of the girl you love. And Mr. Onselm and I pure poison hated each other. That's how love and hate are alike.

He was what country folks call a low man, more than calling him short or small; a low man is low otherwise than by inches. Mr. Onselm's shoulders didn't wide out as far as his big ears, and they sank and sagged. His thin legs bowed in at the knee and out at the shank, like two sickles point to point. On his carrot-thin neck, his head looked like a swollen pale gourd. Thin, moss-gray hair. Loose mouth, a bit open to show long, even teeth. Not much chin. The right eye squinted, mean and dark, while the hike of his brow twitched the left one wide. His good clothes fitted his mean body like they were cut to it. Those good clothes were almost as much out of match to the rest of him as his long, soft, pink hands, the hands of a man who never had to work a tap.

You see what I mean, I can't say how he looked, only he was hateful.

I first met him when I came down from the high mountain's comb, along an animal trail—maybe a deer made it. Through the trees I saw, here and there in the valley below, patch-places and cabins and yards. I hoped I'd get fed at one of them, for I'd run clear out of eating some spell back. I had no money. Only my hickory shirt and blue duckin pants and torn old army shoes, and my guitar on its sling cord. But I knew the mountain folks. If they've got ary thing to eat, a decent spoken stranger can get the half part of it. Towns aren't always the same way.

Downslope I picked, favoring the guitar in case I slipped and fell, and in an hour made it to the first patch. Early fall was browning the corn out of the green. The cabin was two-room, dog-trotted open in the middle. Beyond was a shed and a pigpen. In the yard the man of the house talked to who I found out later was Mr. Onselm.

"No meat at all?" said Mr. Onselm. His voice was the last you'd expect him to have, full of broad low music, like an organ in a town church. I decided against asking him to sing when I glimpsed him closer sickle-legged and gourd-headed and pale and puny in his fine-fitting clothes. For he looked mad and dangerous; and the man of the place, though he was a big, strong old gentlemen with a square jaw, looked afraid.

"I been short this year, Mr. Onselm," he said, begging like. "The last bit of meat I fished out of the brine on Tuesday. And I don't want to have to kill the pig till December."

Mr. Onselm tramped over to the pen. The pig was a friendly one, it reared its front feet against the boards and grunted up to him. Mr. Onselm spit into the pen. "All right," he said, "but I want some meal."

He sickle-legged back to the cabin. A brown barrel stood in the dog trot. Mr. Onselm lifted the cover and pinched some meal between his pink fingertips. "Get me a sack," he told the man.

The man went indoors and brought out the sack. Mr. Onselm held it open while the man scooped out meal enough to fill it. Then Mr. Onselm held it tight shut while the man lashed the neck with twine. Finally Mr. Onselm looked up and saw me standing there.

"Who are you?" he asked, sort of crooning.

"My name's John," I said.

"John what?" Then, without waiting for my answer, "Where did you steal that guitar?"

"It was given to me," I replied. "I strung it with silver wires myself."

"Silver," he said, and opened his squint eye by a trifle.

With my left hand I clamped a chord. With my right thumb I picked a whisper from the silver strings. I began to make a song:

> "Mister Onselm,
>   They do what you tell 'em—"

"That will do," said Mr. Onselm, not so musically, and I stopped playing. He relaxed. "They do what I tell 'em," he said, half to himself. "Not bad."

We studied each other a few ticks of time. Then he turned and tramped out of the yard in among the trees. When he was out of sight the man of the place asked, right friendly, what he could do for me.

"I'm just walking through," I said. I didn't want to ask right off for some dinner.

"I heard you name yourself John," he said. "So happens my name's John too, John Bristow."

"Nice place you've got," I said, looking around. "Cropper or tenant?"

"I own the house and the land," he told me, and I was surprised; for Mr. Onselm had treated him the way a mean boss treats a cropper.

"Then that Mr. Onselm was just a visitor," I said.

"Visitor?" Mr. Bristow snorted. "He visits everybody here around. Let's them know what he wants, and they pass it to him. Thought you knew him, you sang about him so ready."

"Shucks, I made that up." I touched the silver strings again. "I sing a many a new song that comes to me."

"I love the old songs better," he said, and smiled, so I sang one:

> "I had been in Georgia
>   Not a man more weeks than three,
>   When I fell in love with a pretty fair girl,
>   And she fell in love with me.

"Her lips were red as red could be,
Her eyes were brown as brown,
Her hair was like the thundercloud
Before the rain comes down."

You should have seen Mr. Bristow's face shine. He said: "By God you sure enough can sing it and play it."

"Do my possible best," I said. "But Mr. Onselm don't like it." I thought a moment, then asked: "What way can he get everything he wants in this valley?"

"Shoo, can't tell you way. Just done it for years, he has."

"Anybody refuse him?"

"Once Old Jim Desbro refused him a chicken. Mr. Onselm pointed his finger at Old Jim's mules, they was plowing. Them mules couldn't move ary foot, not till Mr. Onselm had the chicken. Another time, Miss Tilly Parmer hid a cake when she seen him come. He pointed a finger and dumbed her. She never spoke one mumbling word from that day to when she died. Could hear and understand, but when she tried to talk she could just wheeze."

"He's a hoodoo man," I said, "which means the law can't do anything."

"Not even if the law worried about anything this far from the county seat." He looked at the meal back against the cabin. "About time for the Ugly Bird to fetch Mr. Onselm's meal."

"What's the Ugly Bird?" I asked, but he didn't have to answer.

It must have hung over us, high and quiet, and now it dropped into the yard like a fish hawk into a pond.

First out I saw it was dark, heavy-winged, bigger than a buzzard. Then I saw the shiny gray-black of the body, like wet slate, and how it seemed to have feathers only on its wide wings. Then I made out the thin snaky neck, the bulgy head and long stork beak, the eyes set in front of its head—man-fashion in front, not to each side.

The feet that taloned onto the sack showed pink and smooth with five graspy toes. The wings snapped like a tablecloth in a wind, and it churned away over the trees with the meal sack.

"That's the Ugly Bird," said Mr. Bristow. I barely heard him. "Mr. Onselm has companioned with it ever since I recollect."

"I never saw such a bird," I said. "Must be a scarce one. You know what struck me while I watched it?"

"I do know, John. Its feet look like Mr. Onselm's hands."

"Might it be," I asked, "that a hoodoo man like Mr. Onselm knows what way to shape himself into a bird?"

He shook his head. "It's known that when he's at one place, the Ugly Bird's been sighted at another." He tried to change the subject. "Silver strings on your guitar—never heard of any but steel strings."

"In the olden days," I told him, "silver was used a many times for strings. It gives a more singy sound."

In my mind I had it the subject wouldn't be changed. I tried a chord on my guitar, and began to sing:

> "You all have heard of the Ugly Bird
> So curious and so queer,
> That flies its flight by day and night
> And fills folks' hearts with fear.

> "I never come here to hide from fear,
> And I give you my promised word
> That I soon expect to twist the neck
> Of the God damn Ugly Bird."

When I finished, Mr. Bristow felt in his pocket.

"I was going to bid you eat with me," he said, "but—here, maybe you better buy something."

He gave me a quarter and a dime. I about gave them back, but I thanked him and walked away down the same trail Mr. Onselm had gone. Mr. Bristow watched me go, looking shrunk up. My song had scared him, so I kept singing it.

> "Oh Ugly Bird! O Ugly Bird!
> You snoop and sneak and thieve!
> This place can't be for you and me,
> And one of us got to leave."

Singing, I tried to remember all I'd heard or read or guessed that might help toward my Ugly Bird study.

Didn't witch people have partner animals? I'd read and heard tell about the animals called familiars—mostly cats or black dogs or the like, but sometimes birds.

That might be the secret, or a right much of it for the Ugly Bird wasn't Mr. Onselm's other self. Mr. Bristow had said the two of them were seen different places at one time. Mr. Onselm didn't turn into the Ugly Bird then. They were just close partners. Brothers. With the Ugly Bird's feet like Mr. Onselm's hands.

I awared of something in the sky, the big black V of a flying creature. It quartered over me, half as high as the highest woolly scrap of cloud. Once or twice it seemed like it would stoop for me, like a hawk for a rabbit, but it didn't. Looking up and letting my feet find the trail, I rounded a bunch of bushes and there, on a rotten log in a clearing, sat Mr. Onselm.

His gourd-head sank on his thin neck. His elbows set on his knees, and the soft, pink, long hands hid his face, as if he was miserable. His look made me feel disgusted. I came toward him.

"You don't feel so brash, do you?" I asked.

"Go away," he sort of gulped, soft and sick.

"Why?" I wanted to know. "I like it here." Sitting on the log, I pulled my guitar across me. "I feel like singing, Mr. Onselm."

> "His father got hung for horse stealing.
> His mother got burned for a witch,
> And his only friend is the Ugly Bird,
> The dirty son of—"

Something hit me like a shooting star from overhead.

It hit my back and shoulder, and knocked me floundering forward on one hand and one knee. It was only the mercy of God I didn't fall on my guitar and smash it. I crawled forward a few scrambles and made to get up, shaky and dizzy.

The Ugly Bird had flown down and dropped the sack of meal on me. Now it skimmed across the clearing, at the height of the low branches, its eyes glinting at me, and its mouth came open a little. I saw teeth, sharp and mean, like a garpike's teeth. It swooped for me, and the wind of its wings was colder than a winter storm.

Without stopping to think, I flung up my both hands to box it off from me, and it gave back, flew backward like the biggest, devilishest humming bird ever seen in a nightmare. I was too dizzy and scared to wonder why it gave back; I had barely the wit to be thankful.

"Get out of here," moaned Mr. Onselm, who hadn't stirred.

I shame to say that I got. I kept my hands up and backed across the clearing and into the trail beyond. Then I half realized where my luck had been. My hands had lifted the guitar toward the Ugly Bird, and somehow it hadn't liked the guitar.

Just once I looked back. The Ugly Bird was perching on the

log and it sort of nuzzled up to Mr. Onselm, most horrible. They were sure enough close together. I stumbled off away.

I found a stream, with stones to make steps across. I turned and walked down to where it made a wide pool. There I knelt and washed my face—it looked pallid in the water image—and sat with my back to a tree and hugged my guitar and rested. I shook all over. I must have felt as bad for a while as Mr. Onselm looked like he felt, sitting on the log waiting for his Ugly Bird and—what else?

Had he been hungry? Sick? Or just evil? I couldn't say which.

After a while I walked back to the trail and along it again, till I came to what must have been the only store thereabouts.

It faced one way on a rough road that could carry wagon and car traffic, and the trail joined on and reached the door. The building wasn't big but it was good, made of sawed planks well painted. It rested on big rocks instead of posts, and had a roofed open front like a porch, with a bench where people could sit.

Opening the door, I went in. You'll find a many such stores in back country places through the land. Counters. Shelves of cans and packages. Smoked meat hung one corner, a glass-front icebox for fresh meat another. One point, sign says U.S. POST OFFICE, with half a dozen pigeonholes for letters and a couple of cigar boxes for stamps and money-order blanks. The proprietor wasn't in. Only a girl, scared and shaking, and Mr. Onselm, there ahead of me, telling her what he wanted.

He wanted her.

"I don't care if Sam Heaver did leave you in charge here," he said with the music in his voice. "He won't stop my taking you with me."

Then he swung around and fixed his squint eye and wide-open eye on me, like two mismated gun muzzles. "You again," he said.

He looked hale and hearty. I strayed my hands over the guitar strings, and he twisted up his face as if it colicked him.

"Winnie," he said to the girl, "wait on him and get him out of here."

Her eyes were round in her scared face. I never saw as sweet a face as hers, or as scared. Her hair was dark and thick. It was like the thundercloud before the rain comes down. It made her paleness look paler. She was small, and she cowered for fear of Mr. Onselm.

"Yes, sir?" she said to me.

"Box of crackers," I decided, pointing to a near shelf. "And a can of those sardine fish."

She put them on the counter. I dug out the quarter Mr. Bristow had given me, and slapped it down on the counter top between the girl and Mr. Onselm.

"Get away!" he squeaked, shrill and mean as a bat. He had jumped back, almost halfway across the floor. And for once both of his eyes were big.

"What's the matter?" I asked him purely wondering. "This is a good silver quarter." And I picked it up and held it out for him to take and study.

But he ran out of the store like a rabbit. A rabbit with the dogs after it.

The girl he'd called Winnie just leaned against the wall as if she was tired. I asked: "Why did he light out like that?"

She took the quarter. "It doesn't scare me much," she said, and rung it up on the old cash register. "All that scares me is—Mr. Onselm."

I picked up the crackers and sardines. "He's courting you?"

She shuddered, though it was warm. "I'd sooner be in a hole with a snake than be courted by Mr. Onselm."

"Why not just tell him to leave you be?"

"He'd not listen. He always does what pleases him. Nobody dares stop him."

"I know, I heard about the mules he stopped and the poor lady he dumbed." I returned to the other subject. "Why did he squinch away from money? I'd reckon he loved money."

She shook her head. The thundercloud hair stirred. "He never needs any. Takes what he wants without paying."

"Including you?"

I laid down my dime I had left. "Let's have a coke drink, you and me."

She rang up the dime too. There was a sort of dry chuckle at the door, like a stone rattling down the well. I looked quick, and saw two long, dark wings flop away from the door. The Ugly Bird had spied.

But the girl Winnie smiled over her coke drink. I asked permission to open my fish and crackers on the bench outside. She nodded yes. Out there, I worried open the can with my pocket knife and had my meal. When I finished I put the trash in a garbage barrel and tuned my guitar. Winnie came out and harked while I sang about the girl whose hair was like the thundercloud before the rain comes down, and she blushed till she was pale no more.

Then we talked about Mr. Onselm and the Ugly Bird, and how they had been seen in two different places at once—

"But," said Winnie, "who's seen them together?"

"Shoo, I have," I told her. "Not long ago." And I told how Mr. Onselm sat, all sick and miserable, and the conjer bird crowded up against him.

She heard all that, with eyes staring off, as if looking for something far away. Finally she said, "John, you say it crowded up to him."

"It did that thing, as if it studied to get right inside him."

"Inside him!"

"That's right."

"Makes me think of something I heard somebody say about hoodoo folks," she said. "How the hoodoo folks sometimes put a stuff out, mostly in dark rooms. And it's part of them, but it takes the shape and mind of another person—once in a while, the shape and mind of an animal."

"Shoo," I said again, "now you mention it, I've heard the same thing. It might explain those Louisiana stories about werewolves."

"Shape and mind of an animal," she repeated herself. "Maybe the shape and mind of a bird. And they call it echo—no, ecto—ecto—"

"Ectoplasm," I remembered. "That's right. I've even seen pictures they say were taken of such stuff. It seems to live—it'll yell, if you grab it or hit it or stab it."

"Could maybe—" she began, but a musical voice interrupted.

"He's been around here long enough," said Mr. Onselm.

He was back. With him were three men. Mr. Bristow, and a tall, gawky man with splay shoulders and a black-stubbled chin, and a soft, smooth-grizzled man with an old fancy vest over his white shirt.

Mr. Onselm acted like the leader of a posse. "Sam Heaver," he crooned at the soft, grizzled one, "can tramps loaf at your store?"

The soft old storekeeper looked dead and gloomy at me. "Better get going, son," he said, as if he'd memorized it.

I laid my guitar on the bench. "You men ail my stomach," I said, looking at them. "You let this half-born, half-bred hoodoo man sic you on me like hound dogs when I'm hurting nobody and nothing.''

"Better go," he said again.

I faced Mr. Onselm, and he laughed like a sweetly played horn. "You," he said, "without a dime in your pocket! You can't do anything to anybody."

Without a dime . . . the Ugly Bird had seen me spend my silver money, the silver money that ailed Mr. Onselm. . . .

"Take his guitar, Hobe," said Mr. Onselm, and the gawky man, clumsy but quick, grabbed the guitar from the bench and backed away to the door.

"That takes care of him," Mr. Onselm sort of purred, and he fairly jumped and grabbed Winnie by the wrist. He pulled her along toward the trail, and I heard her whimper.

"Stop him!" I bawled, but they stood and looked, scared and dumb. Mr. Onselm, still holding Winnie, faced me. He lifted his free hand, with the pink forefinger sticking out like the barrel of a pistol.

Just the look he gave me made me weary and dizzy. He was going to hoodoo me, like he'd done the mules, like he'd done the woman who tried to hide her cake from him. I turned from him, sick and afraid, and I heard him giggle, thinking he'd won already. In the doorway stood the gawky man called Hobe, with the guitar.

I made a long jump at him and started to wrestle it away from him.

"Hang onto it, Hobe," I heard Mr. Onselm sort of choke out, and, from Mr. Bristow:

"There's the Ugly Bird!"

Its wings flapped like a storm in the air behind me. But I'd torn my guitar from Hobe's hands and turned on my heel.

A little way off, Mr. Onselm stood stiff and straight as a stone figure in front of a courthouse. He still held Winnie's wrist. Between them the Ugly Bird came swooping at me, its beak pointing for me like a stabbing bayonet.

I dug in my toes and smashed the guitar at it. Full-slam I struck its bulgy head above the beak and across the eyes, and I heard the polished wood of my music-maker crash to splinters.

And down went the Ugly Bird!

Down it went.

Quiet it lay.

Its great big wings stretched out on either side, without a

flutter. Its beak was driven into the ground like a nail. It didn't kick or flop or stir once.

But Mr. Onselm, standing where he stood holding Winnie, screamed out the way you might scream if something had clawed out all your insides with a single tearing grab.

He didn't move, I don't even know if his mouth came open. Winnie gave a pull with all her strength and tottered back, clear of him. And as if only his hold on her had kept him standing, Mr. Onselm slapped over and down on his face, his arms flung out like the Ugly Bird's wings, his face in the dirt like the Ugly Bird's face.

Still holding my broken guitar by the neck like a club, I ran to him and stooped. "Get up," I said, and took hold of what hair he had and lifted his face up.

One look was enough. From the war, I know a dead man when I see one. I let go his hair, and his face went back into the dirt as if it belonged there.

The others moved at last, tottering a few steps closer. And they didn't act like enemies now, for Mr. Onselm who had made them act so was down and dead.

Then Hobe gave a scared shout, and we looked that way.

The Ugly Bird all of a sudden looked rotten mushy, and was soaking into the ground. To me, anyhow, it looked shadowy and misty, and I could see through it. I wanted to move close, then I didn't want to. It was melting away like snow on top of a stove; only no wetness left behind.

It was gone, while we watched and wondered and felt bad all over.

Mr. Bristow knelt and turned Mr. Onselm over. On the dead face ran sick lines across, thin and purple, as though he'd been struck down by a blow of a toaster or a gridiron.

"The guitar strings," said Mr. Bristow. "The silver guitar strings. It finished him, like any hoodoo man."

That was it. Won't a silver bullet kill a witch, or a silver knife a witch's cat? And a silver key locks out ghosts, doesn't it?

"What was the word you said?" whispered Winnie to me.

"Ectoplasm," I told her. "Like his soul coming out—and getting struck dead outside his body."

More important was talk about what to do now. The men decided. They allowed to report to the county seat that Mr. Onselm's heart had stopped on him, which it had. They went over the tale three or four times to make sure they'd all tell it the same. They cheered up as they talked. You never saw gladder people to get rid of a neighbor.

"And, John," said Mr. Bristow, "we'd sure enough be proud if you stayed here. You took this curse off us."

Hobe wanted me to come live on his farm and help him work it on shares. Sam Heaver offered me all the money out of his old cash register. I thanked him and said no, sir, to Hobe I said thank you kindly, I'd better not. If they wanted their story to stick with the sheriff, they'd better forget that I'd been around when Mr. Onselm's heart stopped. All I was sorry for was my broken guitar.

But while we'd talked, Mr. Bristow was gone. He came back, with a guitar from his place, and he acted honored if I'd take it in place of mine. So I tightened my silver strings on it and tried a chord or two.

Winnie swore she'd pray for me by name each night of her life, and I told her that would sure see me safe from any assaults of the devil.

"Assaults of the devil, John!" she said, almost shrill in the voice, she was so earnest. "It's you who drove the devil from this valley."

The others all said they agreed on that.

"It was foretold about you in the Bible," said Winnie, her voice soft again. "There was a man sent from God, whose name was John."

But that was far too much for her to say, and I was that abashed, I said goodbye all around in a hurry. I strummed my new guitar as I walked away, until I got an old song back into my mind. I've heard tell that the song's written in an old-time book called *Percy's Frolics,* or *Relics,* or something:

> "Lady, I never loved witchcraft,
>   Never dealt in privy wile,
>   But evermore held the high way
>   Of love and honor, free from guile. . . ."

And though I couldn't bring myself to look back to the place I was leaving forever I knew that Winnie watched me, and that she listened, listened, till she had to strain her ears to catch the last, faintest end of my song.

FIG. I
Ganymedeus sapiens standardensis

Skiametric Morphology and Behaviorism of Ganymedeus Sapiens

A Summary of Neoteric Hypotheses
By Kenneth R. Deardorf

Subsequent to the initial intrusion of Ganymedean skiagrams[1] into the scanning specula of early polydimensional exploratory apparatus, a number of theories have been postulated to account for their appearance. These have varied from the original assumption that the profiles were merely aberrations in the crystalline structure of the focussing vector of the apparatus[2] to the extreme sophism that they were revelatory in nature.[3] The equations of Gräf-Hemmler were for a time overlooked.[4]

FIG. II
Ganymedean hurrying

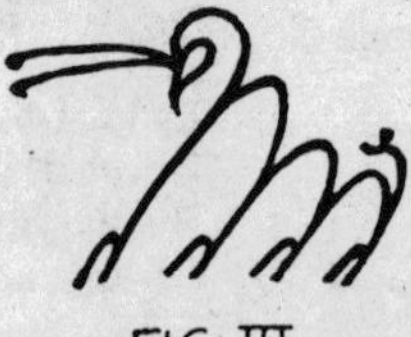

FIG. III
Making sudden stop

There is no longer any divergence from the opinion that the skiagrams are occulted reflections of living organisms. Their incompleteness (they manifest only as mono-line profiles, or cross sections, on the scanning screen—Figure I) is explained by the probability that the conning apparatus as so far developed is able to contact only two of the unknown number of dimensions in which *Ganymedeus* is known to exist. The complete form is a matter for conjecture. In all probability it no more resembles the visible skiagram than the human form resembles a cross section of it obtained, for example, laterally through the thoracic region. Ganymedean cross sections are, however, much more expressive than cross sections of anthropoid anatomies would be.

It is this expressiveness, with its concomitant implication of sagacity, which has led Bruce[5] to append the designation *sapiens* to the original cognomen *Ganymedeus,* a practice adopted wholeheartedly by subsequent investigators. And it is this same expressiveness which has permitted the amassing of a significant body of knowledge concerning this remarkable species. The skiagrams express not only physical activity (Figures II and III), but abstract personality characteristics as well (Figures IV and V).

Within the profuse polymorphism exhibited, a distinct duality of basic types is distinguishable, apparently analogous to the binate sexuality of the homodimensional primates and other mammals.[6] A typical specimen of the female category is illustrated in Figure VI. Male and female duads occasionally occur, as in Figure VII, which portrays a pair of Ganymedes engaged in what appears to be osculation, intimating that courtship procedures are not dissimilar to those of *Homo sapiens.*

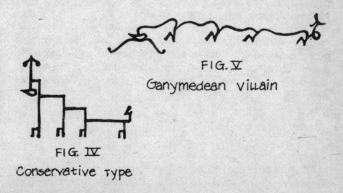

FIG. V

Ganymedean villain

FIG. IV

Conservative type

In other ways, the extraordinary parallelism of Ganymedean life-patterns with those of contemporary *Hominidae* is well documented. Skiagrams are recorded demonstrating a highly developed interest in athletics (Figure VIII). Terpsichorean attitudes also are frequent (Figure IX).

A considerable field for research remains. Additional skiagrams are being recovered, and cataloguing and classifying techniques and categories are still matters of controversy among investigators, awaiting needed clarification and standardization. It is to be hoped that more complete and better collated data will be available in the near future.

FIG. VI

Ganymedeus feminis

REFERENCES

[1] *Variable Resonance Interference Patterns in Porphyrindizine Crystallogy*. P. B. Penticton and John R. H. Murphy, Brin Univ. Monograph Press, July, '47, pp. 372–381.

[2] *Les conséquences de l'agitation des cristaux porphyrindizines dans l'origine des caractères uniques Ganymèdes*. Jean Chevalier, Rapport présenté au cours des séances de la Société des Sciences Physiques, Sorbonne, Sep. '47, pour le bulletin de la Société, 1947.

[3] *Symbolismus Ganymedeus Propheticus*. Elder VJ, Temple Gateway, Aug. '48, pp. 76–425.

FIG. VII
Ganymedeans osculating

[4]*Vorwurf zur Entwickelung anderswoher gekommener intellektueller Geschöpftypen in irdlischer Naturerscheinung.* Karl Gräf-Hemmler, Die Zeitung zur Forderung neuester Zwischenraumgewissenschaften, Stuttgart, N.F., Bd. 12, Heft 1, '49, pp. 1–48.
[5]*Further Observations Regarding Cultural and Social Aspects of* Ganymedeus sapiens. W. Muller Bruce, Annals of the Tennyson Science Foundation, 1948, pp. 142–8.
[6]*Les différences constitutives entre la mâle et la femelle dans les animaux Ganymèdes.* Jean Chevalier, Bulletin de la Société des Sciences Physiques, June '49, pp. 547–551.

FIG. VIII
Ganymedean Acrobats

FIG. IX
Ganymedean performing
light fantastic

Define Your Terms

Again and again in the editors' voluminous correspondence, I noticed how the question of "defining fantasy" kept arising. Of course, the effort to define "fantasy"—or "science fiction" as far as that goes—has been going on since the earliest days when the magazines devoted to these forms caught the fancy of their reading public. Many authors, editors, aficionados, academicians and just readers are still arguing the issue vigorously and vehemently. McComas and Boucher were no exceptions. They had positive and definite opinions. These letters catch them establishing fantasy laws for promising but misguided writers, or answering a specific query from a reader, another editor, an author. It is interesting to measure their views with one's own.

Here is one of the earliest examples of editorial effort to clue the writer into the Boucher/McComas definitions and understanding of "fantasy."

5 November 1949

Dear Mr. Vandegrift:

Although JOHNNY is certainly not, in its present form, suitable to The Magazine of FANTASY, its essential idea is so exactly the sort of concept we like that we want to go into much more detail than on the average rejection.

The chief difficulties are all of a sort that is fatal to fantasy—inconsistency. For fantasy, as you know, is a far more stringently logical and self-consistent form than naturalistic fiction.

A) It's impossible to believe that a sub in wartime would casually pick up a man who happened to be without a berth—all personnel assignments would be controlled and specific.

B) The build-up about Johnny's mysteriousness in the present is unconvincingly grounded on too little; and besides, is from roughly the point of view of one of his shipmates, which makes for an abrupt jerk at the time shift.

C) The significance of the episode of the girl and the dove is not at all clear nor well tied into the rest.

D) And most important—the story doesn't jibe with what we do know of the biblical Jonah—who did not appear out of nowhere, but was a known, existing Jew before he set out for Nineveh.

The answer to the last seems to be that Johnny was not simply projected into the past, but returned to it. That Jonah set out on his flight to Tarshish and was hurled overboard, as recounted in the Bible—and there encountered a time warp which thrust him into our era. His consciousness is warped by the experience. He remembers only that he has an unfulfilled mission . . . something to do with a sea trip . . . which accounts for his maritime life and for his being considered odd, a crackpot monomaniac. When he returns his consciousness does not adjust at once completely—but there is a flood of memory with his final realization that he is the servant of the God who is Master of the heights and depths, not only of Space, but of Time.

It's possible that this concept was in your mind—if so, it is certainly not clearly projected. We feel that reconstruction, clarification along these lines would answer most of our objections—if you'd also make us see what you mean by the dove.

AB

The baffling aspects of trying to differentiate between "fantasy" and "science fiction" really worries the editors as demonstrated in the following letter.

12 December 1952

Dear Mr. Fisher:

In reply to your letter of Dec 9—I suppose it all depends on where you draw the line between "science fiction" and "fantasy." Frankly, we think the line cannot be drawn—

an opinion in which we are supported by such authorities as Fletcher Pratt and John W. Campbell Jr.

One man's s f is another's f, and vice versa. Very few of the books labeled s f which we read as reviewers seem to us to deserve the label. On the other hand we're constantly surprised when stories which we have published under the impression that we were running "pure" f receive awards from s f societies or are chosen by such strict s f anthologists as Groff Conklin.

It's all very baffling. We'd love to run some "pure" s f of the Heinlein type . . . but so far as we can discover, nobody's writing any. We certainly don't feel we're deluding our readers as to the s f content when 7 of the 18 stories in Bleiler-Bikty's annual BEST volume for 1952 appeared in F&SF (more than twice as many as from any other magazine), or when 8 out of 11 stories in our current (Jan) issue and 7 out of 10 in the previous issue fall into one or another of the infinite definitions of s f.

Sincerely,

AB

This excerpt speaks clearly for itself.

Dear Carl:

Trends (as requested by our publishers and our readers): More s f, less "fantasy" (if anybody knows where to draw the line*); more originals, fewer reprints.

*Best definition yet is by Campbell in latest ASF: "A science fiction story is the kind of story I want to read when I feel like reading science fiction."

J. F. McComas

Kay Rogers was to become a valued and valuable contributor to the publication. Here's an analysis of fantasy for her benefit.

20 November 1950

Dear Miss Rogers:

NAKED HEART has some smooth, perceptive writing, but it is *not* fantasy. Rather, it's a very nice psychological study, just a bit slow-paced in spots.

What, then, is fantasy . . . as practised by our editors? First and foremost, it's a story with a situation that can't be explained away by normal, rational hypothesis! It must be literally out of this world . . . as we know it. Your fantasy situation must have its own logic, and that logic must be strictly adhered to! There must be a reason for the happenings in a story. While he reads, the ''impossible'' reasons must be made convincing to the reader.

As illustration, you write a vampire story and have it so that the vampire can see his reflection in a mirror. No. The fantasy logic of the vampire situation has been established; a vampire *can't* be reflected in a mirror.

Get original. You want to write a story about a man who's suddenly able to see through brick walls; not concrete, glass, steel—just brick. Well, you can't just say he does and go on from there. You've got to concoct a series of plausible circumstances, that for the reading time of the story convince the reader that such behavior is proper and right. Perhaps your hero, coming from a long line of Irish bricklayers, was given this gift of brick-sight by one of the little people who owed his family a favor. Only, don't spoil it by having this little person a leprechaun—that's not their tradition.

Remember, a fantasy may be weird, comic, ghostly or what-have-you. But it's no good if you can't achieve suspension of disbelief on the part of the reader!

I have run on! My excuse is that Boucher and I believe you're a comer, and we don't want you to get off on the wrong foot!

Sincerely,

J. Francis McComas

What does ''modern'' science fiction demand as its basis?

2 December 1952

Dear Mr. Fineman:

We're in complete agreement with you that "medical science . . . has been neglected in fiction" and particularly in science fiction. We'd very much like to get more exploration of its possibilities.

But I'm afraid THE WAY THINGS ARE DISCOVERED is, for us at least (or any s f magazine), the wrong approach. It's too impersonal, remote, documentary—almost like a few pp from a medical history on the background of a discovery.

Modern science fiction no longer lays stress solely on the *making* of a discovery. The discovery, to be sure, must be made plausible; but the essential *story* lies in its effect upon society and upon specific human characters.

In other words, science fiction must have, in addition to its scientific background, all the elements of any other *fiction*.

AB

This very early Ron Goulart item demonstrates a fictional aspect of science fiction terminology.

Almost all the most stimulating letters we receive end with the request: ". . . and please don't waste space on a letter column." But for the small minority who occasionally request such a feature, we offer this special page, in which a bright new humority of the University of California Pelican *imagines the letter column of* Fantastic Space Tales.

Anthony Boucher
J. F. McComas

Letters to the Editor

LIKES STORY

Dear Ed: Boy, *Vampires of the Lunar Asteroid Gulf* was some story. I liked it. I read it eleven times and enjoyed it. Although the last two or three times I began to get the idea that I'd read a similar story somewhere before. Print more by Prufrock. I like him. He writes like the great Edgar Rice Burroughs. By the way I have twenty-seven copies of *Tarzan and the City of Gold* which I will swap or trade for back issues of *Spicy Weird Stories*. Liked Carthoff's illos for *Vampires of the Martian Pits*. Except in the story Valkor is described as having three heads and in the picture he had two. Carthoff should watch stuff like that. I enjoyed that babe on the cover. That two piece Terra-Gravitronic suit was fine. What there was of it. Heh, heh. *(Heh, heh, yourself. Ed.)*

Stanley J. Hoff
Apt. C, Devil's Island

READ MARCH ISSUE
Editor: Wow. Gosh. Gee. Yeah, man!

Sam

Editor's note: That was Poe's story, *Vampires of the Rue Morgue*. Yes, we will print more of Poe's stories just as soon as he writes them, although we haven't heard from him for quite some time now. Let us hear from you again, Sam. We enjoy your mature and intelligent comments.

TROUBLE WITH PEN NAMES

Dear Editor: How about a hint as to who some of your authors really are? Is F. Stan Metz really Metz F. Stan? Does William Van Williams write under the name of Williams van William and Sam van Sam? Also isn't Harry C. Nordenhoffer really Max Glutz? And by the way, aren't you really Arnold Silver who escaped from Ohio State Prison in 1922?

Mrs. Emily Harkins

Editor's note: None of your damn business.

PLEASED WITH MARCH ISSUE

Dear Ed: I don't suppose you'll print this because I never wrote a letter to a mag before, but anyway I felt I had to because I like *Vampires of the Martian Woods*. I have been reading science fiction for forty-two years and have never been more pleased with a yarn. I would compare it favorably with A. Merritt's *Vampires of the Venusian Woods*. And those pics by Rogoff. That inky blotch in the left hand corner really looked like Asgor, the Mad Ruler of the Sunken City. By the way, I would like to know what a BEM is. My friends won't tell me. Is it a dirty word?

General Arthur MacDouglas
U.S. Army, Retired

Editor's Note: A BEM is a bugeyed-monster. The word was invented by Jules Verne in *Vampires Under the Sea*.

A COMPLAINT

Dear slob of an editor: What's the big idea? In *Vampires of South Dakota* the hero doesn't get the girl in the last paragraph. You trying to ruin good science fiction? After paying fifteen cents for your lousy mag I expect good writin. I hope this ain't becomin a literary mag like *Amazing Gore Stories*.

Max Sprool

Editor's note: Don't worry, Max. We don't like none of that smart writing anymore than you don't. Read *Vampires of the Terra Mines* in the next issue. Even the vampire gets a girl in that one.

Ron Goulart

This letter is a particularly delightful illumination of Asimov's reaction to his poem "The Foundation of S. F. Success" which follows it.

26 June 1954

Dear Tony:

I love you, too. Do you realize that in sixteen years of professional writing, this will be the first time I have ever had any poetry published. Of course, you are given *carte blanche* in any smoothing polish the thing needs. My pride in my writing does not extend to the care and protection of limping feet and imperfect rhymes.

Do you think the fans will accuse me of anti-Asimov bias? Incidentally, don't forget to put my name on the poem in clear, distinct, and unblurred letters. I wouldn't want the fans to think that anyone else would be so unkind to me.

Yours,

Isaac

The Foundation of S. F. Success

If you ask me how to shine in the science fiction line as a pro of luster bright,
I say, brush up on the lingo of the sciences, by jingo (never mind if not quite right).
You must talk of Space and Galaxies and tesseractic fallacies in slick and mystic style,
Though the fans won't understand it, they will all the same demand it with a softly hopeful smile.

And all the fans will say,
As you walk your spatial way,

"If that young man indulges in flights through all the Galaxy,
Why, what a most imaginative type of man that type of man
    must be!"

So success is not a mystery, just brush up on your history, and
    borrow day by day.
Take an Empire that was Roman and you'll find it is at home in
    all the starry Milky Way.
With a drive that's hyperspatial, through the parsecs you will
    race, you'll find that plotting is a breeze,
With a tiny bit of cribbin' from the works of Edward Gibbon and
    that Greek, Thucydides.

And all the fans will say,
As you walk your thoughtful way,

"If that young man involves himself in authentic history,
Why, what a very learned kind of high IQ his high IQ must be!"

Then eschew all thoughts of passion of a man-and-woman fash-
    ion from your hero's thoughtful mind.
He must spend his time on politics, and thinking up his knavish
    tricks,* and outside that he's blind.
It's enough he's had a mother, other females are a bother,
    though they're jeweled and glistery,
They will just distract his dreaming and his necessary scheming
    with that psychohistory.

And all the fans will say
As you walk your narrow way,

"If all his yarns restrict themselves to masculinity,
Why, what a most particularly pure young man that pure young
    man must be!"

                                        —Isaac Asimov

Asimov comments on Boucher's story:

*If this rime seems questionable, *cf.* "God Save the Queen." —A.B.

February 6 1953

Dear Tony (and/or Mick)

I've just read THE OTHER INAUGURATION in the March issue of F&SF and felt that I had to do something about it—like patting you on the back.

It's pretty obvious that you began writing it on 5 November last and I wish to applaud your principles in writing it and your courage in printing it. It was a good story, too. Only one flaw. You have Lanroyd say "Had enough, Stu? (Hist slogan current ca 1948)"

Actually, it was the slogan of 1946, preceding the election of the infamous 80th Congress. Still, he was writing in 1984 and he said *ca* 1948, so maybe I'm splitting hairs.

Yours,

Asimov

6 March 1953

Dear Isaac:

Of course, you're absolutely right about the dating of "Had enough?" in OTHER INAUG. and I shan't take refuge in the excuses you so kindly and ingeniously provide for me.

Groff's thinking of reprinting the story, so I've dropped him a note to make the change if he does so.

Very glad you liked the story.

Hope Fred (Pohl) will condescend to let us see some Asimov soon.

Best,

A.B.

On April 30, 1789, in the city of New York, George Washington
was inaugurated as the first President of the United States, and
the best working democracy the world has yet known began to
function. Since then, dates, places and circumstances of the inauguration of a President-elect have altered: after several changes,
its date was fixed by Constitutional amendment as January
20; beginning with Jefferson's taking office in 1800, all our
Presidents have been inaugurated in our capital, Washington,
D.C.; the inaugural address of Calvin Coolidge was the first to
be broadcast on a nationwide hook-up; and, in January, 1953,
any American citizen who could get near a TV set was able to
see his President take the oath of office. But despite all these
refinements, underneath all its pomp and ceremony, a Presidential inauguration has one simple meaning for the citizen: it is,
after all, the end product of a chain of effort that began with the
activity of free Americans working and voting within their own
neighborhoods. Anthony Boucher knows from precinct-worker
experience the practical meaning of democracy—local democracy—
in action. Thinking about this year's inauguration he began to
speculate about a problem that our Constitution has not provided
for: should chronokinesis be allowed to affect the voter's choice?

J.F. McC.

The Other Inauguration
By Anthony Boucher

From the Journal of Peter Lanroyd, Ph. D.:
  Mon Nov 5 84: To any man even remotely interested in
politics, let alone one as involved as I am, every 1st Tue of
every 4th Nov must seem like one of the crucial *if*-points of
history. From every American presidential election stem 2 vitally
different worlds, not only for U S but for world as a whole.
  It's easy enough, esp for a Prof of Polit Hist, to find examples—

1860, 1912, 1932 . . . & equally easy, if you're honest with yourself & forget you're a party politician, to think of times when it didn't matter much of a special damn who won an election. Hayes-Tilden . . . biggest controversy, biggest outrage on voters in U S history . . . yet how much of an *if*-effect?

But this is different. 1984 (damn Mr Orwell's long-dead soul! he jinxed the year!) is *the* key *if*-crux as ever was in U S hist. And on Wed Nov 7 my classes are going to expect a few illuminating remarks—wh are going to have to come from me, scholar, & forget about the County Central Comm.

So I've recanvassed my precinct (looks pretty good for a Berkeley Hill precinct, too; might come damn close to carrying it), I've done everything I can before the election itself; & I put in a few minutes trying to be non-party-objective on why this year of race 1984 is so *if*-vital.

Historical b g:

A) U S always goes for 2-party system, whatever the names.

B) The Great Years 1952/76 when we had, almost for 1st time, honest 2-partyism. Gradual development (started 52 by Morse, Byrnes, Shivers, etc) of cleancut parties of "right" & "left" (both, of course, to the right of a European "center" party). Maybe get a class laugh out of how both new parties kept both old names, neither wanting to lose New England Repub votes or Southern Demo, so we got Democratic American Republican Party & Free Democratic Republican Party.

C) 1976/84 God help us growth of 3rd party, American. (The bastards! The simple, the perfect name . . . !) Result: Gradual withering away of DAR, bad defeat in 1980 presidential, total collapse in 82 congressional election. Back to 2-party system: Am vs FDR.

So far so good. Nice & historical. But how tell a class, without accusations of partisanship, what an Am victory means? What a destruction, what a (hell! let's use their own word) subversion of everything American. . . .

Or am I being partisan? Can anyone be as evil, as anti-American, as to me the Senator is?

Don't kid yrself Lanroyd. If it's an Am victory, you aren't going to lecture on Wed. You're going to be in mourning for the finest working democracy ever conceived by man. And now you're going to sleep & work like hell tomorrow getting out the vote.

* * *

It was Tuesday night. The vote had been got out, and very thoroughly indeed. In Lanroyd's precinct, in the whole state of California, and in all 49 other states. The result was in, and the TV commentator, announcing the final electronic recheck of results from 50 state-wide electronic calculators, was being smug and happy about the whole thing. ("Conviction?" thought Lanroyd bitterly. "Or shrewd care in holding a job?")

". . . Yessir," the commentator was repeating gleefully, "it's such a landslide as we've never seen in all American history— and the *American* history is what it's going to be from now on. For the Senator, five . . . hundred . . . and . . . eighty . . . nine electoral votes from forty . . . nine states. For the Judge, four electoral votes from one state.

"Way back in 1936, when Franklin Delano Roosevelt" (he pronounced the name as a devout Christian might say Judas Iscariot) "carried all but two states, somebody said, 'As Maine goes, so goes Vermont.' Well, folks, I guess from now on we'll have to say—ha! ha!—'As Maine goes . . . so goes Maine.' And it looks like the FDR party is going the way of the unlamented DAR. From now on, folks, it's Americanism for Americans!

"Now let me just recap those electoral figures for you again. For the Senator on the American ticket, it's five eighty-nine— that's five hundred and eighty-nine—electoral—"

Lanroyd snapped off the set. The automatic brought up the room lighting from viewing to reading level.

He issued a two-syllable instruction which the commentator would have found difficult to carry out. He poured a shot of bourbon and drank it. Then he went to hunt for a razor blade.

As he took it out of the cabinet, he laughed. Ancient Roman could find a good use for this, he thought. Much more comfortable nowadays, too, with thermostats in the bathtub. Drift off under constantly regulated temperature. Play hell with the M.E.'s report, too. Jesus! Is it hitting me so bad I'm thinking stream of consciousness? Get to work, Lanroyd.

One by one he scraped the political stickers off the window. There goes the FDR candidate for State Assembly. There goes the Congressman—twelve-year incumbent. There goes the United States Senator. State Senator not up for reelection this year, or he'd be gone too. There goes NO ON 13. Of course in a year like this State Proposition # 13 passed too; from now on, as a Professor at a State University, he was forbidden to criticize publicly an incumbent government official, and compelled to submit the reading requirements for his courses to a legislative committee.

There goes the Judge himself . . . not just a sticker but a full lumino-portrait. The youngest man ever appointed to the Supreme Court; the author of the great dissenting opinions of the '50s; later a Chief Justice to rank beside Marshall in the vitality of his interpretation of the Constitution; the noblest candidate the Free Democratic Republican Party had ever offered . . .

There goes the last of the stickers. . . .

Hey, Lanroyd, you're right. It's a symbol yet. There goes the last of the political stickers. You'll never stick 'em on your window again. Not if the Senator's boys have anything to say about it.

Lanroyd picked up the remains of the literature he'd distributed in the precincts, dumped it down the incinerator without looking at it, and walked out into the foggy night.

If . . .

All right you're a monomaniac. You're 40 and you've never married (and what a sweet damn fool you were to quarrel with Clarice over the candidates in 72) and you think your profession's taught you that politics means everything and so your party loses and it's the end of the world. But God damn it *this* time it *is*. This *is* the key-point.

If . . .

Long had part of the idea; McCarthy had the other part. It took the Senator to combine them. McCarthy got nowhere, dropped out of the DAR reorganization, failed with his third party, because he attacked and destroyed but didn't *give*. He appealed to hate, but not to greed, no what's-in-it-for-me, no porkchops. But add the Long technique, every-man-a-king, fuse 'em together: "wipe out the socialists; I'll give you something better than socialism." That does it, Senator. Coming New Year: "wipe out the democrats; I'll give you something better than democracy."

IF . . .

What was it Long said? "If totalitarianism comes to America, it'll be labelled *Americanism*." Dead Huey, now I find thy saw of might . . .

IF

There was a lighted window shining through the fog. That meant Cleve was still up. Probably still working on temporomagnetic field-rotation, which sounded like nonsense but what did you expect from a professor of psionics? Beyond any doubt the most unpredictable department in the University . . . and yet Lanroyd was glad he'd helped round up the majority vote when the Academic Senate established it. No telling what might come of it . . . *if* independent research had any chance of continuing to exist.

The window still carried a sticker for the Judge and a NO ON 13. This was a good house to drop in on. And Lanroyd needed a drink.

Cleve answered the door with a full drink in his hand. "Have this, old boy," he said; "I'll mix myself another. Night for drinking, isn't it?" The opinion had obviously been influencing him for some time; his British accent, usually all but rubbed off by now, had returned full force as it always did after a few drinks.

Lanroyd took the glass gratefully as he went in. "I'll sign that petition," he said. "I need a drink to stay sober; I think I've hit a lowpoint where I can't get drunk."

"It'll be interesting," his host observed, "to see if you're right. Glad you dropped in. I needed drinking company."

"Look, Stu," Lanroyd objected. "If it wasn't for the stickers on your window, I'd swear you were on your way to a happy drunk. What's to celebrate for God's sake?"

"Well as to God, old boy, I mean anything that's to celebrate is to celebrate for God's sake, isn't it? After all . . . Pardon. I *must* be a bit tiddly already."

"I know," Lanroyd grinned. "You don't usually shove your Church of England theology at me. Sober, you know I'm hopeless."

"Point not conceded. But God does come into this, of course. My rector's been arguing with me—doesn't approve at all. Tampering with Divine providence. But A: how can mere me tamper with anything Divine? And B: if it's possible, it's part of the Divine plan itself. And C: I've defied the dear old boy to establish that it involves in any way the Seven Deadly Sins, the Ten Commandments, or the Thirty-Nine Articles."

"Professor Cleve," said Lanroyd, "would you mind telling me what the hell you are talking about?"

"Time travel, of course. What else have I been working on for the past eight months?"

Lanroyd smiled. "O.K. Every man to his obsession. My

world's shattered and yours is rosy. Carry on, Stu. Tell me about it and brighten my life.''

"I say, Peter, don't misunderstand me. I am . . . well, really dreadfully distressed about . . .'' He looked from the TV set to the window stickers. "But it's hard to think about anything else when . . .''

"Go on.'' Lanroyd drank with tolerant amusement. "I'll believe anything of the Department of Psionics, ever since I learned not to shoot craps with you. I suppose you've invented a time machine?''

"Well, old boy, I think I have. It's a question of . . .''

Lanroyd understood perhaps a tenth of the happy monolog that followed. As an historical scholar, he seized on a few names and dates. Principle of temporomagnetic fields known since discovery by Arthur McCann circa 1941. Neglected for lack of adequate power source. Mei-Figner's experiment with nuclear pile 1959. Nobody knows what became of M-F. Embarrassing discovery that power source remained chrono-stationary; poor M-F stranded somewhere with no return power. Hasselfarb Equations 1972 established that any adequate external power source must possess too much temporal inertia to move with traveler.

"Don't you see, Peter?'' Cleve gleamed. "That's where everyone's misunderstood Hasselfarb. 'Any *external* power source . . .' Of course it baffled the physicists.''

"I can well believe it,'' Lanroyd quoted. "Perpetual motion, or squaring the circle, would baffle the physicists. They're infants, the physicists.''

Cleve hesitated, then beamed. "Robert Barr,'' he identified. "His Sherlock Holmes parody. Happy idea for a time traveler: Visit the Reichenback Falls in 1891 and see if Holmes really was killed. I've always thought an imposter 'returned.' ''

"Back to your subject, psionicist . . . which is a hell of a word for a drinking man. Here, I'll fill both glasses and you tell me why what baffles the physicists fails to baffle the ps . . .''

" 'Sounds of strong men struggling with a word,' '' Cleve murmured. They were both fond of quotation; but it took Lanroyd a moment to place this muzzily as Belloc. "Because the power source doesn't have to be *external*. We've been developing the *internal* sources. How can I regularly beat you at craps?''

"Psychokinesis,'' Lanroyd said, and just made it.

"Exactly. But nobody ever thought of trying the effect of PK power on temporomagnetic fields before. And it works and the Hasselfarb Equations don't apply!''

''You've done it?''

''Little trips. Nothing spectacular. Tiny experiments. *But*—and this, old boy, is the damnedest part—there's every indication that PK can *rotate* the temporomagnetic stasis!''

''That's nice,'' said Lanroyd vaguely.

''No, of course. You don't understand. My fault. Sorry, Peter. What I mean is this: We can not only travel in time; we can rotate into another, an alternate time. A world of If.''

Lanroyd started to drink, then abruptly choked. Gulping and gasping, he eyed in turn the TV set, the window stickers and Cleve. ''*If* . . .'' he said.

Cleve's eyes made the same route, then focused on Lanroyd. ''What we are looking at each other with,'' he said softly, ''is a wild surmise.''

From the Journal of Peter Lanroyd, Ph. D.:

Mon Nov 12 84: So I have the worst hangover in Alameda County, & we lost to UCLA Sat by 3 field goals, & the American Party takes over next Jan; but it's still a wonderful world.

Or rather it's a wonderful universe, continuum, whatsit, that includes both this world & the possibility of shifting to a brighter alternate.

I got through the week somehow after Black Tue. I even made reasonable-sounding non-subversive noises in front of my classes. Then all week-end, except for watching the game (in the quaint expectation that Cal's sure victory wd lift our spirits), Stu Cleve & I worked.

I never thought I'd be a willing lab assistant to a psionicist. But we want to keep this idea secret. God knows what a good Am Party boy on the faculty (Daniels, for inst) wd think of people who prefer an alternate victory. So I'm Cleve's factotum & busbar-boy & I don't understand a damned thing I'm doing but—

It works.

The movement in time anyway. Chronokinesis, Cleve calls it, or CK for short. CK . . . PK . . . sounds like a bunch of executives initialing each other. Cleve's achieved short CK. Hasn't dared try rotation yet. Or taking me with him. But he's sweating on my ''psionic potential.'' Maybe with some results: I lost only 2 bucks in a 2 hour crap game last night. And got so gleeful about my ps pot that I got me this hangover.

Anyway, I know what I'm doing. I'm resigning fr the County Committee at tomorrow's meeting. No point futzing around w politics any more. Opposition Party has as much chance under the Senator as it did in pre-war Russia. And I've got something else to focus on.

I spent all my non-working time in politics because (no matter what my analyst might say if I had one) I wanted, in the phrase that's true the way only corn can be, I wanted to make a better world. All right; now I can really do it, in a way I never dreamed of.

CK . . . PK . . . *OK!*

Tue Dec 11: Almost a month since I wrote a word here. Too damned magnificently full a month to try to synopsize here. Anyway it's all down in Cleve's records. Main point is development of my psionic potential (Cleve says anybody can do it, with enough belief & drive—wh is why Psionics Dept & Psych Dept aren't speaking. Psych claims PK, if it exists wh they aren't too eager to grant even now, is a mutant trait. OK so maybe I'm a mutant. Still . . .

Today I made my first CK. Chronokinesis to you, old boy. Time travel to you, you dope. All right, so it was only 10 min. So nothing happened, not even an eentsy-weentsy paradox. But I did it; & when we go, Cleve and I can go together.

So damned excited I forgot to close parenth above. Fine state of affairs. So:)

Sun Dec 30: Used to really keep me a journal. Full of fascinating facts & political gossip. Now nothing but highpoints, apptly. OK: latest highpoint:

Sufficient PK power *can* rotate the field.

Cleve never succeeded by himself. Now I'm good enough to work with him. And together . . .

He picked a simple one. Purely at random, when he thought we were ready. We'd knocked off work & had some scrambled eggs. 1 egg was a little bad, & the whole mess was awful. Obviously some alternate in wh egg was *not* bad. So we went back (CK) to 1 p m just before Cleve bought eggs, & we (how the hell to put it?) we . . . *worked.* Damnedest sensation. Turns you inside out & then outside in again. If that makes sense.

We bought the eggs, spent the same aft working as before, knocked off work, had some scrambled eggs . . . delicious!

Most significant damned egg-breaking since Columbus!

Sun Jan 20 85: This is the day.

Inauguration Day. Funny to have it on a Sun. Hasn't been since 57. Cleve asked me what's the inaugural augury. Told him the odds were eve. Monroe's 2d Inaug was a Sun . . . & so was Zachary Taylor's 1st & only, wh landed us w Fillmore.

We've been ready for a week. Waiting till today just to hear the Senator get himself inaugurated. 1st beginning of the world we'll never know.

TV's on. There the smug bastard is. Pride & ruin of 200,000,000 people.

"Americans!"

Get that. Not "fellow Americans . . ."

"Americans! You have called me in clarion tones & I shall answer!"

Here it comes, all of it. ". . . my discredited adversaries . . ." ". . . strength, not in union, but in unity . . ."

". . . as you have empowered me to root out these . . ."

The one-party system, the one-system state, the one-man party-system-state . . .

Had enough, Stu? (Hist slogan current ca 48) OK: let's *work*!

Damn! Look what this pencil did while I was turning inside out & outside in again. (Note: Articles in contact w body move in CK. For reasons cf Cleve's notebooks.) Date is now

Tues Nov 6 84: TV's on. Some cheerful commentator:

". . . Yessir, it's 1 of the greatest landslides in American history. 524 electoral votes from 45 states, to 69 electoral votes from 5 states, all Southern, as the experts predicted. I'll repeat: That's 524 electoral votes for the Judge . . ."

We've done it. We're *there*. . . . then . . . whatever the hell the word is. I'm the first politican in history who ever made the people vote right against their own judgment!

Now, in this brighter better world where the basic tenets of American democracy were safe, there was no nonsense about Lanroyd's resigning from politics. There was too much to do. First of all a thorough job of party reorganization before the Inauguration. There were a few, even on the County and State Central Committees of the Free Democratic Republican Party, who had been playing footsie with the Senator's boys. A few well-planned parliamentary maneuvers weeded them out; a new set of by-laws took care of such contingencies in the future; and the Party was solidly unified and ready to back the Judge's administration.

Stuart Cleve went happily back to work. He no longer needed a busbar-boy from the History Department. There was no pressing need for secrecy in his work; and he possessed, thanks to physical contact during chronokinesis, his full notebooks on experiments for two and a half months which, in this world, hadn't happened yet—a paradox which was merely amusing and nowise difficult.

By some peculiar whim of alternate universes, Cal even managed to win the UCLA game 33–10.

In accordance with the popular temper displayed in the Presidential election, Proposition 13, with its thorough repression of all academic thought and action, had been roundly defeated. A short while later, Professor Daniels, who had so actively joined the Regents and the Legislature in backing the measure, resigned from the Psychology Department. Lanroyd had played no small part in the faculty meetings which convinced Daniels that the move was advisable.

At last Sunday, January 20, 1985, arrived (or, for two men in the world, returned) and the TV sets of the nation brought the people the Inaugural Address. Even the radio stations abandoned their usual local broadcasts of music and formed one of their very rare networks to carry this historical highpoint.

The Judge's voice was firm, and his prose as noble as that of his dissenting or his possibly even greater majority opinions. Lanroyd and Cleve listened together, and together thrilled to the quietly forceful determination to wipe out every last vestige of the prejudices, hatreds, fears and suspicions fostered by the so-called American Party.

"A great man once said," the Judge quoted in conclusion, " 'We have nothing to fear but fear itself.' Now that a petty and wilful group of men have failed in their effort to undermine our very Constitution, I say to you: 'We have one thing to destroy. And that is destruction itself!' "

And Lanroyd and Cleve beamed at each other and broached the bourbon.

From the journal of Peter Lanroyd, Ph. D.:

Sun Oct 20 85: Exactly 9 mos. Obstetrical symbolism yet?

Maybe I shd've seen it then, at this other inauguration. Read betw the lines, seen the meaning, the true inevitable meaning.

Realized that the Judge was simply saying, in better words (or did they sound better because I thought he was on My Side?), what the Senator said in the inaugural we escaped: "I have a commission to wipe out the opposition."

Maybe I shd've seen it when the Senator was arrested for inciting to riot. Instead I cheered. Severed the sonofabitch right. (And it did, too. That's the hell of it. It's all confused. . . .)

He still hasn't been tried. They're holding him until they can nail him for treason. Mere matter of 2 constitutional amendments: Revise Act III Sec 3 Par 1 so "treason" no longer needs direct-witness proof of an overt act of war against the U S or adhering to their enemies, but can be anything yr Star Chamber wants to call it; revise Art I Sec 9 Par 3 so you can pass an ex post facto law. All very simple; the Judge's arguments sound as good as his dissent in U S vs Feinbaum. (I shd've seen, even in the inaug, that he's not the same man in this world—the same mind turned to other ends. My ends? My end . . .) The const ams'll pass all right . . . except maybe in Maine.

I shd've seen it last year when the press began to veer, when the dullest & most honest columnist in the country began to blether about the "measure of toleration"—when the liberal Chronical & the Hearst Examiner, for the 1st time in S F history, took the same stand on the Supervisors' refusal of the Civic Aud to a pro-Senator rally—when the NYer satirized the ACLU as something damned close to traitors. . . .

I began to see it when the County Central Committee started to raise hell about a review I wrote in the QPH. (God knows how a Committeeman happened to read that learned journal.) Speaking of the great old 2-party era, I praised both the DAR & the FDR as bulwarks of democracy. Very unwise. Seems as a good Party man I shd've restricted my praise to the FDR. Cd've fought it through, of course, stood on my rights—hell, a County Committeeman's an elected representative of the people. But I resigned because . . . well, because that was when I began to see it.

Today was what did it, though. 1st a gentle phone call fr the Provost—in person, no secty—wd I drop by his office tomorrow? Certain questions have arisen as to some of the political opinions I have been expressing in my lectures. . . .

That blonde in the front row with the teeth & the busy notebook & the D's & F's . . .

So Cleve comes by & I think I've got troubles . . . !

He's finally published his 1st paper on the theory of CK & PK-induced alternates. It's been formally denounced as "dangerous" because it implies the existence of better worlds. And guess who denounced it? Prof Daniels of Psych.

Sure, the solid backer of # 13, the strong American Party boy. He's a strong FDR man now. *He* knows. And he's back on the faculty.

Cleve makes it all come out theological somehow. He says that by forcibly setting mankind on the alternate *if*-fork that *we* wanted, we denied man's free will. Impose "democracy" against or without man's choice, & you have totalitarianism. Our only hope is what he calls "abnegation of our own desire"—surrender to, going along with, the will of man. We must CK & PK ourselves back to where we started.

The hell with the theology; it makes sense politically too. I was wrong. Jesus! I was wrong. Look back at every major election, every major boner the electorate's pulled. So a boner to me is a triumph of reason to you, sir. But let's not argue which dates were the major boners. 1932 or 1952, take your pick.

It's always worked out, hasn't it? Even 1920. It all straightens out, in time. Democracy's the craziest, most erratic system ever devised . . . & the closest to perfection. At least it keeps coming closer. Democratic man makes his mistakes—& he corrects them in time.

Cleve's going back to make his peace with his ideas of God & free will. I'm going back to show I've learned that a politician doesn't clear the hell&gone out of politics because he's lost. Nor does he jump over on the winning side.

He works & sweats as a Loyal Opposition—hell, as an Underground if necessary, if things get as bad as that—but he holds on & works to make men make their own betterment.

Now we're going to Cleve's, where the field's set up . . . & we're going back to the true world.

Stuart Cleve was weeping, for the first time in his adult life. All the beautifully intricate machinery which created the temporomagnetic field was smashed as thoroughly as a hydrogen atom over Novosibirsk.

"That was Winograd leading them, wasn't it?" Lanroyd's voice came out oddly through split lips and missing teeth.

Cleve nodded.

"Best damn coffin-corner punter I ever saw . . . Wondered why our friend Daniels was taking such an interest in athletics recently."

"Don't oversimplify, old boy. Not all athletes. Recognized a couple of my best honor students. . . ."

"Fine representative group of youth on the march . . . and all wearing great big FDR buttons!"

Cleve picked up a shard of what had once been a chronostatic field generator and fondled it tenderly. "When they smash machines and research projects," he said tonelessly, "the next step is smashing men."

"Did a fair job on us when we tried to stop them. Well . . . These fragments we have shored against our ruins. . . . And now, to skip to a livelier maker for our next quote, it's back to work we go! Hi-Ho! Hi-Ho! Need a busbar-boy, previous experience guaranteed?"

"It took us ten weeks of uninterrupted work," Cleve said hesitantly. "You think those vandals will let us alone that long? But we have to try, I know." He bent over a snarled mess of wiring which Lanroyd knew was called a magnetostat and performed some incomprehensibly vital function. "Now this looks almost servicea—" He jerked upright again, shaking his head worriedly.

"Matter?" Lanroyd asked.

"My head. Feels funny. . . . One of our young sportsmen landed a solid kick when I was down."

"Winograd, no doubt. Hasn't missed a boot all season."

Perturbedly Cleve pulled out of his pocket the small dice-case which seemed to be standard equipment for all psionicists. He shook a pair in his fist and rolled them out in a clear space on the rubbage-littered floor.

"*Seven!*" he called.

A six turned up, and then another six.

"Sometimes," Cleve was muttering ten unsuccessful rolls later, "even slight head injuries have wiped out all psionic potential. There's a remote possibility of redevelopment; it *has* happened. . . ."

"And," said Lanroyd, "it takes both of us to generate enough PK to rotate." He picked up the dice. "Might as well check mine." He hesitated, then let them fall. "I don't think I want to know. . . ."

They stared at each other over the ruins of the machinery that would never be rebuilt.

" 'I, a stranger and afraid . . .' " Cleve began to quote.

" 'In a world,' " Lanroyd finished, "I damned well made."

Anderson-Editors Correspondence:

24 March 1950

Dear Mr. Boucher:

It tickles me no end to appear in so excellent a magazine as yours—if it were only larger, it'd replace the lamented Unknown.

Writing is fun, especially science-fiction writing. I don't necessarily believe the thesis of a story, but it's great sport to assume it and follow out the logical consequences. Someday when I get around to it, there's a couple of historical novels and a whole slew of essays waiting to be written.

Sincerely,

Poul Anderson

Editorial notes between McC. and A.B.

12 March 1952

Anderson: When Half-Gods Go

This strikes me as pretty much all right.

A.B.

Don't think "his unsupported word. . . . etc.", is quite right. Surely he cd talk someone else into looking at the plates. But we can fix.

McC

Let's say that after the reporter's visit, the ships either A) came under top-classified UN control; or B) "returned" to their "native" planet.

AB

OK, yes. But I still want to cut like crazy, esp pp 8/10. It'll probably end up closer to 3000 or even a little less. But let's say $100 anyway.

McC

16 March 1953

Dear Mick and Tony,

I should like here to express a very real appreciation of your policy of letting the author do his own rewriting. No other s-f editor does this, damn their eyes, and writers weep bitter tears at seeing their carefully constructed prose ripped to shreds . . . even if nobody ever seems to notice the difference. Like you, I shall never understand the type of mentality which can't take straight fantasy, and at the same time labels stories containing phrases like "variable truth" as *science*-fiction, save the mark! (Not that I didn't like "The Fairy Chessmen") I'm tempted to imitate old what's-his-name and add about two pages of differential equations and circuit diagrams at the end of a story, so that the reader may pepper and salt as he pleases.

Sincerely,

Poul

Science fiction deals largely with Utopias, but very rarely with how they come into being. They are usually presented simply as inevitable results of man's constant striving toward a better world; but supposing Utopia, the ideal world of the far future, were offered to this earth today? Would we have the sense to accept it, or even to recognize it? It is this novel problem which confronts the galactic emissaries in Mr. Anderson's new story—a problem which illustrates the fact that the most highly trained missionary may sometimes need to seek the advice of the bushman.

A.B./J.F. McC

When Half-Gods Go
By Poul Anderson

Morton, of the Harvard Astronomy department, knocked the dottle from his notoriously evil-smelling pipe and looked around the room. There were a dozen or so men gathered here in his home, all professors at his university and neighboring schools, all old friends who could be trusted to keep their mouths shut.

"I hope I wasn't too melodramatic," he said, "but then this whole business is so fantastic that I've long ago given up my usual standards of normality. All you know is that I called each of you up and asked you to come here tonight as discreetly as possible. Now that we're gathered, there really isn't much more I can tell you."

His eyes traveled around the group which sat quietly smoking and sipping his brandy, and he wondered how to continue. "You remember," he went on as dryly as possible, "that a couple of weeks ago our little discussion club wrote to these *soi-disant* Sagittarians, this couple which claims to be envoys from an interstellar civilization, inviting them to come and speak. We were interested in them and their claims, we hoped to find out how they did their tricks. . . . Well, they wrote back politely

194

saying we were too small a bunch for their purposes, and I thought that was the end of it. When they got in trouble with the law the other day and were officially denounced, I was merely disappointed. Another pair of Cagliostros, eh?

"Then yesterday afternoon they appeared in my office," Morton smiled, a shy smile pleading for belief. "I was sitting alone, the door was closed, and suddenly there they were. They requested me to assemble the club—such members, at least, as I knew wouldn't blab—and said they'd talk to us after all. When I agreed, they vanished again."

The astronomer shrugged. "That's it, gentlemen. Are you game?"

"Certainly," rumbled Johns, the M.I.T. cybernetics man. "For the kind of show they put on, I don't mind harboring a fugitive."

"Y'think they're the genuine article?" asked Foxxe, the British anthropologist currently on loan to Harvard.

"I don't know," said Morton. "I honestly don't know. Maybe we'll find out tonight. We're supposed to think at them simultaneously when we're ready. They're hiding somewhere nearby and will, uh, hear us. Telepathy."

"Rum go," said Foxxe. "One day they're just another show, the next they're wanted for every crime from high treason to selling peanuts without a license. I shall never understand you Americans."

"Sometimes," said Morton, "we don't understand ourselves." He looked around the shabby, comfortable room again. The shades were pulled; night lay beyond the windows. "All set? Okay, let's get on with the seance."

They thought the invitation, feeling a little silly about the whole affair. With a faint whooshing of displaced atmosphere, the Sagittarians stood among them.

There were two, and they looked quite human on the outside, an ordinariness increased by the conventional Earthly garments they wore. They had admitted to having only four toes on each foot—shoes hid that fact—and their ears lacked the intricate Terrestrial convolutions. An X-ray would have shown other differences, and a physiologist would have been surprised by a number of internal details. But all in all, the foreignness was not great. Evolution on Earth-like planets tends to follow very similar patterns.

The man, En-Shan Khorokum, was of medium height, slender

and graceful, with high cheekbones and sleek black hair, olive skin and dark eyes. Chi Balkhai, his wife or equivalent thereof, had the same racial characteristics, and was lovely to look on, slim and supple as a finely bred cat. Both seemed young—ageless might be a better term, for there was a vibrant strength and aliveness in them, a depth of mature wisdom under the weary desperation of the hunted.

"Ah . . . how do you do," said Morton.

Khorokum smiled, a flash of white teeth in his mobile face, but the eyes were mostly on Chi. Voices murmured at the newcomers, greetings, good wishes. If they could really scan minds, thought Morton, they'd find here the friendliness they needed—a high degree of tentative acceptance of their story, with no dogmatic rejection such as had cursed them elsewhere.

He looked awkwardly around. "Please don't try to do anything special," said Chi. "We're simply old friends who had dropped in for a visit."

"Well, sit down then, sit down and have some of this brandy," bellowed Johns. "Our host keeps the best cellar this side of—what did you say your home star was called?—this side of Urukand."

"Thank you, thank you." The guests found chairs, and the professors crowded their own seats close.

"There is nothing overly melodramatic about this," said Khorokum. "My wife and I are in no danger of our lives, not when with an effort of will we can teleport ourselves off the planet altogether. But we are in a certain amount of professional jeopardy. This is our first big job as an independent team, and we'd hate to mess it up."

"You mean," said Gray, who taught history, "that there are many planets in our situation? That it's a function of your society to—convert them?"

"Well, quite a few such worlds," replied Khorokum. "You see, the Galactic Union originated in the Sagittarian star clusters about a half million years ago and has since been spreading outward, its aim being ultimately to bring all inhabited planets into itself. Urukand was civilized 10,000 years or so in the past. But it's a big job, you can readily see that, so we concentrate on worlds which have reached approximately your stage of technology. Their science is then sufficiently highly developed to understand the concepts involved, while at the same time they are far behind us and so grasp eagerly at the gifts we offer—the parapsychic powers replacing machines for all but the most routine work, the conquest of age and disease and social ills like war and poverty, membership in the glorious federation of stars—oh, it was a straightforward sort of thing till Earth came along. But there's something unique in your human psychology. You don't believe the evidence of your own senses—I wonder if you *want* a higher civilization. When our scouts reported heavy neutrino emission from your planet, Chi and I were sent on what seemed an easy mission. And we failed. We failed completely." His face twisted a little.

"Our jobs are a very small matter compared to the danger all Earth is in," said Chi softly. "Your unstable society is moving inevitably toward annihilating war and cruel tyranny. Any nation of Earth which joined the Union could no longer wage war, but it would be safe from all attack—but nobody believes that! They've seen what we can do, and still they won't believe. What we want, gentlemen, is advice."

"The savages advise the missionaries?" Van Tyne, of Boston University's English department, raised his shaggy brows.

"You are humans and we are not," said Chi. "One of you may have the vital fact we need."

Foxxe nodded. "I always claimed that the only white men who ever really understood a primitive folk were those who went native," he said. "Trouble always was, y'know, that kind of person just doesn't write for the journals."

Khorokum leaned forward, clasping his hands between his knees. "Suppose," he said, "that I give you the whole situation—from the very beginning."

At first it had seemed easy. Teleporting across a thousand light years was no more mysterious than willing your arm to move, once you understood the psychophysiological applications of wave mechanics. They took along no equipment except some small powerpacks, the size of cigaret cases, with which to equalize gravitational potentials and trigger the vast cosmic-force flows which their nervous systems could direct to control matter and energy. There had been a month or two of inconspicuous flitting about Earth and reading minds, learning the history, language, mores, filling their trained memories with the key facts. The, quite simply, they had gone to the leaders of the important nations.

The Union was not a conqueror. That was ruled out by the

relative smallness of its population in an enormous Galaxy, by a total lack of any economic necessity for tribute, and by the very structure of a society based on individual development. New planets had to join of their own free will, if they were not to become a dangerous and disruptive element in a carefully balanced civilization. Even the field agents could not exert compulsion of any sort, including hypnosis, except in self-defense; and even after a state had become a member the necessary internal changes were best carried out, gradually, by its own government. The immediate alterations ran in the direction of libertarianism, universal equality, total disarmament—the obvious reforms. After that, field agents would gently guide further development, and give training in the fantastic parapsychic powers to qualified natives. The standards therefore weren't impossibly high—apart from physical and mental potentiality, there was simply the ethic of civilized behavior. Usually it took only four or five generations for all normal dwellers on a planet to become full citizens; and meanwhile the benefits of reform, peace, order, higher production for less work, medicine, interstellar trade and exploration were freely available to everyone. A nation, a world, would leap at the chance.

Only Earth didn't.

Skepticism, laughter, alarm, malignant slyness . . . Chi shuddered, there in the quiet Cambridge room, as she remembered what had been in the mind of a dictator who had believed. After they refused him and made it plain what the Union meant, they had never been quite safe from his assassins.

America had seemed the best bet. If it joined, the dam was broken. And while the President had not accepted them as anything but a pair of bunco artists, there were the people. Convince enough of them, and the government of a democratic country would have to yield. Barnstorming!

Money was no problem. With a slight mental effort, they could duplicate the currency of any nation, atom by atom. Auditoriums could be hired, advertisements bought—and a free show had never lacked for an audience.

It should have worked. Khorokum teleported himself across the stage. He floated automobiles and tractors onto the scene, and duplicated them there from piles of sand. He extracted seventh roots in his head. He turned the lights on and off by a thought. He identified individuals and told them what they were thinking. He asked them to invent tricks for him, and could almost always perform as directed, from controlling the throw of dice to whisking an elephant onstage. At the conclusion of the show, he materialized the full instrument ensemble of an orchestra to play him a grand finale.

It was good. The applauded wildly and shouted for encores. But they didn't believe him. His accompanying lecture about his true nature and purposes, his earnest request that they write their Congressmen and their President, struck them as a smart new line of patter. That was all.

The pyschology of it was unique in the known Galaxy. Khorokum could understand some of the reasons. After all, humanity had been exposed to lunatics of one sort or another for centuries, self-styled prophets of this and that, fakers, as well as magicians who never claimed to be more than experts at deception—to say nothing of the visionary fiction which had worn the Galactic Union story a little thin ahead of the reality. Yes, they'd had to develop skepticism, a sort of racial immunity to fantastic claims.

But even so, to reject the evidence of the senses and plain logic . . . !

Then finally, on the blank edge of discouragement, the G-men arriving, an escort to the White House, an interview with the President and his important military and political associates . . .

Khorokum's smile was bitter as he related that part of the story. Almost no one at the conference had believed that the visitors were from outer space, and those who did considered the fact irrelevant. The pair had extraordinary powers. As spies, as projectors of atomic bombs, as shields for advancing troops, the Urukandians could perhaps be useful. But as emissaries . . . the United States government could hardly accept formal ambassadors from a country no one had ever seen!

"Someone wanted to be taken back with us," said Chi. "It wasn't a bad idea, except that on a long hop an untrained mind could distort things, would probably kill us all. Besides, they didn't really want to join, even if they were sure. It would have upset the status quo, in which they had attained success."

"The present situation has made them pathologically suspicious and xenophobic," added Khorokum. "It presages ill for your world if you don't get outside help."

"You have become a political issue, you know," said Van Tyne. "Russia at once denies that you exist and accuses us of making a secret weapon of you. Norway is up in arms because you didn't go direct to the U.N. but said it was neither a government nor even a good debating society. France thinks it's some kind of plot to pry her colonies loose from her. Questions have been asked in the British House of Commons. It's that way all over the world: nobody is sure what you are, but many are aware that you represent some new factor. You may end up precipitating the very crisis you're trying to avoid."

. "When we refused to help them with their plans," said Khorokum, "they pointed out that we're technically guilty of counterfeiting, to say nothing of illegal entry, subversion, inciting to riot, and I don't know what else. They demanded our passports, birth certificates, draft cards, income tax returns . . . The land of the free and the home of the brave!"

"And then—?"

"We said we'd go right on taking our case to the people. They replied that we were outlaws; and while they can't successfully hold us in jail, they can break up all our meetings and deluge us under such a barrage of official denunciation that no one will ever listen to us. That's what they've been doing for the past few days, as you know.

"All right, gentlemen." En-Shan Khorokum leaned back in his chair and smiled bleakly. "If you accept our story, you are our last hope. You have to tell us. *How can we convince Earth?*"

The vision went around the circle of men, rapt eyes, indrawn breaths, the realization that they would partake in the rewards the whole planet would have and that most likely all of them could qualify for immediate mind training. Morton said at last, slowly: "If you aren't telling the truth, you're at least the most extraordinary phenomenon science has yet encountered. I, for one, am going to take your truthfulness as a working hypothesis."

"Occam's razor," said Johns, fingering his beard.

"Its application is sometimes a matter of dispute," said the mathematician Lucasczewski. "It is simpler to believe that these people are from an advanced civilization or that they are merely terrestrial mutants with unusual powers?"

"I'll take the interstellar hypothesis any day," said the geneticist Phillips. "All that ability in one mutation? Hah!"

"I suppose so," said Morton, "though we'll certainly have to revise our physics." His eyes glowed. "God, but we can learn!"

"This is getting us nowhere," said Van Tyne impatiently. "These young people have a problem. Who has a solution?"

"Another country?" suggested Johns. "Some nation at once more stable and more progressive than ours—oh, say Sweden or Switzerland?"

"Maybe we should have tried that at first," admitted Khorokum gloomily. "But certainly not after the United States government has formally branded us as charlatans and criminals."

"I fail to understand," said Phillips. "How people can be so stupid, I mean. I never was too unbearable an intellectual snob, I hope, but when the much-touted Common Man can't see what's as plain as Mendel's law—when he can't reason from the facts that it's at least probable that you two are from outer space— gracious, Foxxe, I often wonder why you Britishers didn't keep your aristocracy in power."

"Oh, Joe Average isn't so very stupid," said Morton. "What the devil, I'll bet half our fathers were from the lower economic brackets. But he's been fooled too often. He knows, or thinks he knows, that all these amazing effects can be produced by perfectly ordinary means. In any case, how many people have actually *seen* you two perform, not over a TV screen but with their own eyes? What you need is something that everyone can see directly."

"Even then they'd call it a fake," said Johns darkly. "You could light up the sky with letters ten miles tall asking them to join your Galactic Union, and they'd look for a cigaret ad underneath the message. Psychologists would probably call it mass delusion!"

"It's a common enough phenomenon, really," said Foxxe. "I've seen it happen time and again. Primitive peoples, isolated, hardly seen a white man in living memory, y'know. Somebody flies an airplane in. They may be a little scared at first, though more often than not they'll shoot at it. But then it's accepted. Just isn't a marvel, y'know, or rather it's simply another part of a mysterious and surprising world. It's accepted. Nobody wonders very much. What really gets a tribe like that excited, a genuine never-ending wonder, something to be almost worshiped, that's not one of our clever technical gadgets, oh, no. It's something just a little beyond what they have but not so far advanced that the bally old mind refuses to try t'understand it. An airplane . . . bah, just a large metal bird, what of it? A truck

. . . int'resting. A horse and cart . . . oh, there's where they bring out the brass band and the keys to the village!''

"And we're the primitive tribe, eh?'' chuckled Lucasczewski.

"I've read a lot of these science fiction stories,'' said Van Tyne. "Far advanced psychology, subtle trickery making a population do anything the hero wanted. How about it?''

"The stories never went into detail, did they?'' asked Khorokum dryly.

"Big impressive fleet, robots, all that sort of thing?'' suggested Foxxe.

"We don't have them,'' said Chi. "The Union left such devices behind hundreds of millennia ago.''

"The most fantastic part of this business is its irony,'' said Johns. "Here you are, like gods almost, and you can't do a thing. You're *too* powerful!'' He chuckled heavily. "Like a man who has a sixteen-inch naval rifle but no fly swatter. Looks as if you'll just have to let us stew in our bed or whatever the saying is.''

Phillips sighed. "Damn it, anyway! I'd give my right arm to the left shoulder for a chance to see—learn—Oh, well . . .''

Khorokum got out of his chair and paced the floor. "I'm tired,'' he admitted. "It's been a fearful strain. I'm worn down too far to think. Maybe Chi and I had better go into hiding for a few months—that would be easy—and try to think of something in that time.''

"Judging by the world situation,'' said Morton grimly, "you maybe not have that long.''

"What to do, what to do?'' Chi buried her face in her hands.

"A tribe,'' said Khorokum between his teeth. "An isolated tribe of savages, needing the spectacular but not very advanced proof, too blind to understand—''

Of a sudden he stopped. Chi sat bolt upright, and the same thought flamed between them.

"A primitive tribe—''

The circle of humans edged away, uncertain, dimly aware of the sudden mighty surge of will.

Then Foxxe was having his hand shaked almost off the wrist by Khorokum, who was babbling about the natives of Orkhuzan and mass production via atom-by-atom duplication of a covertly prepared prototype—and somewhat to the Englishman's surprise, and very much to his gratification, Chi Balkhai ran up and kissed him.

*   *   *

Four months later the spaceships came.

They blazed mightily out of the sky, filling heaven with flame and thunder. There were three of them, each a good thousand feet long, and they rounded the world six times before settling into a Wisconsin cornfield.

The crews were fairly humanoid, though they had green skins and antennae and seven fingers to a hand. They received visitors graciously and set themselves to learning English, which they did with astonishing ease. As soon as possible, they explained that they were from Orkhuzan, a member planet of the Galactic Union.

When asked about the now almost forgotten pair who had disappeared four months ago, they seemed a little excited and consulted their files. Then they informed the inquirer that, yes, this En-Shan Khorokum and Chi Balkhai were notorious "traders." What was a "trader"? Oh, a petty criminal who traveled ahead of the Galactic Exploratory Service, reaching new planets first and trying to bilk the innocent natives. Fortunately, Earth's wise leaders had seen through this cheap scheme and the evil pair had fled. Alas, the Union was far from perfect.

Still, there were advantages to be gained by joining. The explorers showed copious files of pictures, statistics, specimens. They appeared on radio and television programs and answered all queries with charming frankness. They showed visitors through their ships and let them handle the mighty engines.

Yes, the Galactic Union was anxious to admit all the nations of Earth. There would be gains—well, nothing spectacular, obvious things which a science a couple of hundred years older than that of humanity would be expected to have. Cures for most diseases, regeneration of lost limbs and some organs, improved mental health, tripled lifespan—things like that.

Of course, the offer was not really disinterested. The Union wanted the technical genius of Earth. Why, even now humanity had three varieties of fission pile which nobody in the Union had ever thought of!

Would the honorable leaders and citizens of Earth care to consider it?

The United States, Great Britain, India, and several European and Latin American countries had joined, and a number of other lands were undergoing revolutions which would soon lead to their admission, when an eager young cub reporter contrived a

chance to give one of the great spaceships a really detailed
investigation. What he saw made him attempt some detective
work, but those he was checking up on had covered their tracks
too thoroughly. And since no more orthodox investigator was
able (or eager) to pierce the security regulations surrounding the
mighty ships, his unsupported word could never convince his
editor that several items of control equipment had borne neat
brass plates with the legend

GENERAL ELECTRIC
Schenectady, New York, U.S.A.

Dick-Editors
Correspondence

8 November 1951

Gentlemen,

I'm glad that ROOG pleased you. Certainly, the new title is all right.

Writing is a major event for me, and I am beginning to find ways of arranging my life around it, rather than squeezing in a few hours after work or on Sunday. Oddly, most of my writing tends to be fantasy of a religious, drifting nature, ill-suited for worldly things or large publications. All I can say to defend it is that people who read it are disturbed, and go off brooding, very puzzled and unhappy.

ROOG, as you slyly guessed, is my first acceptance. Needless to say, I feel that an unusual honor is involved in having one's first published story appear in F&SF; and thank God I won't have to see it filtered between RUPTURED? ads and BREAST CREAM ads and TEETH SLIPPING? ads.

Thank you very much for all your kindness and help. I appreciate it a very great deal.

Very truly yours,

Philip K. Dick

19 March 1952

Dear Sirs:

THE LITTLE MOVEMENT—a brand new pretty typed-up version with a few minor changes only, all for the good, I think. It's much smoother.

(If LITTLE MOVEMENT comes back with a rejection slip, I'll have a stroke.)

Hoping to hear from you, I remain,

Yours very truly,

Philip K. Dick

The Little Movement
By Philip K. Dick

The man was sitting on the sidewalk, holding the box shut with his hands. Impatiently the lid of the box moved, straining up against his fingers.

"All right," the man murmured. Sweat rolled down his face, damp, heavy sweat. He opened the box slowly, holding his fingers over the opening. From inside a metallic drumming came, a low insistent vibration, rising frantically as the sunlight filtered into the box.

A small head appeared, round and shiny, and then another. More heads jerked into view, peering, craning to see. "I'm first," one head shrilled. There was a momentary squabble, then quick agreement.

The man sitting on the sidewalk lifted out the little metal figure with trembling hands. He put it down on the sidewalk and began to wind it awkwardly, thick-fingered. It was a brightly

207

painted soldier with helmet and gun, standing at attention. As the man turned the key the little soldier's arms went up and down. It struggled eagerly.

Along the sidewalk two women were coming, talking together. They glanced down curiously at the man sitting on the sidewalk, at the box and the shiny figure in the man's hands.

"Fifty cents," the man muttered. "Get your child something to—"

"Wait!" a faint metallic voice came. "Not them!"

The man broke off abruptly. The two women looked at each other and then at the man and the little metal figure. They went hurriedly on.

The little soldier gazed up and down the street, at the cars, the shoppers. Suddenly it trembled, rasping in a low, eager voice.

The man swallowed. "Not the kid," he said thickly. He tried to hold onto the figure, but metal fingers dug quickly into his hand. He gasped.

"Tell them to stop!" the figure shrilled. "Make them stop!" The metal figure pulled away and clicked across the sidewalk, its legs stiff and rigid.

The boy and his father slowed to a stop, looking down at it with interest. The sitting man smiled feebly; he watched the figure approach them, turning from side to side, its arms going up and down.

"Get something for your boy. An exciting playmate. Keep him company."

The father grinned, watching the figure coming up to his shoe. The little soldier bumped into the shoe. It wheezed and clicked. It stopped moving.

"Wind it up!" the boy cried.

His father picked up the figure. "How much?"

"Fifty cents." The salesman rose unsteadily, clutching the box against him. "Keep him company. Amuse him."

The father turned the figure over. "You sure you want it, Bobby?"

"Sure! Wind it up!" Bobby reached for the little soldier. "Make it go!"

"I'll buy it," the father said. He reached into his pocket and handed the man a dollar bill.

Clumsily, staring away, the salesman made change.

*   *   *

The situation was excellent.

The little figure lay quietly, thinking everything over. All circumstances had conspired to bring about optimum solution. The Child might not have wanted to stop, or the Adult might not have had any money. Many things might have gone wrong; it was awful even to think about them. But everything had been perfect.

The little figure gazed up in pleasure, where it lay in the back of the car. It had correctly interpreted certain signs: the Adults were in control, and so the Adults had money. They had power, but their power made it difficult to get to them. Their power, their size. With the Children it was different. *They* were small, and it was easier to talk to them. They accepted everything they heard, and they did what they were told. Or so it was said at the factory.

The little metal figure lay, lost in dreamy delicious thoughts.

The boy's heart was beating quickly. He ran upstairs and pushed the door open. After he had closed the door carefully he went to the bed and sat down. He looked down at what he held in his hands.

"What's your name?" he said. "What are you called?"

The metal figure did not answer.

"I'll introduce you around. You must get to know everybody. You'll like it here."

Bobby laid the figure down on the bed. He ran to the closet and dragged out a bulging carton of toys.

"This is Bonzo," he said. He held up a pale stuffed rabbit. "And Fred." He turned the rubber pig around for the soldier to see. "And Teddo, of course. This is Teddo."

He carried Teddo to the bed and laid him beside the soldier. Teddo lay silent, gazing up at the ceiling with glassy eyes. Teddo was a brown bear, with wisps of straw poking out of his joints.

"And what shall we call you?" Bobby said. "I think we should have a council and decide," He paused, considering. "I'll wind you up so we can all see how you work."

He began to wind the figure carefully, turning it over on its face. When the key was tight he bent down and set the figure on the floor.

"Go on," Bobby said. The metal figure stood still. Then it began to whirr and click. Across the floor it went, walking with

stiff jerks. It changed directions suddenly and headed toward the
door. At the door it stopped. Then it turned to some building
blocks lying about and began to push them into a heap.

Bobby watched with interest. The little figure struggled with
the blocks, piling them into a pyramid. At last it climbed up onto
the blocks and turned the key in the lock.

Bobby scratched his head, puzzled. "Why did you do that?"
he said. The figure climbed back down and came across the
room toward Bobby, clicking and whirring. Bobby and the
stuffed animals regarded it with surprise and wonder. The figure
reached the bed and halted.

"Lift me up!" it cried impatiently, in its thin, metallic voice.
"Hurry up! Don't just sit there!"

Bobby's eyes grew large. He stared, blinking. The stuffed
animals said nothing.

"Come on!" the little soldier shouted.

Bobby reached down. The soldier seized his hand tightly.
Bobby cried out.

"Be still," the soldier commanded. "Lift me up to the bed. I
have things to discuss with you, things of great importance."

Bobby put it down on the bed beside him. The room was
silent, except for the faint whirring of the metal figure.

"This is a nice room," the soldier said presently. "A very
nice room." Bobby drew back a little on the bed.

"What's the matter?" the soldier said sharply, turning its head
and staring up.

"Nothing."

"What is it?" The little figure peered at him. "You're not
afraid of me, are you?"

Bobby shifted uncomfortably.

"Afraid of *me*?" The soldier laughed. "I'm only a little metal
man, only six inches high." It laughed again and again. It
ceased abruptly. "Listen. I'm going to live here with you for
awhile. I won't hurt you; you can count on that. I'm a friend—a
good friend."

It peered up a little anxiously. "But I want you to do things
for me. You won't mind doing things, will you? Tell me: how
many are there of them in your family?"

Bobby hesitated.

"Come, how many of *them*? Adults."

"Three. . . . Daddy, and Mother, and Foxie."

"Foxie? Who is that?"

"My grandmother."

"Three of them." The figure nodded. "I see. Only three. But others come from time to time? Other Adults visit this house?"

Bobby nodded.

"Three. That's not too many. Three are not so much of a problem. According to the factory—"

It broke off. "Good. Listen to me. I don't want you to say anything to them about me. I'm *your* friend, your secret friend. They won't be interested in hearing about me. I'm not going to hurt you, remember. You have nothing to fear. I'm going to live right here, with you."

It watched the boy intently, lingering over the last words.

"I'm going to be a sort of private teacher. I'm going to teach you things, things to do, things to say. Just like a tutor should. Will you like that?"

Silence.

"Of course you'll like it. We could even begin now. Perhaps you want to know the proper way to address me. Do you want to learn that?"

"Address you?" Bobby stared down.

"You are to call me . . ." The figure paused, hesitating. It drew itself together, proudly. "You are to call me—My Lord."

Bobby leaped up, his hands to his face.

"My Lord," the figure said relentlessly. "My Lord. You don't really need to start now. I'm tired." The figure sagged. "I'm almost run down. Please wind me up again in about an hour."

The figure began to stiffen. It gazed up at the boy. "In an hour. Will you wind me tight? You will, won't you?"

Its voice trailed off into silence.

Bobby nodded slowly. "All right," he murmured. "All right."

It was Tuesday. The window was open, and warm sunlight came drifting into the room. Bobby was away at school; the house was silent and empty. The stuffed animals were back in the closet.

My Lord lay on the dresser, propped up, looking out the window, resting contentedly.

There came a faint humming sound. Something small flew suddenly into the room. The small object circled a few times and then came slowly to rest on the white cloth of the dresser-top, beside the metal soldier. It was a tiny toy airplane.

"How is it going?" the airplane said. "Is everything all right so far?"

"Yes," My Lord said. "And the others?"

"Not so good. Only a handful of them managed to reach Children."

The soldier gasped in pain.

"The largest group fell into the hands of Adults. As you know, that is not satisfactory. It is very difficult to control Adults. They break away, or they wait until the spring is unwound—"

"I know." My Lord nodded glumly.

"The news will most certainly continue to be bad. We must be prepared for it."

"There's more. Tell me!"

"Frankly, about half of them have already been destroyed, stepped on by Adults. A dog is said to have broken up one. There's no doubt of it: our only hope is through Children. We must succeed there, if at all."

The little soldier nodded. The messenger was right, of course. They had never considered that a direct attack against the ruling race, the Adults, would win. Their size, their power, their enormous stride would protect them. The toy vender was a good example. He had tried to break away many times, tried to fool them and get loose. Part of the group had to be wound at all times to watch him, and there was that frightening day when he failed to wind them tight, hoping that—

"You're giving the Child instructions?" the airplane asked. "You're preparing him?"

"Yes. He understands that I'm going to be here. Children seem to be like that. As a subject race they have been taught to accept; it's all they can do. I am another teacher, invading his life, giving him orders. Another voice, telling him that—"

"You've started the second phase?"

"So soon?" My Lord was amazed. "Why? Is it necessary, so quickly?"

"The factory is becoming anxious. Most of the group has been destroyed, as I said."

"I know." My Lord nodded absently. "We expected it, we planned with realism, knowing the chances." It strode back and forth on the dresser-top. "Naturally, many would fall into their hands, the Adults. The Adults are everywhere, in all key positions, important stations. It's the psychology of the ruling race to control each phase of social life. But as long as those who reach Children survive—''

"You were not supposed to know, but outside of yourself, there's only three left. Just three."

"Three?" My Lord stared.

"Even those who reached Children have been destroyed right and left. The situation is tragic. That's why they want you to get started with the second phase."

My Lord clenched its fist, its features locked in iron horror. Only three left. . . . What hopes they had entertained for this band, venturing out, so little, so dependent on the weather—and on being wound up tight. If only they were larger! The Adults were so huge.

But the Children. What had gone wrong? What had happened to their one chance, their one fragile hope?

"How did it happen? What occurred?"

"No one knows. The factory is in a turmoil. And now they're running short of materials. Some of the machines have broken down and nobody knows how to run them." The airplane coasted toward the edge of the dresser. "I must be getting back. I'll report later to see how you're getting on."

The airplane flew up into the air and out through the open window. My Lord watched it, dazed.

What could have happened? They had been so certain about the Children. It was all planned—

It meditated.

Evening. The boy sat at the table, staring absently at his geography book. He shifted unhappily, turning the pages. At last he closed the book. He slid from his chair and went to the closet. He was reaching into the closet for the bulging carton when a voice came drifting to him from the dresser-top.

"Later. You can play with them later. I must discuss something with you."

The boy turned back to the table, his face listless and tired. He nodded, sinking down against the table, his head on his arm.

"You're not asleep, are you?" My Lord said.

"No."

"Then listen. Tomorrow when you leave school I want you to go to a certain address. It's not far from the school. It's a toy store. Perhaps you know it. Don's Toyland."

"I haven't any money."

"It doesn't matter. This has all been arranged for long in advance. Go to Toyland and say to the man: 'I was told to come for the package.' Can you remember that? 'I was told to come for the package.' "

"What's in the package?"

"Some tools, and some toys for you. To go along with me." The metal figure rubbed its hands together. "Nice modern toys, two toy tanks and a machine gun. And some spare parts for—"

There were footsteps on the stairs outside.

"Don't forget," My Lord said nervously. "You'll do it? This phase of the plan is extremely important."

It wrung its hands together in anxiety.

The boy brushed the last strands of hair into place. He put his cap on and picked up his school books. Outside, the morning was gray and dismal. Rain fell, slowly, soundlessly.

Suddenly the boy set his books down again. He went to the closet and reached inside. His fingers closed over Teddo's leg, and he drew him out.

The boy sat on the bed, holding Teddo against his cheek. For a long time he sat with the stuffed bear, oblivious to everything else.

Abruptly he looked toward the dresser. My Lord was lying outstretched, silent. Bobby went hurriedly back to the closet and laid Teddo into the carton. He crossed the room to the door. As he opened the door the little metal figure on the dresser stirred.

"Remember Don's Toyland. . . ."

The door closed. My Lord heard the Child going heavily down the stairs, clumping unhappily. My Lord exulted. It was working out all right. Bobby wouldn't want to do it, but he would. And once the tools and parts and weapons were safely inside there wouldn't be any chance of failure.

Perhaps they would capture a second factory. Or better yet: build dies and machines themselves to turn out larger Lords. Yes, if only they could be larger, just a little larger. They were so small, so very tiny, only a few inches high. Would the Movement fail, pass away, because they were too tiny, too fragile?

But with tanks and guns! Yet, of all the packages so carefully secreted in the toyshop, this would be the only one, the only one to be—

Something moved.

My Lord turned quickly. From the closet Teddo came, lumbering slowly.

"Bonzo," he said. "Bonzo, go over by the window. I think it came in that way, if I'm not mistaken."

The stuffed rabbit reached the window-sill in one skip. He huddled, gazing outside. "Nothing yet."

"Good." Teddo moved toward the dresser. He looked up. "Little Lord, please come down. You've been up there much too long."

My Lord stared. Fred, the rubber pig, was coming out of the closet. Puffing, he reached the dresser. "I'll go up and get it," he said. "I don't think it will come down by itself. We'll have to help it."

"What are you doing?" My Lord cried. The rubber pig was settling himself on his haunches, his ears down flat against his head. "What's happening?"

Fred leaped. And at the same time Teddo began to climb swiftly, catching onto the handles of the dresser. Expertly, he gained the top. My Lord was edging toward the wall, glancing down at the floor, far below.

"So this is what happened to the others," it murmured. "I understand. An Organization, waiting for us. Then everything is known."

It leaped.

When they had gathered up the pieces and had got them under the carpet, Teddo said:

"That part was easy. Let's hope the rest won't be any harder."

"What do you mean?" Fred said.

"The package of toys. The tanks and guns."

"Oh, we can handle them. Remember how we helped next door when the first little Lord, the first one we ever encountered—"

Teddo laughed. "It did put up quite a fight. It was tougher than this one. But we had the panda bears from across the way."

"We'll do it again," Fred said. "I'm getting so I rather enjoy it."

"Me, too," Bonzo said from the window.

The Naming of Names

When they settled the nightside of Mercury,
    It was May, and they called the dome *Mayfair*;
But the colonists soon had rechristened it *June*,
    Because what is so rare as a day there?

HERMAN W. MUDGETT*

*An alias for one, Anthony Boucher.

Lists

Here are three lists for people who like lists. They have little in common, but represent some unusual titles, some personal editorial preferences. The last list showing reader preference is interesting historically. It was compiled in compliance with a request by William Nolan who asked the question about reader preference for the pamphlet he was preparing about the magazine.

21 July 1950

Dear Joe [Ferman]:

As a personal favor (which will result in pleasant and valuable publicity) Joseph Henry Jackson, literary editor of the San Francisco *Chronicle*, has asked us to list for him the ten most neglected classics of fantasy and/or science fiction. This will be part of a general feature Jackson is doing on "neglected classics" and is indicative of the special attention he is paying to our specialty.

It is, further, indicative of the recognition Jackson gives to the current boom in science fiction.

Ever,

Mick

19 July 1950

Mr. Joseph Henry Jackson
San Francisco Chronicle
San Francisco 19, Calif

Dear Joe:

Mick and I have been doing some extensive brooding on Great Neglecteds in fantasy and sf, and come up (in addition to Anstey & Nesbit already discussed) with the following, out of print, all pretty much forgotten, which still seem to us fresh stimulating delightful reading—a damned sight fresher, in fact, than most of the current crop:

Michael Arlen: MAN'S MORTALITY (1933) Excellent science fiction of a future under a Pax Aeronautica, written in straight un-Arlen style.

Norman Douglas: THEY WENT (1920). Opulent and ironic satire-romance of the inundation of Ys—a work on which N D could be famous if he'd never seen Capri or collected a limerick.

George du Maurier: THE MARTIAN (1897) Least known but possibly most imaginative and touching of the DuM novels.

H Rider Haggard: ERIC BRIGHTEYES (1891) Haggard's own favorite, now forgotten—a stirring Scandinavian saga.

Storm Jameson: IN THE SECOND YEAR (1936) A novel of a future England under fascism, which got lost in the excitement concerning the much inferior (in thinking or writing) IT CAN'T HAPPEN HERE.

Leo Perutz: THE MASTER OF THE DAY OF JUDGMENT (1930). Beautifully poised between supernatural terror and the psychological murder novel; also all of the other excellent Perutzes, especially THE MARQUES OF BOLIBAR.

R C Sheriff: THE HOPKINS MANUSCRIPT (1939) Beautifully detailed study of world catastrophe seen through a petty mind.

Wallace Smith: THE HAPPY ALIENIST (1936) Bubbling fantasy-satire on psychiatry.

Mervyn Wall: THE UNFORTUNATE FURSEY (1946)
A monk-and-devil story with medieval authenticity and
modern wit.

Sylvia Townsend Warner: LOLLY WILLOWES: or,
THE LOVING HUNTSMAN (1926) Perhaps the one
perfect story on the nature of being a witch.

Interesting to notice, I think, (it didn't strike us until
after compiling) that none of these is by a specialized
"fantasy" writer, and that most of them are by pretty big
general-literary names.
   We've restricted this to novels—for great neglected short
stories see, of course, any issue of F&SF. (We think you
might like the splendid Fitz-James O'Brien in our # 5 for
September.)
   Very curious to see how other suggestions turn out on
this.

                           Best—and to Fee too,

                           A.B.

                           16 December 1949

Mr. Peter Godfrey
Cape Town
South Africa

Dear Mr. Godfrey:
   Your letter indicates so definitely a man of our tastes
that I'm tempted to lay by more pressing editorial duties to
answer it.
   You'll have realized, of course, that our use twice in the
same issue of "one of the three most terrifying" was pure
damned editorial carelessness. That first issue well outdid
the elephant by having a period of gestation of over 3
years; and various introductions were written at wide inter-
vals apart. You might be interested to know that Ted

Sturgeon is the only other hawk-eyed hawkshaw who spotted the awkward position we'd put ourselves in.

I'll give you the lists that John Dickson Carr and Bill Baring-Gould and I compiled one afternoon over many bottles of Prior's Double Dark, a Pennsylvania beer which justifies the state's existence. The conditions were: *Name the 6 most terrifying supernatural stories*. Results:

2 votes:

M R James: CASTING THE RUNES (JDC, B-G)

Perceval Landon: THURNLEY ABBEY (AB, JDG)

Oliver Onions: THE BECKONING FAIR ONE (AB, JDC)

May Sinclair: WHERE THEIR FIRE IS NOT QUENCHED (AB, JDC)

1 vote:

Martin Armstrong: THE PIPE SMOKER (B-G)

F Marion Crawford: THE UPPER BERTH (B-G)

L P Hartley: THE VISITOR FROM DOWN UNDER (JDC)

W W Jacobs: THE MONKEY'S PAW (AB)

M R James: CANON ALBRICH'S SCRAPBOOK (AB)
            MARTIN'S CLOSE (JDC)

Vernon Lee: AMOUR PURE (JDC)

H P Lovecraft: THE RATS IN THE WALLS (B-G)

E Nesbitt: Story, title forgotten by B-G, in Summers' SUPERNATURAL OMNIBUS

Fitz-James O'Brien: WHAT WAS IT? (JDC & AB protested that this was para-normal, science-fictional rather than supernatural; B-G conceded)

H R Wakefield: PROFESSOR POWNALL'S OVERSIGHT (AB)

Certainly IT belongs on the list—I keep begging Ted to do something in the same mood again. Various others occur to one haphazardly:

Fritz Leiber: SMOKE GHOST

H R Wakefield: THE FRONTIER GUARDS

W F Harvey: AUGUST HEAT

D K Broster: COUCHING AT THE DOOR

G P Gilman: THE YELLOW WALLPAPER (though strictly not supernatural)

Michael Arlen: THE GENTLEMAN FROM AMERICA
   (again not strictly)
Robert Hickens: HOW LOVE CAME TO PROFESSOR
   GUILDEA
W W Hodgson: THE WHISTLING ROOM
and of course every single story in the collected works
   of M R James.

Thanks very much for your warm words about the first
issue. I'm startled about the S A customs, especially since
someone recently sent a paid subscription from South Africa; but I trust that your ingenuity will triumph.

Sincerely yours,

A.B.

The question was asked by William Nolan in August 1952.
What stories, he asked, drew the most reader mail.

Very hard to answer. Reader-mail fluctuates according
to no known laws; hate to make an average-estimate. One
important note: it's almost all from unfamiliar names.
Most actifen write only to mags who'll give them ogoboo
by publishing the letters. Stories that have drawn most mail:

Philip MacDonald: PRIVATE—KEEP OUT!
R Bretner: THE GNURRS COME FROM THE
   VOODVORK OUT
Richard Matheson: BORN OF MAN & WOMAN
Howard Schoenfeld: BUILT UP LOGICALLY
Idris Seabright: THE LISTENING CHILD
Will Stanton: BARNEY
Cornell Woolrich: JANE BROWN'S BODY (50/50 vio-
   lently pro or con)
Zenna Henderson: COME ON, WAGON!
Mildren Clingerman: MINISTER WITHOUT PORT-
   FOLIO
Anthony Boucher: THE ANOMALY OF THE EMPTY
   MAN (largely because of a technical error)
Anthony Boucher: NINE-FINGER JACK
Zenna Henderson: ARARAT
Ward Moore: BRING THE JUBILEE
I don't have exact statistics, but that's a fair guess.

I am constantly amazed at the number and variety of lists and breakdowns these two men put together. However, I know that doing so was a source of pleasure as well as editorial necessity.

Smith-Editors Correspondence

9 January 1952

Dear Mr. Boucher and Mr. McComas:

Since I admitted in my letter that I've never had a story published, I don't have to pretend to be blasé about your having accepted my story (especially with my typewriter obviously jumping up and down for joy). I am utterly delighted and am making Hydras' lives even more hideous by phoning them at odd hours to say "Nyaaa!"

I'm afraid I can't be of much help to Mr. McComas in his search for a group name to designate female writers, as all those I can think of would seem either too complimentary (to a male, anyhow), or much too un-. Lord Peter Wimsey called his collection of females a "cattery," but I imagine that would cause more dissension in the ranks than even "harem."

Confusion or purporting to confuse me with Dr. Smith seems to be an idiosyncrasy of all great minds. When I'm allowed in sf circles here, I am invariably introduced as E. E. Smith, to which the standard retort is, "But what have you done with your beard, Dr. Smith?" And so homopsychic are sf fans everywhere that, when I arrived in London this fall, I was put on display at the White Horse (a pub where the sf intelligentsia foregather and drink—ugh—ginger beer) as E. E. Smith, all the way from America; whereupon a choir of angel voices piped, "But what 'ave you done with your beard, Dr. Smith?" I think, though, that some of the smaller British fans still aren't sure that I *am* E. E. Smith. Ph.D.

Effusively yours,

Evelyn E. Smith

11 September 1952

Dear Miss Smith:

THE LAST OF THE SPODE is utterly delightful! I trust you will recognise it as a compliment when I say I couldn't have laughed more violently if it had been written by the Old Master, P. G. Wodehouse.

I thought the piece in AR & SC very powerful. It displayed your prose at its lean and muscular best. You built skillfully and subtly to a series of climaxes that were utterly devastating. One very mild carping note: at times, your imagery was just a shade obscure. I could not decide whether the portrayal of the child weaving a nest in its mother's hair implied the excellence of shingling or was intended to demonstrate the primal urge for cover which is the psychic heritage of Man. But this, of course, is a minor complaint and one that may well be peculiar to this reviewer.

Enough of this foolery. I must get back to work.

Cordially,

McComas

There is a peculiar endemic madness in the British Isles which persuades otherwise rational authors, particularly of detective stories and science fiction, that they can write as Americans and nobody will notice the difference. (We well recall a novel written by one of our favorite British authors and edited by one of our favorite American editors, in which the characters drove lorries around the streets of New York and effected repairs on those lorries with spanners.) "The British are so fond," Evelyn Smith *writes us, "of writing science fiction in the American idiom that I felt it only courteous for an American (me) to write one with a British flavour." The result is as deadly as only true courtesy can be.*

A.B./J.F. McC

The Last of the Spode
By Evelyn E. Smith

"It is my theory," said the Professor, sipping his tea thoughtfully, "that the character of a people can be discerned from its linguistic analogies."

"Really?" Angela murmured as she dissected a scone. "The butter looks rather foul, doesn't it? I do hope the freezer hasn't gone wonky on us. That would be the absolute end."

"Now rhyming is of course," he continued, "primarily a mnemonic device. However, I would extend this to include not only actual verse but the essential character of the words themselves. Why is it that certain particular words agree in terminal sound; what semantic relationships did their speaker find between or among them? . . . Now *custard* and *mustard* I can understand. They are both edible and—ah—glutinous. But why *bustard?*"

"Perhaps a bustard is glutinous when it's cooked," Angela

226

replied vaguely. "I shouldn't think one would want to eat it raw."

"Once I have discovered precisely why the creators of the English language chose—even though the choice was, of course, hardly on a conscious level—to rhyme *bustard* with *custard* and, of course, *mustard*," the Professor went on, "I feel I shall discover the key to the English character. Undoubtedly the same theory would apply to other languages . . . French, Arabic, Swahili. Through semantics one would achieve a true understanding of all the peoples of the world." He frowned. "Don't know what one would do about the Americans, though, with no proper language of their own."

"But you can't understand the peoples of the world, in any case," Angela pointed out as she covered the dubious butter thickly with jam. "Because there aren't any people any more. Just us."

"There is that difficulty. But perhaps you and Eric will reproduce. After all, it will be 50 years before the radiations die down enough for Them to cross over here. By then we should have been able to establish at least two generations, although, of course, they would hardly have time to formulate any linguistic variants."

"I don't think I should care to reproduce with Eric," Angela said, brushing crumbs off her frock onto the barren ground. "I think I shall let the race die with me. Rather a pretty thought."

"Not the sporting thing to do at all," he reproached her. "You must look at the matter from the larger viewpoint."

"Why?" she asked. "I have no urge to provide the components of a zoo—and that seems to be the only future open to the human race."

"Sonics, anyone?" Eric asked, as he came up swinging a sonics rod against his immaculate white sports tunic.

"Oh no, Eric!" Angela said. "The radiations are still giving off too much heat. Besides, it would be a waste of power. We're going to need all we've got, you know, and there are just so many tins."

"I daresay you're right," he replied manfully, but he could not quite hide his disappointment. "What's that you have there? Tea? I do think you might have called a chap." Settling himself at Angela's feet, he put out a hand for the cup. "You haven't done at all well by the bread, old girl. It's fearfully thick."

"I haven't managed to get the hang of slicing it. But then, I haven't had a fearful lot of practice yet. Remember, Nora got blasted only day before yesterday."

"Only day before yesterday? That's right. Seems as if you'd been cooking for us for an eternity—Not," Eric added with speed, "that I mean to hint anything of a derogatory nature about your cooking, pet. It's just that some have the gift and others haven't."

"But will there be enough food?" the Professor asked, absent-mindedly slipping a handful of sandwiches into his pocket. "There isn't much use conserving power if there won't be enough food."

Eric brightened. "You're quite right, Professor. So why don't we have a round of sonics after all?" His face fell. "Oh, I forgot, I've already started my tea. Must wait an hour or frightful things happen to the jolly old viscera."

"We have plenty of food," Angela said. "Enough for 50 years."

"Fifty years! Think we'll be here as long as that?" Eric slammed his cup petulantly on the ground.

"Watch out, Eric," Angela warned. "This is the last of the Spode."

"But it's going to be frightfully dull here," Eric murmured. "Especially if I can't run down to London now and then. You're sure London got it too?"

"Quite sure," Angela replied gently. "Every place got it. Every place but here. We're the only three people left in the world, Eric."

"I do wonder why we escaped," the Professor speculated. "Something to do with the soil, I should say. You know nothing ever would grow here. Probably some sort of natural force field. Interesting."

"If one of us were scientific," Angela remarked, "he could occupy himself for the next 50 years trying to determine just what the reason was."

"No point to it," Eric muttered. "No point to anything, really."

"We must face the facts, lad," the Professor said. "Pity about the Bodleian, though."

Eric slewed his lissome body around until he faced the Professor. "And at the end of 50 years? Then what happens?"

The old scholar held out his cup for more tea. "The radiations will die down enough for Them to cross, I expect."

"Remember, Angela," Eric assured her, "I have a disintegrator. When They come, I shall use it on you."

"But why?" Angela asked, shaking the pot to make sure there was enough tea for her before she served the Professor. "They're not human, you know."

"Never thought of that," Eric agreed. "And after 50 years I daresay it wouldn't matter even if They were." He looked up at her. "But I'm human, you know."

She sighed. "No, I don't know. Sorry, Eric, but it's utterly out of the question."

He flung his sonics rod on the ground peevishly. "The whole thing is a crashing bore. I shouldn't be surprised if after ten years or so I use the disintegrator on myself."

The other two shook their heads in unison. "Not the sort of thing one does, you know," the Professor reproved him. "We must face things. Come, try one of Angela's scones. They're not half bad considered in the light of a scientific experiment."

"Don't want a scone," Eric muttered. "I wish I were dead like everyone else."

The blatant bad taste of this took both the others' breath away.

"He's not himself, you know," Angela finally whispered to the Professor. "After all, it has been a bit nerve-racking, and he always was a sensitive lad."

"We all have our feelings," the Professor grumbled, "but we don't wash them in public."

"Come, Eric," Angela tempted him, "do try one of my scones. If you do, I'll open a tin of power and play a set of sonics with you as soon as our tea has settled."

Eric brightened. "Oh, that'll be wizard! But I'd rather have a chocolate biscuit."

"Come now," smiled the Professor, "try a scone. Let it never be said that an Englishman was a coward." He wiggled one eyebrow, a sign that he was about to perpetrate a witticism. "It'll probably have the same effect on you as a disintegrator."

All three laughed.

A frown creased Eric's smooth brow. "I've just thought of something absolutely ghastly."

"What is it?" Angela asked, rising to take the pot back to the scullery for more hot water.

"Supposing the tea doesn't hold out for 50 years?"

There was a dead silence.

With the rays of the setting sun tangled in her golden curls and glinting on the teapot which she proudly bore aloft, Angela looked like more than a splendid figure of young English womanhood; she looked like a goddess. "The tea must hold out," she said.

Asimov-Editors Correspondence

17 January 1951

Dear Mr. Boucher:

Thank you for your letter of 9 January, and for the kind words for my robot stories, MOTHER EARTH and NO CONNECTION. My early days as a writer back in 1939 and 1940 created permanent scars on my soul and editorial kindness is still mighty soothing.

I have enjoyed F. and S. F. tremendously (still do) but must admit that I always thought your editorial bent leant strongly towards fantasy and the emotional or "Ray Bradbury" type of science-fiction. It is therefore exceedingly good news to me that you consider my sort of stuff favorably.

What stands in the way of the fulfillment of your request at the moment is the chronic shortage of time. Unfortunately I am strictly a spare-time writer (having a full-time biochemical research job) so that my output is necessarily small. I can only say that I'll try.

Very truly yours,

Isaac Asimov

18 January 1952

Dear Mr. Boucher,

I am anxious to write for Fantasy and Science Fiction since it is the one major magazine my byline has not yet appeared in. Once the Doubleday novel is out of the way then (say May 1) I would like to make a F&SF yarn the first matter of business. There is this provision, though. I rather like to write to order. It soothes me to know that I know exactly what the editor wants. In the case of the

Healy anthology, for instance, I was told: Write a story on
political science with an optimistic ending. So I did so.
Therefore, would you care to give me a small idea as to
the kind of Asimov story you would most like to see; what
angles to avoid because you are overstocked with them at
the moment, and so on. I'll answer with my own ideas on
the subject and by May 1 we ought to have the thing
pinned down and there will be small delay thereafter.

Yours,

Isaac Asimov

20 February 1952

Dear Mick,

Enclosed is the new version of what was "King LEAR,
IV, 1, 36". I did a complete retyping job (I hate patching
it up with pen and ink—makes it look so sloppy) so I'll
describe what changes I made.

1—You wanted a better title. I thought of lots of possibilities: "Beelzebub," "Thy will, O Lord," "Moloch,"
"Lord of Flies," "Insecticide," and so on. I finally decided
on the shortest, most straightforward and most non-committal
possibility; FLIES. (I was afraid that by being too cute I
would give the story away.) However, be it understood
that if you still dislike the title, you have carte blanche to
make it anything you please. You can even name it "?"
and ask the readers to name it. I do think though, that
FLIES is satisfactory.

2—You wanted a more subtly phrased ending. I tried to
do that by a device which usually works. The final climax
which was about 150 words long in the original version,
has been cut down to 50 words. Same ending but more
economically and suddenly arrived at. I think the real
sock even comes in the final word. Here again if you
are still unsatisfied and think that changing a sentence
or so might make you happier, go ahead. Again, I think it
is satisfactory.

Thank you again for accepting the story and I hope you
find my changes have set it up for you as you want. Please

send the check to Fred Pohl who will send it to me, the bum, outrageously docked as he always does. (You know the old story. Nobody loves an agent.)

Yours,

Isaac

27 February 1953

Dear Tony,

I'm so glad you wrote to me about FLIES. I was getting quite dismal about it. Every month I'd buy F&SF and look—quick—at the contents page and then riffle through and find the "in the next issue" spot, and then feel very low indeed.

Every once in a while, I'd sit down to write you a letter asking about it and then tear it up because I *do* know about the jig-saw each issue of a magazine is.

Anyway, for your amusement, I'm sending you the carbon of a letter I wrote you on 6 February (the original of which I tore up, *after* I had sealed it into a stamped envelope). I thought you had enough troubles without being plagued by cases of "author's melancholia." This disease attacks most authors mildly when written stories are not accepted and virulently when accepted stories are not published.

Yours,

Asimov

This is the letter to which Asimov refers, above, written on February 6, 1953.

Dear Tony:

. . . Incidentally, while I'm writing to you, I wonder whatever has happened to my story FLIES which you bought months and months ago. I keep watching for it every issue.

Of course, I know that each issue has to be put together like a jigsaw and that the turn of FLIES may not have come

up, but—call this crazy, if you like—I keep thinking,
"Gee, maybe they changed their minds about the yarn and
decided it isn't printable after all."

If that has happened, I wouldn't want you to be out any
money. I'll be willing (not glad, but willing) to buy it back
from you.

May I hear from you?

Yours,

Asimov

Isaac Asimov has written just about every kind of science fiction that you can think of (in addition to much perfectly serious straight science), from weighty sociological extrapolations to intergalactic E. Phillips Oppenheim, from a lastingly influential series on robots to the best deadpan "factual" hoax on record, from a movingly believable study of an ursine civilization to a charmingly human time-travel story without a word of science. But Mr. Asimov's versatility is by no means exhausted: this curious view of the relationship between one man and the genus Musca *is like no other story in the Asimov canon.*

A.B./J.F. McC

Flies
by Isaac Asimov

"Flies!" said Kendell Casey, wearily. He swung his arm. The fly circled, returned and nestled on Casey's shirt-collar.

From somewhere there sounded the buzzing of a second fly.

Dr. John Polen covered the slight uneasiness of his chin by moving his cigarette quickly to his lips.

He said, "I didn't expect to meet you, Casey. Or you, Winthrop. Or ought I call you Reverend Winthrop?"

"Ought I call you Professor Polen?" said Winthrop, carefully striking the proper vein of rich-toned friendship.

They were trying to snuggle into the cast-off shell of twenty years back, each one of them. Squirming and cramming and not fitting.

Damn, thought Polen, fretfully, why do people attend college reunions?

Casey's hot blue eyes were still filled with the aimless anger of the college sophomore who has discovered intellect, frustration, and the tag-ends of cynical philosophy all at once.

Casey! Bitter man of the campus!

He hadn't outgrown that. Twenty years later and it was Casey, bitter ex-man of the campus! Polen could see that in the way his finger tips moved aimlessly and in the manner of his spare body.

As for Winthrop? Well, twenty years older, softer, rounder. Skin pinker, eyes milder. Yet no nearer the quiet certainty he would never find. It was all there in the quick smile he never entirely abandoned, as though he feared there would be nothing to take its place, that its absence would turn his face into a smooth and featureless flush.

Polen was tired of reading the aimless flickering of a muscle's end; tired of usurping the place of his machines; tired of the too much they told him.

Could they read him as he read them? Could the small restlessness of his own eyes broadcast the fact that he was damp with the disgust that had bred mustily within him?

Damn, thought Polen, why didn't I stay away?

They stood there, all three, waiting for one another to say something, to flick something from across the gap and bring it, quivering, into the present.

Polen tried it. He said, "Are you still working in chemistry, Casey?"

"In my own way, yes," said Casey, gruffly. "I'm not the scientist you're considered to be. I do research on insecticides for E. J. Link at Chatham."

Winthrop said, "Are you really? You said you would work on insecticides. Remember, Polen? And with all that, the flies dare still be after you, Casey?"

Casey said, "Can't get rid of them. I'm the best proving ground in the labs. No compound we've made keeps them away when I'm around. Someone once said it was my odor. I attract them."

Polen remembered the someone who had said that.

Winthrop said, "Or else—"

Polen felt it coming. He tensed.

"Or else," said Winthrop, "it's the curse, you know." His smile intensified to show that he was joking, that he forgave past grudges.

Damn, thought Polen, they haven't even changed the words. And the past came back.

"Flies," said Casey, swinging his arm, and slapping. "Ever see such a thing? Why don't they light on you two?"

Johnny Polen laughed at him. He laughed often then. "It's something in your body odor, Casey. You could be a boon to science. Find out the nature of the odorous chemical, concentrate it, mix it with DDT, and you've got the best fly-killer in the world."

"A fine situation. What do I smell like? A lady fly in heat? It's a shame they have to pick on me when the whole damned world's a dung heap."

Winthrop frowned and said with a faint flavor of rhetoric, "Beauty is not the only thing, Casey, in the eye of the beholder."

Casey did not deign a direct response. He said to Polen, "You know what Winthrop told me yesterday? He said those damned flies were the curse of Beelzebub."

"I was joking," said Winthrop.

"Why Beelzebub?" asked Polen.

"It amounts to a pun," said Winthrop. "The ancient Hebrews used it as one of their many terms of derision for alien gods. It comes from *Ba'al*, meaning *lord* and *zevuv*, meaning *fly*. The lord of flies."

Casey said, "Come on, Winthrop, don't say you don't believe in Beelzebub."

"I believe in the existence of evil," said Winthrop, stiffly.

"I mean Beelzebub. Alive. Horns. Hooves. A sort of competition deity."

"Not at all." Winthrop grew stiffer. "Evil is a short-term affair. In the end it must lose—"

Polen changed the subject with a jar. He said, "I'll be doing graduate work for Venner, by the way. I talked with him day before yesterday, and he'll take me on."

"No! That's wonderful." Winthrop glowed and leaped the subject-change instantly. He held out a hand with which to pump Polen's. He was always conscientiously eager to rejoice in another's good fortune. Casey often pointed that out.

Casey said, "Cybernetics Venner? Well, if you can stand him, I suppose he can stand you."

Winthrop went on, "What did he think of your idea? Did you tell him your idea?"

"What idea?" demanded Casey.

Polen had avoided telling Casey so far. But now Venner had considered it and had passed it with a cool, "Interesting!" How could Casey's dry laughter hurt it now?

Polen said, "It's nothing much. Essentially, it's just a notion that emotion is the common bond of life, rather than reason or intellect. It's practically a truism, I suppose. You can't tell what a baby thinks or even *if* it thinks, but it's perfectly obvious that it can be angry, frightened or contented even when a week old. See?

"Same with animals. You can tell in a second if a dog is happy or if a cat is afraid. The point is that their emotions are the same as those we would have under the same circumstances."

"So?" said Casey. "Where does it get you?"

"I don't know yet. Right now, all I can say is that emotions are universals. Now suppose we could properly analyze all the actions of men and certain familiar animals and equate them with the visible emotions. We might find a tight relationship. Emotion A might always involve Motion B. Then we could apply it to animals whose emotions we couldn't guess at by common-sense alone. Like snakes, or lobsters."

"Or flies," said Casey, as he slapped viciously at another and flicked its remains off his wrist in furious triumph.

He went on. "Go ahead, Johnny. I'll contribute the flies and you study them. We'll establish a science of flychology and labor to make them happy by removing their neuroses. After all, we want the greatest good of the greatest number, don't we? And there are more flies than men."

"Oh, well," said Polen.

Casey said, "Say, Polen, did you ever follow up that weird idea of yours? I mean, we all know you're a shining cybernetic light, but I haven't been reading your papers. With so many ways of wasting time, something has to be neglected, you know."

"What idea?" asked Polen, woodenly.

"Come on. You know. Emotions of animals and all that sort of gug. Boy, those were the days. I used to know madmen. Now I only come across idiots."

Winthrop said, "That's right, Polen. I remember it very well. Your first year in graduate school you were working on dogs and rabbits. I believe you even tried some of Casey's flies."

Polen said, "It came to nothing in itself. It gave rise to certain new principles of computing, however, so it wasn't a total loss."

Why did they talk about it?

Emotions! What right had anyone to meddle with emotions? Words were invented to conceal emotions. It was the dreadfulness of raw emotion that had made language a basic necessity.

Polen knew. His machines had by-passed the screen of verbalization and dragged the unconscious into the sunlight. The boy and the girl, the son and the mother. For that matter, the cat and the mouse or the snake and the bird. The data rattled together in its universality and it had all poured into and through Polen until he could no longer bear the touch of life.

In the last few years he had so painstakingly schooled his thoughts in other directions. Now these two came, dabbling in his mind, stirring up its mud.

Casey batted abstractedly across the tip of his nose to dislodge a fly. "Too bad," he said. "I used to think you could get some fascinating things out of, say, rats. Well, maybe not fascinating, but then not as boring as the stuff you would get out of our somewhat-human beings. I used to think—"

Polen remembered what he used to think.

Casey said, "Damn this DDT. The flies feed on it, I think. You know, I'm going to do graduate work in chemistry and then get a job on insecticides. So help me. I'll personally get something that *will* kill the vermin."

They were in Casey's room, and it had a somewhat keroseny odor from the recently applied insecticide.

Polen shrugged and said, "A folded newspaper will always kill."

Casey detected a non-existent sneer and said instantly, "How would you summarize your first year's work, Polen? I mean aside from the true summary any scientist could state if he dared, by which I mean: 'Nothing.' "

"Nothing," said Polen. "There's your summary."

"Go on," said Casey. "You use more dogs than the physiologists do and I bet the dogs mind the physiological experiments less. I would."

"Oh, leave him alone," said Winthrop. "You sound like a piano with 87 keys eternally out of order. You're a bore!"

You couldn't say that to Casey.

He said, with sudden liveliness, looking carefully away from Winthrop. "I'll tell you what you'll probably find in animals, if you look closely enough. Religion."

"What the dickens!" said Winthrop, outraged. "That's a foolish remark."

Casey smiled. "Now, now, Winthrop. *Dickens* is just a euphemism for *devil* and you don't want to be swearing."

"Don't teach me morals. And don't be blasphemous."

"What's blasphemous about it? Why shouldn't a flea consider the dog as something to be worshipped? It's the source of warmth, food, and all that's good for a flea."

"I don't want to discuss it."

"Why not? Do you good. You could even say that to an ant, an anteater is a higher order of creation. He would be too big for them to comprehend, too mighty to dream of resisting. He would move among them like an unseen, inexplicable whirlwind, visiting them with destruction and death. But that wouldn't spoil things for the ants. They would reason that destruction was simply their just punishment for evil. And the anteater wouldn't even know he was a deity. Or care."

Winthrop had gone white. He said, "I know you're saying this only to annoy me and I am sorry to see you risking your soul for a moment's amusement. Let me tell you this," his voice trembled a little, "and let me say it very seriously. The flies that torment you are your punishment in this life. Beelzebub, like all the forces of evil, may think he does evil, but it's only the ultimate good after all. The curse of Beelzebub is on you for *your* good. Perhaps it will succeed in getting you to change your way of life before it's too late."

He ran from the room.

Casey watched him go. He said, laughing, "I told you Winthrop believed in Beelzebub. It's funny the respectable names you can give to superstition." His laughter died a little short of its natural end.

There were two flies in the room, buzzing through the vapors toward him.

Polen rose and left in heavy depression. One year had taught him little, but it was already too much, and his laughter was thinning. Only his machines could analyze the emotions of animals properly, but he was already guessing too deeply concerning the emotions of men.

He did not like to witness wild murder-yearnings where others could see only a few words of unimportant quarrel.

Casey said, suddenly, "Say, come to think of it, you did try some of my flies, the way Winthrop says. How about that?"

"Did I? After twenty years, I scarcely remember," murmured Polen.

Winthrop said, "You must. We were in your laboratory and

you complained that Casey's flies followed him even there. He suggested you analyze them and you did. You recorded their motions and buzzings and wing-wiping for half an hour or more. You played with a dozen different flies.''

Polen shrugged.

''Oh, well,'' said Casey. ''It doesn't matter. It was good seeing you, old man.'' The hearty hand-shake, the thump on the shoulder, the broad grin—to Polen it all translated into sick disgust on Casey's part that Polen was a ''success'' after all.

Polen said, ''Let me hear from you sometimes.''

The words were dull thumps. They meant nothing. Casey knew that. Polen knew that. Everyone knew that. But words were meant to hide emotion and when they failed, humanity loyally maintained the pretence.

Winthrop's grasp of the hand was gentler. He said, ''This brought back old times, Polen. If you're ever in Cincinnati, why don't you stop in at the meeting-house? You'll always be welcome.''

To Polen, it all breathed of the man's relief at Polen's obvious depression. Science too, it seemed, was not the answer, and Winthrop's basic and ineradicable insecurity felt pleased at the company.

''I will,'' said Polen. It was the usual polite way of saying, I won't.

He watched them thread separately to other groups.

Winthrop would never know. Polen was sure of that. He wondered if Casey knew. It would be the supreme joke if Casey did not.

He *had* run Casey's flies, of course, not that once alone, but many times. Always the same answer! Always the same unpublishable answer.

With a cold shiver he could not quite control, Polen was suddenly conscious of a single fly loose in the room, veering aimlessly for a moment, then beating strongly and reverently toward Beelzebub.

Dickson-Editors Correspondence

13 October 1950

Dear Mr. Boucher:

Thanks for the compliments on LISTEN!—and by all means keep the story. Aside from the payment, which is generous, and the purchase of first rights only, which is damn fine, the prestige resultant on appearing in your magazine is going to do me more than a little good.

I'm twenty-seven. So it was twenty years ago I decided to be a writer.

I quit graduate school last June (without any advanced degree gained), and got a job driving a bakery truck. After four weeks they fired me and as a result I finally stopped talking about writing and started to do it.

To tell you the honest-to-God truth, I'm not a real short story writer at all. What I want to write is novels—huge thick things that take a year or two apiece to do and which have pages of description about the sun coming through a streetcar window and making a beery-faced old man look like a patriarch; and, because I am incredibly lucky in some ways, I'll probably end up doing just that. Meanwhile, I write short stories like trying to cram a parachute into a thimble. In fact, up to July, the mechanics and structure of the short story were Greek to me. The first ones I did were Holy Horrors. I've still got a kind-hearted but firm rejection slip from Mr. McComas in which he points out that the subject of my story was too big to be dealt with by a short-short. It was like (he said) making an anecdote of the Trojan War. It was an understatement. In my innocence, I had tried to convey the tragedy of the extermination of the human race in eight hundred words.

Sincerely,

Gordon R. Dickson

6 March 1951

Dear Tony:

Thanks for everything, including and especially the nice things you continue to say about LISTEN! How to say my thanks properly. I don't know. You lead the editorial field—at least, of my acquaintance—by a good ten miles in the matter of being friendly and thoughtful where your writers are concerned. I never saw anything like it. First and last—from the first letter suggesting revisions on LISTEN! down to this postcard you must have written me as many words as there originally were in that little pipsqueak of a story of mine.

I don't, in all seriousness, see how you do it, where you find the time, the energy, and the postage—to say nothing of the fact that grunts rather than graciousness are what I've armored myself to expect from editors. You're as rare a bird as the ancient dodo and I'm half-afraid you're liable to become equally extinct if you keep on spending your energies this lavishly. Anyway, all I can say is thanks.

Yours,

Gordy [Dickson]

PS:—the above thanks also for Mike McComas (or have I got his name wrong again?)

In most science fiction stories, the men of earth have successfully established an impervious empire over all the lesser breeds of the Galaxy, ruling as a sort of cross between Pukka Sahibs and Roman procurators . . . only of course in a strictly new American version. In the reports of a few subversive dissenters, earth men are baffled by totally alien civilizations and retire in frustration. These two alternatives are not, however, the only answer to the question of the relation between Terran conquerors and subject native races, as Gordon Dickson—a Minnesotan of 28 who says he decided to be a writer twenty-one years ago, and has certainly implemented his decision ably in the past couple of years—subtly demonstrates in this sensitive story.

A.B./J.F. McC

Listen!
by Gordon R. Dickson

Reru did not like to see humans eat. So he was waiting in the living room while Taddy and his parents finished breakfast.

"—And quite right, too," boomed Taddy's father. "He has as much right to his own ways as we have to ours. Remember that, Taddy, when you grow up. The only reason humans have been successful conquerors throughout the galaxy is because they have always respected the attitudes and opinions of the people they conquered."

"Oh, Harry!" said Taddy's mother. "He's too young to understand all that."

"I am not young," said Taddy defensively, through a mouthful of breakfast food. "I'm four years old."

"See there, Celia," said Taddy's father, laughing. "He's four years old—practically grown up. But seriously, honey, he's going to be growing up into a world in which the great majority

244

of thinking beings are Mirians like Reru. He should start to understand the natives early.''

"Well, I don't know," said Taddy's mother, worriedly. "After all, he was born in space on the way here and he's a delicate child—''

"Delicate, nonsense!'' boomed Taddy's father. "He comes from the toughest race in the galaxy. Look at these Mirians, chained to their planet by a symbiosis so extensive that our biologists haven't reached the end of the chain, yet. Look at Reru himself, gentle, non-combative, unenergetic, a stalwart example of the Mirian Race and therefore—the ideal nursemaid for our son.''

"Oh, I don't have a word of complaint to say against Reru," answered Taddy's mother. "He's been just wonderful with Taddy. But I can't help it—when he cocks his head on one side and starts *listening* the way they all do, I get a little bit scared of him.''

"Damn it, Celia!'' said Taddy's father. "I've told you a thousand times that he's just hearing one of their cows calling that it wants to be milked.''

Taddy squirmed in his chair. He knew all about the cows. They were six-legged Mirian animals that roamed around much as Reru and his kind roamed around. When they were full of milk they would start making a high, whistling sound, and Reru or some other Mirian would come along and attach his suckers to them and drink the milk. But the cows were no longer interesting. Reru was; and Taddy had finished his breakfast food.

"I'm all through,'' he broke in suddenly on his parents' conversation. "Can I go now? Can I?''

"I guess so,'' said Taddy's mother and Taddy scrambled from the chair and ran off toward the living room.

"Don't go too far!'' his mother's voice floated after him, followed by his father's deep bass.

"Let him go. Reru will bring him back all right. And, anyway, what on this planet of vegetarians could harm him?''

But Taddy had already forgotten his mother's words. For Reru was waiting for him, and Reru was fascinating.

He looked, at first glance, like a miniature copy of an old Chinese Mandarin, with robe, bald head, and little wispy beard. It was only when you got to know him that you realized that there were tentacles beneath the robe, that he had never had hair on his head, and that the wispy beard hid and protected the suckers with which he milked the *cows* that were his source of food.

But Taddy liked him very much; and Taddy didn't think that there was anything the least bit strange about him.

"Where are we going today, Reru?" demanded Taddy, bouncing up and down before the little Mirian who was not quite twice as tall as he was.

Reru's voice was like the voice of a trilling bird, and it sang more than it spoke.

"Good morning, Taddy," it trilled. "Where would you like to go?"

"I want to go to the silver and green place," cried Taddy. "Can we go?"

Reru's dark little mandarin face did not smile because it did not have the muscles to do so. But the mouth opened and the Mirian gave a short wordless trill expressive of happiness and pleasure.

"Yes, small Taddy," Reru answered. "We can go." And, turning with a kind of stately dignity, he led the way out of the dwelling and into the soft yellow Mirian sunlight.

"Oh, good, good, good!" sang Taddy, skipping along beside him.

They went away from the buildings of the humans, out across the low rolling grassland of Miria, Taddy bounding and leaping in the light gravity and Reru gliding along with effortless ease. And if that dignified glide was the result of twisting tentacles hidden beneath the robe, what of it? Where older humans might have felt squeamish at the thought of the twisting ropes of white muscle, Taddy took it entirely for granted. To him, Reru was beautiful.

They went on across the grasslands. Several times Reru stopped to *listen* and each time Taddy tried to imitate him, standing with his tousled head cocked on one side and an intent expression on his baby face. After one of these stops his brow furrowed and he seemed to be thinking. The little Mirian noticed him.

"What is it, Taddy?" he trilled.

"Daddy says that when you listen, you're listening to the cows," Taddy answered. "You hear more than that, don't you, Reru?"

"Yes, Taddy," said Reru, "I am listening to all my brothers."

"Oh," said the boy, wisely. "I thought so."

*   *   *

As they went on, the grasslands began to dip, and after a while a patch of deeper green came into sight in the distance.

"There it is," trilled the Mirian. Taddy broke into a run.

"Let's hurry, Reru," cried the boy, pulling at the mandarin robe. "Come *on*, Reru!"

Reru increased his glide and they hurried forward until they came to the silver-and-green place.

It was fairy-like in its beauty. Little green islands and clumps of vegetation were interspersed with flashing slivers of water, so that no matter where you stood, some small reflective surface caught the yellow light of the sun and sent it winking into your eyes. It looked, for all the world, like a toy landscape on which some giant had broken his mirror and left the bits to sparkle and shine in the daytime brightness. Reru squatted and Taddy sat down on the edge of one of the pools.

"What does it say?" asked the boy. "Tell me what it says, Reru."

The Mirian trilled again his little trill of pleasure; then composed himself. For a long time he sat silent, *listening*, while the boy squirmed, impatient, yet not daring to say anything that might interrupt or delay what Reru was about to say. Finally, the Mirian spoke.

"I can hear my brother the cow down in the tall grass at the edge of a pool. I can hear him as he moves among the grass; and I hear what he hears, his little brother, the dweller in the ground who stores up rich food for my brother the cow. And I can hear still further to all the other little brothers of the world as they go about their appointed tasks, until the air is thick with the sound of their living and their memories are my memories and their thoughts my thoughts.

"So the green-and-silver place is filled with a mighty thought; and this is what that thought says:

" 'The green-and-silver place is coming together of waters that have traveled a long way. Our brothers in the earth have told us that there are three waters that come together here, and none flow in the light of day. Our brothers of the waters have told us that these waters run far, for they have traveled the waters.

" 'One comes from the south, but the other two from the north. And the ones from the north travel side by side for a long way, with the dark and silent earth between and around them, until they come out in a colder land to the far north of here. And, in the far north, the two come together and their source is a single river that comes from a high mountain where the winds blow over bare rock. And in that place there is a brother who lives on the stones of the hillside and watches the stars at night. He has listened along the water and heard us down here in the warm grasslands; and he dreams of the green-and-silver place as he lies at night on the bare rock, watching the stars.

" 'But the water that comes from the south comes from deep beneath the mountains of the south, from a silent lake in the heart of the rock. The lake is filled by the water that trickles down the veins of the mountains; and in it lives another brother who is blind and has never seen the yellow sun. But he lies in the dark on a rock shelf above the silent lake and listens to the grumbling of the world as it talks to itself deep in the heart of the planet. And he, too, has heard us here in the warm grasslands, under the light of the yellow sun, and he dreams of the green-and-silver place as he lies on his rock ledge listening to the grumbling of the world.' "

Reru ceased talking and opened his eyes.

"That is only one story, Taddy," he said, "of the green-and-silver place."

"More," begged the boy. "Tell me more, Reru."

And he looked up into the alien face with eyes glowing in the wonder and excitement of what he had just heard. And Reru told him more.

The morning was nearly gone when they returned to Taddy's home, and Taddy's father and mother were already seated at the table eating lunch.

"Late again, Taddy," said his mother, with mock anger.

"No, I'm not," Taddy retorted, sliding into his place. "You're early."

"You are a little early at that, Celia," said Taddy's father. "How come?"

"Oh, I promised to go over to visit Julia this afternoon," answered Taddy's mother. "Taddy! Did you wash your hands?"

"Uh-huh," said Taddy with a vigorous nod, his mouth already full. "Look!" He displayed them at arms' length.

"Where did you go today, anyway?" asked his mother.

"To the green-and-silver place," answered Taddy.

"Green-and-silver place?" She looked across at her husband. "Where's that, Harry?"

"Darned if I know," answered Taddy's father. "Where is it, son?"

Taddy pointed in a southwesterly direction.

"Out there," he said. "There's lots of little pieces of water and lots of little bushes and things."

"Why," said Harry, "he must mean the swamp."

"The swamp!" echoed Taddy's mother. "He spent the whole morning at at a swamp! Harry, you have to do something. It isn't healthy for a boy to go mooning around like these Mirians."

"Now, Celia," grumbled Taddy's father. "The Mirians put their planet before everything else. It's almost a form of worship with them. But that can't possibly affect Taddy. Humans are just too big and strong to be seduced into that dead-end sort of philosophy. Anyway, that swamp's going to be drained shortly and they're going to put a building in its place."

He leaned across the table toward Taddy.

"You'd like that better, now, wouldn't you, son?" he said. "A big new building to run around in instead of that water and muck!"

The boy's face had gone completely white and his mouth was open.

"You can get Reru to take you over and watch it go up," his father went on.

"No!" said the boy, suddenly and violently.

"Why, Taddy!" said his mother. "Is that any way to talk to your father? Now, you apologise at once."

"I won't," said Taddy.

"Taddy!" his father's big voice rumbled dangerously.

"I don't care!" cried Taddy. Suddenly the words were tumbling out of him all at once. "I hate you! I hate your old buildings! When I grow up I'm going to tear down that old building and put all the water and things back." He was crying now, and his words came interspersed with sobs. "I don't like you here. Nobody else likes you either. Why don't you go 'way? Why don't you all go 'way?"

Taddy's father sat dumbfounded. But Taddy's mother got quickly up from her chair and around to Taddy's. She took him by his arm and pulled him away from the table.

"It's his nerves," she said. "I knew all this running around was bad for him." And she led him off in the direction of his room, his wails diminishing with distance and the closing of a door.

After a little while she came back.

"You see?" she said triumphantly to her husband. "Now he'll have to stay in bed all afternoon and I can't go over to Julia's because I'll have to stay here and watch him."

But Taddy's father had recovered his composure.

"Nonsense, Celia," he said. "It's just a case of nerves, like you said. Every boy has them one time or another. We can let the young pioneer kick up a few fusses without worrying too much about it. It won't hurt his character any. Now, you go on over to Julia's as you planned. He'll stay put."

"Well," said Taddy's mother slowly, wanting to be convinced, "if you say so—I don't suppose it would do any harm to run over for a few minutes. . . ."

Up in his room, Taddy's sobs diminished until they no longer racked his small body. He got up and went to the window and looked out at the rolling grasslands.

"I will, too," he said to himself, "I will too tear down all their old buildings when I grow up."

And, immediately he said it, a strange thing seemed to happen. A wave of peace flooded over him and he stopped crying. It was as if all the brothers that Reru had been talking about were here in the room and just outside his window, comforting him. He felt them all around him; and at the same time he sensed that they were all waiting for him to say something, waiting and listening. For just a few seconds he could feel all of Miria listening to him, to Taddy.

And he knew what they wanted; for he stretched both his arms out the window to them, a love filling his heart like no love he had ever felt before, as he spoke the two words they were waiting to hear.

"I promise," said Taddy.

Porges-Editors Correspondence

27 April 1951

Mr. Anthony Boucher
Editor
The Magazine of Fantasy and Science Fiction

Dear Sir:

Since your stories are getting so short ("Tick-tock," said the clock.) how about this?

FABLE

The Scoffer-at-the-Supernatural was spending a Night in the Deepest Dungeons of a quote Haunted unquote Castle, as per Wager. At about Midnight, certain Remarkable Manifestations having shaken his Skepticism, he sat down upon a Heap of Skulls to reflect.

Essaying the Objective Scientist, nobly abandoning a False Hypothesis, he said: "Apparently my Theory of the Non-Existence of Extra-Normal Phenomena is Untenable. Ah well. It's not the First Time I've been Wrong; and it certainly won't be the Last."

"Oh yes it will!" an Extra-Normal Phenomenon corrected him.

Sincerely yours,

Arthur Porges

P.S. I'm only kidding, so drop that rejection slip! Besides, there's no postage for it! (Your "vacation" will continue; I've nothing you would care for.)

20 August 1951

Dear Sir [A.B.]:

The first story I sent you, two years ago, was "The Devil and Simon Flagg." You liked it very much, except for the ending, and you suggested that I re-submit it later for rewrite advice. Well, after two years, I've finally hit on a different ending which also follows your other suggestion that I get some math in a story! It may be too specialized, but I thought I'd give you a look.

Sincerely yours,

Arthur Porges

15 September 1951

Mr. Anthony Boucher

Dear Sir:

Thank you for the excellent detailed commentary on "Simon Flagg." I agree with practically all the suggestions made, and the only one I've had doubts about is really something only an editor knows about. I refer to your opinion that many readers would never wade past all the early dialog and bargaining. However, I must conclude from the success of F and S-F, that you know what readers like!

All of which means that I've slashed hell out of the story to the extent of over a thousand words, although I had to fight an urge to add them elsewhere. I've followed, I believe, every suggestion to wit:

An early introduction to the question
Explanation of math
More of Simon's wife
More consistent dominating coolness of Simon
Sharpen up the devil's misery
Better (?) dialog at end

I am very willing to work it over further, but wanted to know first if the structure and general development are along the lines you preferred.

A. Porges

10 October 1951

Dear Sir [A.B.]:

One thing troubles me, and that is the perjury I'll be committing by claiming this story* as my own. Honestly, I feel that you should be listed as co-author, although I make the suggestion on the assumption that your standing as a writer won't be injured by such a collaboration!

Sincerely yours,

Arthur Porges

*Simon Flagg

5 June 1952

Dear Tony:

I got quite a bang out of your witty cipher message. You must have had excellent mathematical training to whip through it like that. Although the method is basically quite simple, continued fractions are something of an off-trail topic, and many a college mathematics major knows nothing about their theory.

There was one thing that puzzled me, however, On deciphering the salutation, I found to my surprise, the letters: EFBS BSU! I was momentarily baffled, until it occurred to me to shift one letter back, thus getting DEAR ART. I wondered why you used $A = 1$, $B = 2$, etc., instead of the $A = 2$, $B = 3$, example given in the paper. Even more surprising was the fact that your method *worked*; for the article, you will note, purposely excluded $A = 1$. ($2 \sim \neq 1$ Line 6). The reason for that exclusion will be clear by a glance at the following continued fraction:

$$3 + \cfrac{1}{1 + \cfrac{1}{2 + \cfrac{1}{1}}} \; .$$

A work ending in "A" will lead to a "1" for the last partial quotient, and while not likely to happen often, might make the final quotient ambiguous, since 2 plus 1/1 is the same as 3.

Of course, even my small knowledge of ciphers as such tells me that a choice as simple as that used in the paper would never be tried in practice. But then I don't even know if cipher has practical value anyway; to me it was just an exercise in mathematics!

In any case, you've actually cleared up a mistake of my own; I see now that my restriction that no letter be represented by unity is unnecessary, since a fraction like that above is easily avoided by not ciphering a block of letters ending in "A"; either stop short of the "A" or go past it! The other "1's" won't cause trouble.

Amusingly enough, yours was the second cipher message in two days. My uncle, a math teacher in Chicago, felt kittenish, and sent anonymous greetings in cipher!

My regards to Mick.

Cordially,

Art

Now, while Simon Flagg's acquaintance with spells, incantations, charms and such like was limited, his knowledge of mathematical arcana was most comprehensive . . . which should have been fair warning to the devil.

A.B./J.F. McC

The Devil and Simon Flagg
by Arthur Porges

After several months of the most arduous research, involving the study of countless faded manuscripts, Simon Flagg succeeded in summoning the devil. As a competent medievalist, his wife had proved invaluable. A mere mathematician himself, he was hardly equipped to decipher Latin holographs, particularly when complicated by rare terms from Tenth Century demonology, so it was fortunate that she had a flair for such documents.

The preliminary skirmishing over, Simon and the devil settled down to bargain in earnest. The devil was sulky, for Simon had scornfully declined several of his most dependable gambits, easily spotting the deadly barb concealed in each tempting bait.

"Suppose you listen to a proposition from me for a change," Simon suggested finally. "At least, it's a straightforward one."

The devil irritably twirled his tail-tip with one hand, much as a man might toy with his key chain. Obviously, he felt injured.

"All right," he agreed, in a grumpy voice. "It can't do any harm. Let's hear your proposal."

"I will pose a certain question," Simon began, and the devil brightened, "to be answered within twenty-four hours. If you cannot do so, you must pay me $100,000. That's a modest request compared to most you get. No billions, no Helen of Troy on a tiger skin. Naturally there must be no reprisals of any kind if I win."

"Indeed!" the devil snorted. "And what are *your* stakes?"

"If I lose, I will be your slave for any short period. No torment, no loss of soul—not for a mere $100,000. Neither will I harm relatives or friends. Although," he amended thoughtfully, "there are exceptions."

The devil scowled, pulling his forked tail petulantly. Finally, a savage tug having brought a grimace of pain, he desisted.

"Sorry," he said flatly. "I deal only in souls. There is no shortage of slaves. The amount of free, wholehearted service I receive from humans would amaze you. However, here's what I'll do. If I can't answer your question in the given time, you will receive not a paltry $100,000, but any sum within reason. In addition, I offer health and happiness as long as you live. If I do answer it—well you know the consequences. That's the very best I can offer." He pulled a lighted cigar from the air and puffed in watchful silence.

Simon stared without seeing. Little moist patches sprang out upon his forehead. Deep in his heart he had known what the devil's only terms would be. Then his jaw muscles knotted. He would stake his soul that nobody—man, beast, or devil—could answer *this* question in twenty-four hours.

"Include my wife in that health and happiness provision, and it's a deal," he said. "Let's get on with it."

The devil nodded. He removed the cigar stub from his mouth, eyed it distastefully, and touched it with a taloned forefinger. Instantly it became a large pink mint, which he sucked with noisy relish.

"About your question," he said, "it must have an answer, or our contract becomes void. In the Middle Ages, people were fond of proposing riddles. A few came to me with paradoxes, such as that one about a village with one barber who shaves all those, and only those, who don't shave themselves. 'Who shaves the barber?' they asked. Now, as Russell has noted, the 'all' makes such a question meaningless and so unanswerable."

"My question is just that—not a paradox," Simon assured him.

"Very well. I'll answer it. What are you smirking about?"

"Nothing," Simon replied, composing his face.

"You have very good nerves," the devil said, grimly approving, as he pulled a parchment from the air. "If I had chosen to appear as a certain monster which combines the best features of your gorilla with those of the Venusian Greater Kleep, an animal—I suppose one could call it that—of unique eye appeal, I wonder if your aplomb—''

"You needn't make any tests," Simon said hastily. He took the proffered contract, and satisfied that all was in order, opened his pocketknife.

"Just a moment," the devil protested. "Let me sterilize that; you might get infected." He held the blade to his lips, blew gently, and the steel glowed cherry red. "There you are. Now a touch of the point to some—ah—ink, and we're all set. Second line from the bottom, please; the last one's mine."

Simon hesitated, staring at the moist red tip.

"Sign," urged the devil, and squaring his shoulders, Simon did so.

When his own signature had been added with a flourish, the devil rubbed his palms together, gave Simon a frankly proprietory glance, and said jovially: "Let's have the question. As soon as I answer it, we'll hurry off. I've just time for another client tonight."

"All right," said Simon. He took a deep breath. "My question is this: Is Fermat's Last Theorem correct?"

The devil gulped. For the first time his air of assurance weakened.

"Whose last what?" he asked in a hollow voice.

"Fermat's Last Theorem. It's a mathematical proposition which Fermat, a Seventeenth Century French mathematician, claimed to have proved. However, his proof was never written down, and to this day nobody knows if the theorem is true or false." His lips twitched briefly as he saw the devil's expression. "Well, there you are—go to it!"

"Mathematics!" the devil exclaimed, horrified. "Do you think I've had time to waste learning such stuff? I've studied the Trivium and Quadrivium, but as for algebra—say," he added resentfully, "what kind of a question is that to ask me?"

Simon's face was strangely wooden, but his eyes shone. "You'd rather run 75,000 miles and bring back some object the size of Boulder Dam, I suppose!" he jeered. "Time and space are easy for you, aren't they? Well, sorry. I prefer this. It's a simple matter," he added, in a bland voice. "Just a question of positive integers."

"What's a positive integer?" the devil flared. "Or an integer, for that matter?"

"To put it more formally," Simon said, ignoring the devil's

question, "Fermat's Theorem states that there are no non-trivial, rational solutions of the equation $X^n + Y^n = Z^n$, for n a positive integer greater than two."

"What's the meaning of—"

"You supply the answers, remember."

"And who's to judge—you?"

"No," Simon replied sweetly. "I doubt if I'm qualified, even after studying the problem for years. If you come up with a solution, we'll submit it to any good mathematical journal, and their referee will decide. And you can't back out—the problem obviously is soluble: either the theorem is true, or it is false. No nonsense about multivalued logic, mind. Merely determine which, and *prove* it in twenty-four hours. After all, a man—excuse me—demon, of your intelligence and vast experience surely can pick up a little math in that time."

"I remember now what a bad time I had with Euclid when I studied at Cambridge," the devil said sadly. "My proofs were always wrong, and yet it was all obvious anyway. You could see just by the diagrams." He set his jaw. "But I can do it. I've done harder things before. Once I went to a distant star and brought back a quart of neutronium in just sixteen—"

"I know," Simon broke in. "You're very good at such tricks."

"Trick, nothing!" was the angry retort. "It's a technique so difficult—but never mind, I'm off to the library. But this time tomorrow—"

"No," Simon corrected him. "We signed half an hour ago. Be back in exactly twenty-three point five hours! Don't let me rush you," he added ironically, as the devil gave the clock a startled glance. "Have a drink and meet my wife before you go."

"I never drink on duty. Nor have I time to make the acquaintance of your wife . . . now." He vanished.

The moment he left, Simon's wife entered.

"Listening at the door again?" Simon chided her, without resentment.

"Naturally," she said in her throaty voice. "And darling—I want to know—that question—is it really difficult? Because if it's not—Simon, I'm so worried."

"It's difficult, all right." Simon was almost jaunty. "But most people don't realize that at first. You see," he went on, falling automatically into his stance for Senior Math II, "anybody can find two whole numbers whose squares add up to a square. For example, $3^2 + 4^2 = 5^2$; that is, $9 + 16 = 25$. See?"

"Uh huh." She adjusted his tie.

"But when you try to find two cubes that add up to a cube, or higher powers that work similarly, there don't seem to be any. Yet," he concluded dramatically, "nobody has been able to prove that no such numbers exist. Understand now?"

"Of course," Simon's wife always understood mathematical statements, however abstruse. Otherwise, the explanation was repeated until she did, which left little time for other activities.

"I'll make us some coffee," she said, and escaped.

Four hours later as they sat together listening to Brahm's Third, the devil reappeared.

"I've already learned the fundamentals of algebra, trigonometry, and plane geometry!" he announced triumphantly.

"Quick work," Simon complimented him. "I'm sure you'll have no trouble at all with spherical, analytic, projective, descriptive, and non-Euclidean geometries."

The devil winced. "Are there so many?" he inquired in a small voice.

"Oh, those are only a few." Simon had the cheerful air suited to a bearer of welcome tidings. "You'll like non-Euclidean," he said mendaciously. "There you don't have to worry about diagrams—they don't tell a thing! And since you hated Euclid anyway—"

With a groan the devil faded out like an old movie. Simon's wife giggled.

"Darling," she sang, "I'm beginning to think you've got him over a barrel."

"Sh," said Simon. "The last movement. Glorious!"

Six hours later, there was a smoky flash, and the devil was back. Simon noted the growing bags under his eyes. He suppressed a grin.

"I've learned all those geometries," the devil said with grim satisfaction. "It's coming easier now. I'm about ready for your little puzzle."

Simon shook his head. "You're trying to go too fast. Apparently you've overlooked such basic techniques as calculus, differential equations, and finite differences. Then there's—"

"Will I need all those?" the devil moaned. He sat down and knuckled puffy eyelids, smothering a yawn.

"I couldn't say," Simon replied, his voice expressionless. "But people have tried practically every kind of math there is on that 'little puzzle,' and it's still unsolved. Now, I suggest—" But the devil was in no mood for advice from Simon. This time he even made a sloppy disappearance while sitting down.

"I think he's tired," Mrs. Flagg said. "Poor devil." There was no discernible sympathy in her tones.

"So am I," said Simon. "Let's get to bed. He won't be back until tomorrow, I imagine."

"Maybe not," she agreed, adding demurely, "but I'll wear the black lace—just in case."

It was the following afternoon. Bach seemed appropriate somehow, so they had Landowska on.

"Ten more minutes," Simon said. "If he's not back with a solution by then, we've won. I'll give him credit; he could get a Ph.D. out of my school in one day—with honors! However—"

There was a hiss. Rosy clouds mushroomed sulphurously. The devil stood before them, steaming noisomely on the rug. His shoulders sagged; his eyes were bloodshot; and a taloned paw, still clutching a sheaf of papers, shook violently from fatigue or nerves.

Silently, with a kind of seething dignity, he flung the papers to the floor, where he trampled them viciously with his cloven hoofs. Gradually then, his tense figure relaxed, and a wry smile twisted his mouth.

"You win, Simon," he said, almost in a whisper, eyeing him with ungrudging respect. "Not even I can learn enough mathematics in such a short time for so difficult a problem. The more I got into it, the worse it became. Non-unique factoring, ideals—Baal! Do you know," he confided, "not even the best mathematicians on other planets—all far ahead of yours—have solved it? Why, there's a chap on Saturn—he looks something like a mushroom on stilts—who solves partial differential equations mentally; and even he's given up." The devil sighed. "Farewell." He dislimned with a kind of weary precision.

Simon kissed his wife—hard. A long while later she stirred in his arms.

"Darling," she pouted, peering into his abstracted face, "what's wrong now?"

"Nothing—except I'd like to see his work; to know how close

he came. I've wrestled with that problem for—" He broke off amazed as the devil flashed back. Satan seemed oddly embarrassed.

"I forgot," he mumbled. "I need to—ah!" He stooped for the scattered papers, gathering and smoothing them tenderly. "It certainly gets you," he said, avoiding Simon's gaze. "Impossible to stop just now. Why, if I could only prove one simple little lemma—" He saw the blazing interest in Simon, and dropped his apologetic air. "Say," he grunted, "you've worked on this, I'm sure. Did you try continued fractions? Fermat must have used them, and—move over a minute, please—" This last to Mrs. Flagg. He sat down beside Simon, tucked his tail under, and pointed to a jungle of symbols.

Mrs. Flagg sighed. Suddenly the devil seemed a familiar figure, little different from old Professor Atkins, her husband's colleague at the university. Any time two mathematicians got together on a tantalizing problem . . . Resignedly she left the room, coffee pot in hand. There was certainly a long session in sight. She knew. After all, she was a professor's wife.

Our friend Herman Mudgett is a collector and composer of that noble and neglected form of verse, the science fiction limerick. If you like this sample, we'll use others occasionally.

There was a young man of Cape Horn
Who held his grandparents in scorn;
Time-travel adventury,
He killed them last century—
And found he had never been born!

Herman Mudgett is a pseudonym for a well-known writer of limericks, and a collector too. (?)

Predictions

I'm not at all sure that I can make a valid argument for throwing these few items together in a group. Suggested by the first item, a note from Lord Dunsany to Arthur C. Clarke (September 27, 1951), I have labeled the group "Predictions." Candidly, no one can figure out how a copy of this note came to be included in the folder labeled "Dunsany," incoming correspondence to the editors. Perhaps Dunsany sent it to them. I don't know. I've taken the liberty of including it since the second paragraph is undeniably a prediction delivered with humor. It is the only exception in any of the correspondence, of not being written from the editors or to the editors, but, on the other hand, observe to whom it *is!*

Beefsteak Club,
London

Dear Clarke

Many thanks for the very interesting book. And "salesmanship" & the Gnoles made an amusing contrast of the kind that I think Sime would have loved, for he always made his goblins very earthly.

I tell my younger friends that one day they will see a photograph of the far side of the moon. When I said that, many years ago, to the late Lord Rayleigh he said, "Not a bit more interesting than the near side." But I disagreed with him there.

Yours sincerely,

Dunsany

Flying saucers were very much an item in 1950 and 1951. I guess they constitute conjecture rather than prediction, but I sense some vague link. The recipient of this letter is the author known as Gerald Heard as well as H. F. Heard.

12 February 1951

Dear Mr. Heard:

Yes, McComas & I are very much interested in the saucers, particularly since I spent long hours of hotel-room drinking in Portland last September with Kenneth Arnold—a fascinating and complex, but oddly convincing character.

We read the Keyhoe with great interest and the Scully with unalloyed contempt, and have tried to follow most magazine writing on the subject. (Did you see Bob Considine's *The disgraceful flying saucer hoax!* in Cosmopolitan for this January, in which, it seems to me, Considine offers some interesting evidence precisely contrary to his thesis?)

Just in case we should ever need to express an editorial policy on saucers (aside from the fact that we're deathly sick of them in science fiction), we've formulated the following opinion: There appears to be a significant residuum of saucer data which cannot be explained away by meteorological phenomena, mass hysteria, etc., etc. Interplanetary travel is the *least implausible* thesis so far advanced to cover these data.

Sincerely,

B.

Someone writing an article on science fiction, possibly for a fanzine, asked what science fiction writers were most frequently predicting.

8 November 1952

Dear Mr. Brooke:

As to what science fiction writers are most frequently "predicting," we'd say, as editors and reviewers, that most current writing falls into 3 classes:

A) Writing of the scientific developments of the very immediate future—moon flight, space stations, cybernetics, atomic and bacterial war, etc—in which fictional speculation is hardly to be distinguished from the factual conjectures of scientists, and in which indeed fiction writers may be anticipated by tomorrow's headlines (and are probably already anticipated by secret classified material).

B) Writing of an infinitely remote intergalactic future in which the goddamnedest scientific miracles happen, with guessing so wild that there is almost no known element of extrapolation from present scientific possibility;

C) Exploration of the mental, rather than physical sciences; telekinesis, extra-sensory perception, teleportation, poltergeister, etc—the sort of thing studied by Rhine at Duke . . . what John W Campbell Jr of ASTOUNDING calls *psionics*.

In other words, very little of the sort of technological prophecy of the middle future at which Hugo Gernsback excelled. Chief reason: the factual science of the immediate future is moving too fast.

Hope this is useful. May we please see a copy of your piece?

Sincerely,

A.B.

I first met Mick McComas in a wonderful old bier stubbe in Hollywood in the long ago early thirties. We were introduced by one Anthony Boucher whose first mystery novel had just been published by Simon & Schuster, for whom I was Western Representative.

Mick, Tony and I became fast friends. We had similar tastes . . . good beer, well written fiction, the occult and (in premarital days) lithesome young ladies who also liked beer—and vigorous young men. At that time I knew nothing of science fiction and was surprised to discover that both of these brilliant fellows read what I called "pulp" magazines. However, when I was introduced to ASTOUNDING, then edited by the extraordinary John Campbell, I became enlightened!

Mick soon left a dull office job with a large oil company to become for a good number of years my associate in book peddling. He had become pretty much persona non grata there anyhow, as the scandalous fellow had been trying to unionize his office cohorts! As we pursued our interest in science fiction, it occurred to us that an anthology of such stories by the wonderful young writers of the time might be salable. Bennett Cerf, president of Random House, agreed, and Mick and I put together a volume of science fiction stories titled ADVENTURES IN TIME AND SPACE. It is still in print some thirty-five years later.

Mick and Tony are both gone, but their particular influence is strongly present in current fantasy and science fiction—especially in the best!

Raymond J. Healy

A decade and more ago, McComas used to write science fiction under the pseudonym of Webb Marlowe; but since then his writing has been confined to editorial comments here and elsewhere, a noteworthy essay on capital punishment, and critiques of science-fantasy for the New York Times Book Review. *Now*

*in 1954 he's blossoming out as a fiction-writer again, starting
off with an intelligent analytical study of future penology in
Raymond J. Healy's 9 TALES OF SPACE AND TIME; and I'm as
happy as I'm sure you will be that F&SF has the privilege of
being the first magazine to present a story by The New McComas.
When science fiction turns to the past rather than the future, the
theme of beginnings—of how things came to pass for the first
time—is an especially fascinating one. We've brought you stories
of the first man who consciously uttered a word (by John P.
McKnight) and of the first man who learned to season food (by
me); now McComas takes up another "first" which has been
surprisingly neglected to date and introduces us to the delightful
company of Sleepy Hawk, a tribal leader who knew how to fight
and how to laugh and how to coin words . . . and how fighting
could be replaced by something new and vital and demanding
fresh word-making.*

—A.B.

Brave New Word
by J. Francis McComas

The travelers to the hot country arrived today, carrying many
things, so tonight there will be dancing and all the hearts of The
People will be good. As ever, when the travelers return, I
remember how the thing began with Sleepy Hawk, that great
doer of deeds, that laugher, that maker of words.

Most of The People think the matter had its beginning later;
but I, whose oldest father had the story from the mouth of Sleepy
Hawk himself, think otherwise. The true beginning was when
Long Ax, that angry man, had his new ax handle break in his
hand the very first time he swung the weapon. Long Ax had
chosen the wood with care and knowledge, made it straight with
his knife, and then, in the chosen way, fixed it to the great stone
ax his oldest father had given him.

Then, at the very first trial swing at one of the big trees that
grew by the river where The People were camped, the handle
had splintered, the great stone head had bounced from the tree to
the river water and Long Ax, a splinter driven into his thumb,
danced about, shouting with pain and anger.

Since all this was a very bad sign, the rest of the young men

looked very solemn. All, that is, except Sleepy Hawk, who fell
on his back and laughed. He laughed so loud and so long that the
other four thought he might never stop, but choke himself to
death there by the river.

"Why do you laugh?" cried Long Ax. "Now I must make
another handle! We can't start until I do!"

"Yes," asked Hungry Dog, who was fat and liked to sit in
Long Ax's shadow, "why do you laugh?"

Sleepy Hawk stopped choking himself and said, "I'm sorry.
But you looked so—so—" he looked in his head for a word,
could not find one and said, "so—laugh-making! One moment
you were swinging with your great ax, the next moment you
were dancing about, a little boy with a splinter in your hand!
And the fine new handle for your ax was nothing but wood for
the fire!"

At Sleepy Hawk's words, even Mountain Bear, the quiet man,
laughed softly deep in his throat.

The face of Long Ax colored the angry red and he said, "How
would you like to stay here and laugh while the others follow *me*
on our hunt?"

Sleepy Hawk sat up then and looked at the other. His face did
look something like that of a hawk that sleeps, with his sharp
curved nose and his half-closed eyes. But it was the face of a
hawk just waiting to wake and pounce.

"How would you like to try to make me?" he said very
softly.

Long Ax was still red with anger but he looked away from
Sleepy Hawk, toward the river.

"You have a knife and I have nothing," he growled.

With a move so fast it could barely be seen Sleepy Hawk
jumped to his feet, took the knife from his belt and tossed it
away.

"Now, I have no knife."

"Enough!" cried Mountain Bear, who was a quiet man but
strong like his name animal. "Save your blows for our enemies!
Long Ax, I have a stick for a spear, dry and tough. You may
have it for your ax. Sleepy Hawk, take up your knife. You know
we would not go on a fight or a hunt without you to lead us."

So there was peace but later, while waiting for Long Ax to
bind together haft and head of his weapon, Mountain Bear said
to Sleepy Hawk, "I cannot understand you. Always you laugh.
And there is nothing to smile about in life."

"Yes, there is! Each thing of life, even the worst thing, has a part of it that will make you laugh, if only you will see it."

"Ha! I suppose you laugh even when you are with a woman!"

"Sometimes. If it is the proper woman and her heart is like mine."

But, as I said, most of The People think the matter had its beginning later, there on the ledge in the mountain of the Mud Dwellers, halfway down the great cliff, when the five young men came face to face with six of the little Mud Dwellers and there was no going back for any man.

For, after much thought, the band had decided to go toward the sun and into the mountain of the Mud Dwellers, rather than to the cold mountains and the Dwellers-in-Caves. The young men of The People wanted women. Those Dwellers-in-Caves, who made such queer markings on the walls of their homes, were strong and not easy to surprise. Too, their women were fierce, not kind and pleasing like those of the Mud Dwellers.

So they made a long journey, over a strange country. First, the river had dried into a hot land. After that, they seemed to be in the time of the long sun, come before they had thought, and the skins of animals they wore were hot on their backs. Sleepy Hawk wound into a tight roll his skin of a big cat and wrapped it around his waist. After a while, the others did the same.

Sleepy Hawk looked at them, running slowly along, the water pouring off their bodies, and said, "It is cooler by the side of our river."

Even Long Ax grinned at this although his tongue was swollen in his mouth.

The heat of the long sun fell on them and what little water they found made their hearts sick and their minds weak. So the young men went a day and a night without drinking.

Then, when they felt they could run no longer, they saw before them that great mountain rising straight up from the ground to the sky which held in its heart the little caves of the little men that The People called the Mud Dwellers. They stopped and looked up at the mountain.

"OO-ee!" cried Hungry Dog, "That will be a hard run!"

But Sleepy Hawk found a trickle of water and they drank it without having their bellies cry out against them.

So the five young men of The People climbed the mountain that day and found its top was broad and flat. They moved carefully across the ground, ducking from tree to tree. Once, they found a pile of rocks that had, in the long ago, been a Mud Dwellers' home, before the wars of The People had driven them down inside the mountain, where the little men thought they might live more safely.

"These do not look like rocks," said Mountain Bear, stopping to look at them.

"They are not rocks," said Sleepy Hawk. "I have heard that the Mud Dwellers mix dried grass with mud, shape this into blocks and let the heat of the sun make the blocks hard. They build their caves with these hard blocks."

"That is a foolish waste of time," said Mountain Bear.

"And we waste time," said Sleepy Hawk. "We must reach the edge of their home place before dark."

So, just before the hiding of the sun, the young hunters came to where the top of the mountain suddenly ended. They crouched down and looked over the edge. There was a great cut, going deep to the heart of the mountain; and down, far down at the bottom of the cut, they could see, moving like bugs on a raw hide, a few of the Mud Dwellers.

"We'll rest here until the first morning light," Sleepy Hawk told them.

"Then climb down as far as we can?" asked Mountain Bear. Sleepy Hawk nodded.

"Then we should watch another day, I think," said Long Ax. Sleepy Hawk nodded again.

"We'll have to be quick," said Short Spear.

"Take women only," grunted Long Ax. "Weapons too, if there are any."

"And food!" added Hungry Dog.

"No food!" cried the others.

"They do not eat," Cat-In-The-Mud told Hungry Dog. "Their food is taken from the ground and it is dirty."

Sleepy Hawk smiled a little at this, but said nothing.

Yet it did not work out as they planned. The five young men waked at the first light and slowly, quietly, they climbed down the steep side of the cut in the mountain. But as they crawled around a high rock to a narrow ledge, six men of the Mud Dwellers came up onto the ledge from the down trail. All stopped suddenly and stared at each other.

Then each side took a step forward, raised their weapons, then stopped again, weapons half-lifted in their hands.

"Well," Long Ax growled deep in his throat, "why do we wait?"

"For the same reason they do!" Sleepy Hawk's voice was sharp.

He waved his hand and they all looked quickly about them. There was the long, narrow ledge, with the mountain going straight up from one side and, from the other, straight down in a heart-choking drop. And at each end of the ledge stood a little group of men, angry, uncertain, the length of three steps of a tall man between them.

"Who can win a fight in such a place?" asked Sleepy Hawk.

"We can!" growled Long Ax. "They are but little men!"

"But they are six and we are five, so all is equal."

"Throw spears and after them!" cried Long Ax.

Cat-In-The-Mud and Hungry Dog raised their weapons. As they did so, three of the Mud Dwellers lifted their arms.

"Stop!" cried Sleepy Hawk. Over his shoulder he said to Long Ax, "I am chief here. Now look, all of you. They throw, we throw. None can miss. If any men are left after the throwing, they fight.

"Perhaps one of all here lives. Then what? If that one is of The People, can he, wounded, alone, ever hope to return to our river? No!"

"You are right," said Mountain Bear.

"They will call for help," warned Cat-In-The-Mud.

"Soon enough to fight then," said Sleepy Hawk. "There is little room for more on this ground."

"True enough," said Mountain Bear.

"Now, quiet all of you," ordered Sleepy Hawk, "and let me think."

He watched the Mud Dwellers. They were strange little men. Around their waists they wore belts of dried skin, but in these belts were set little pieces of colored stone. They wore smaller belts around their heads, to keep their long hair from falling over their eyes, and these belts, too, had the pieces of stone in them.

Sleepy Hawk liked these colored stones very much. But he did not think he would get any from the Mud Dwellers, who, though small, stood their ground as bravely as did The People, frowning, with knives and spears ready for the fight.

"Look at their spears," Sleepy Hawk said.

"They have two handles!" There was wonder in Cat-In-The-Mud's voice.

"Yes. One goes back from the hand, then joins the other, which goes forward to the head of the spear."

"I don't understand," Mountain Bear said softly.

"Neither do I." Sleepy Hawk frowned. "Two handles . . . I would like a closer look at those strange spears."

"Enough of this women's chatter!" screamed Long Ax. "Let us fight like men!"

Sleepy Hawk shrugged.

"If the rest of you feel that we should get ourselves killed," he said quietly, "and leave our bones here for Mud Dwellers to hang in their caves, why—let Long Ax begin the fight."

None moved.

Long Ax called out again but still no man of the other four moved and Long Ax closed his mouth tightly.

For a time there was silence on the ledge. Sleepy Hawk watched the Mud Dwellers; he had a wish to talk with them, to learn what they might be thinking. Now, like many of The People, Sleepy Hawk had a woman from the Mud Dwellers in his family, and from her had learned a few of their love words, the words that a mother says to a child that pleases her. But that was all. When The People caught a Mud Dweller woman it was her duty to learn their talk, not theirs to learn her noises.

So there was nothing he could say to them. He watched. They, too, stood as did The People, their leader a little in front of them, staring at his enemies, his men behind him, looking about nervously, their knives and strange two-handled spears ready for blood.

It seemed then to Sleepy Hawk that the two groups of men looked like two deer caught in the trap sands of a river. A deer so caught by the water hiding below the quiet-looking sands cannot step forward, nor can it move backward. So it was with the men. Their legs were caught on the rock. They dared not move either up or down. All of them, The People and Mud Dwellers, could only stand still and wait for what would happen.

And thinking of the men trapped like silly deer, Sleepy Hawk laughed aloud.

"Why do you laugh?" snarled Hungry Dog. Fright was in his voice.

Sleepy Hawk was choking again, as he always did when laughing swelled in his throat.

"This is—this is all very—" He choked and his breath flew out between his lips and he made a word.

"What was that?" cried Mountain Bear. "What did you say?"

"I said *funny*."

"What does *funny* mean?"

"It is a word I have made and it means laugh-making. All this—we and they standing here, of us all none daring to go a step forward or back—it is very laugh-making . . . very *funny*!"

"We have a crazy man for a chief," growled Long Ax. "Or a fool. It takes little to make a fool laugh—"

But Sleepy Hawk was not listening. He was watching the leader of the Mud Dwellers and he was so startled by what that one was doing that he gave no ear to Long Ax's words. For the Mud Dweller was smiling. At first, it was a little smile, on the mouth only, but then, as Sleepy Hawk started to laugh again, the Mud Dweller's smile shone in his eyes, he opened his mouth and laughed as loudly as Sleepy Hawk ever did.

The two of them stood and laughed with each other while their followers looked at them uneasily and Long Ax muttered words of anger that he knew Sleepy Hawk could not hear.

Then, perhaps because his heart was warmed by his laughing, or because he was a great thinker as the later days of his life proved, Sleepy Hawk did a very strange thing. First he put his knife back in his belt, so that his left hand held nothing. Then he dropped his spear from his right hand. Mountain Bear cried out at this, but Sleepy Hawk did not listen. He stepped forward one step and raised his right hand, so that the chief of the Mud Dwellers could see that it was empty.

The Dweller's smile was now on his lips only .He looked very hard at Sleepy Hawk, then he slowly nodded his head. Then he moved his hands slowly so that the two handles of his spear came apart. In one hand, he held a spear with a sharp stone head. In the other, just a simple, harmless stick with a hook at one end. He dropped these to the ground and stepped toward Sleepy Hawk, his right hand raised.

The two of them came close together. Sleepy Hawk said a Mud Dweller word that they all knew, one that a mother uses when her child makes her smile at his play. The Mud Dweller's smile became smaller; the young men saw that he did not like the use of that word between men. So Sleepy Hawk pointed at the young men of The People, then at the Mud Dwellers, making fearful frowns to show each of them angry at the other. Then he pointed to himself and laughed. He pointed to the Mud Dweller and laughed. He swept his arm around the air, pointing at both sides and laughing.

Then, slowly and clearly, Sleepy Hawk said his new word.

The chief of the Mud Dwellers nodded and said it after him.

"Fun—nee!" he said.

Sleepy Hawk held out his empty right hand and the Mud Dweller slowly reached out and touched Sleepy Hawk's hand with his.

"Very funny," answered Sleepy Hawk, grinning. Then, hoping the Mud Dweller might know the tongue of The People, he said, "I am Sleepy Hawk."

But the Mud Dweller did not understand. He said some words, in the high bird voice of the Mud Dwellers. Nor did Sleepy Hawk understand the Mud Dweller's words, so the two men just stood there, their right hands touching, smiling.

"Do any of you know any of the Mud Dwellers' words among men?" asked Sleepy Hawk.

The young men shook their heads.

"Never mind. Put down your weapons."

"Is that wise?" asked Mountain Bear.

"It is. Put them down."

So all the young men except Long Ax lowered their spears and put their knives and axes in their belts.

"Long Ax! I command you—" Sleepy Hawk began, but the chief of the Mud Dwellers turned his head and said a few words to his followers and they, slowly, took apart their two-handled spears and set them on the ground and those that had knives in their hands put these back in their belts. So Long Ax, too, let his weapon rest on the ground.

While their men stood, not at peace, but not ready for war, the two chiefs made talk with their hands; and after a while Sleepy Hawk nodded many times and turned to his followers and said, "Now we may go. With no spears in our backs. I have his promise."

"What is that worth!" cried Long Ax. "I do not turn my back on an enemy."

"Stay here, then," answered Sleepy Hawk. He himself waved at the Mud Dweller, turned and took a step back toward the upward trail.

Then he stopped, so suddenly that Mountain Bear, who was behind him, bumped into Sleepy Hawk.

"What is the matter with you?" cried Mountain Bear.

"Let us stay a little longer. I want one of those spears."

Sleepy Hawk looked again at the Mud Dweller, smiled, and very slowly, took the knife from his belt. The Mud Dweller frowned, but made no move when he saw that Sleepy Hawk held the knife by its blade and offered it to him.

"One does not give presents to an enemy," said Hungry Dog.

"This is no present. Watch and see."

The Mud Dweller took Sleepy Hawk's knife and looked at it. It was a good knife, with a blade of sharp flint and a handle made of the polished horn of old humpback. It was easy to see that the Mud Dweller wanted the knife.

Then Sleepy Hawk pointed to the little head-belt with its polished stones. Then he pointed to himself, then to the knife, and finally, to the Mud Dweller.

The Mud Dweller reached behind his head and took off the belt. Its bright-colored stones sparkled in the sun's light. The Mud Dweller handed it to Sleepy Hawk, who fastened it around his head. The Mud Dweller weighed the knife in his hand, nodded twice, and put the knife in the belt around his waist.

"Ha!" said Mountain Bear. "I thought you wanted a spear."

"Be quiet! I shall get one."

"How?"

"You shall see."

Once more Sleepy Hawk made as if to go. And once more he stopped and turned back to the Mud Dweller. That little man watched with sharp eyes. Sleepy Hawk took his rolled-up skin of a mountain cat from around his waist, shook it out so that the Mud Dweller could see, and spread it on the ground.

The Mud Dweller felt of the skin and his fingers saw how soft it was, having been well-cured by Sleepy Hawk's oldest mother. Sleepy Hawk looked up at the sun, covered his eyes, and shivered. The Mud Dweller watched closely. Sleepy Hawk uncovered his eyes but still shivered. Then he reached for the skin and wrapped it around him. As soon as it covered him all over, he stopped shaking and smiled.

The chief of the Mud Dwellers nodded to show he understood that when the time of little sun came, the skin would keep him warm and dry.

He reached toward Sleepy Hawk for the skin of the big cat.

"Careful!" Mountain Bear called softly.

Sleepy Hawk let the skin fall to the ground. The Mud Dweller reached for it again, but Sleepy Hawk raised his hand, shook his head just a little, and walked over to where the two parts of the chief's spear lay on the ground. A Mud Dweller started for Sleepy Hawk, but his chief called out and the man was quiet. Sleepy Hawk picked up the two parts of the weapon but did not take them away. Instead he carried them back to the chief of the Mud Dwellers.

Sleepy Hawk made slow, careful signs. He lifted in his hand the spear that was no spear, but just a harmless stick. He shook it, held each end of it in turn, very close to his eyes, then, shaking his head, he let that stick fall to the ground. Next, Sleepy Hawk looked at the spear that was a proper spear, felt its sharp point with his thumb and nodded. After that, he picked up the other stick and held both parts out toward the Mud Dweller.

The Mud Dweller shook his head.

Sleepy Hawk stirred the cat's skin with his toe.

The Mud Dweller frowned just a little, then nodded. He moved his hand to show that Sleepy Hawk could have the two spears and reached down for the skin. But Sleepy Hawk shook his head and held out the stick part that was not a spear at all.

The Mud Dweller smiled, took both parts from Sleepy Hawk's hands. He looked around him, then moved to the rim of the ledge and stood there, looking upward.

"Now we shall see how a man throws that spear," Sleepy Hawk said softly.

"Surely he will not throw it *up* the mountain," said Mountain Bear.

But that is what the little man did. The Mud Dweller put the pieces together and raised his arm back to throw. One of the shafts went back from his hand. The queer hook at its end held the haft of the true spear. Then the Mud Dweller threw and, as the stick in his hand made his arm twice as long as any man's, so was his throw twice as strong and the spear flew up the mountain, farther than the farthest spear ever thrown by any of The People. It landed beside the trail down which the young men had come and stood there, its point deep in the ground.

"Oo—ee!" whistled Mountain Bear.

"A stick that throws!" cried Sleepy Hawk.

"The stick throws the spear!" said Cat-In-The-Mud. He grinned sourly at Long Ax. "Their weapons are better than ours. Sleepy Hawk is a very wise chief."

And Hungry Dog nodded and moved away from Long Ax.

Then the chief of the Mud Dwellers took up Sleepy Hawk's spear and showed him how to fit it on the throwing stick. He seemed to think of something new, then, for he pointed to his own spear sticking in the ground high up the mountain. He made a sign to keep Sleepy Hawk's spear, then pointed at Sleepy Hawk and to the spear up by the trail.

"A wise man," Sleepy Hawk said to Mountain Bear. "He wants to keep my spear and I will take his as we pass by it."

"Wait!" cried Mountain Bear. "I want one of those spear-throwers!"

And he unwrapped his bear's skin from where it was wound around his middle and walked over to one of the Mud Dwellers. After him came the rest of the young men of The People, even the angry Long Ax, and The People and the Mud Dwellers stood beside each other, smiling and talking, even though there was no understanding of what was said.

And all of them laughed when a little, fat Mud Dweller offered Hungry Dog some small, round brown things and made signs that Hungry Dog should eat them. Which Hungry Dog did, of course.

"Good!" he cried with his mouth full, as a man should not. "Eat them! They're good!"

"Now, Hungry Dog," said Sleepy Hawk, "give them some dried meat."

Hungry Dog looked unhappy at this but he took some dried flesh of deer and offered it to the Mud Dwellers. After chewing a little bit, they smiled and rubbed their middles to show that the dried meat was good to their insides.

Now the sun was straight up in the sky. The giving and receiving was finished and the men stood about, tired, hot, but peaceful. Sleepy Hawk made signs to the Mud Dweller chief, pointing up the mountain. That man nodded, but he looked sad. Then Sleepy Hawk looked up at the sun, waved his hand across the sky, pointed down at the ledge, held up his fingers many times. The Mud Dweller smiled.

Sleepy Hawk thought a long time, looking hard at the Mud Dweller, then he said a word. Mountain Bear, who was standing by, had never heard this word before.

Sleepy Hawk pointed to the Mud Dwellers and the young men

of The People, at the skins and the weapons, and at the belts with the colored stones.

He said the word again.

The Mud Dweller said the word after Sleepy Hawk.

Sleepy Hawk and the Mud Dweller said the word together.

Then the young men of The People waved to the Mud Dwellers and started the climb back to the top of the mountain.

When they reached the flat top of the mountain and rested a while, Sleepy Hawk laughed softly and said to Mountain Bear, "You know, I have another, better knife at home. And my cat's skin was old. I shall hunt for another one." He laughed again. "But I have never had a stick that throws spears farther than can a man's arms. And when I seek a wife, I shall give her father some of the colored stones. Even the chief of all our chiefs should then be willing to give me his oldest daughter—the beautiful one."

Mountain Bear hefted the throwing stick. "We are coming back?"

"Yes. I want many belts with their stones of many colors. Yes, in three hands of suns I will return to . . ."

"To what?" asked Mountain Bear. "I heard you make a word."

"Yes. I made a word to tell of giving one thing to get another. I taught it to that chief of the Mud Dwellers. So, from now on, unless some fool like Long Ax makes trouble, the Mud Dweller and I will not fight. We will *trade*."

And that is why we go peacefully to the land of Mud Dwellers and bring back many things without war. And that is why the youngest young son of Sleepy Hawk, who is like the old man was, is planning to go up the mountains where the Dwellers-in-Caves are. He thinks they will trade us the strange colors they put on the walls of their caves and other things for our throwing sticks and skins and bright stones.

Norton-Editors
Correspondence

7 April 1953

Dear Miss Norton:

We like MOUSETRAP—nice idea, greatly told, but one thing bothers us. How on earth (or Mars) does Sam know about the puffball action. I don't see how it can be abstractly deduced. He could, of course, easily find out by seeing it happen to a cat or dog or some odd martian beast.

If you can fix this up, we'll be happy to buy it.

Have any of your other shorts sold or will this be a first?

And just incidentally, how come it is Andre and not Andrée or Andrea? It's been bothering me ever since I learned your sex.

Cordially,

Anthony Boucher

9 April 1953

Dear Mr. Boucher:

To say that I am overwhelmed at your reception of "Mousetrap" is putting it very mildly! I can very easily put in a puff-ball discovery for Sam. Think I know just where to insert it and how.

Had two stories published in the "Fantasy Book" under "Andrew North"—"Gifts of Asti" and "People of the Crater". But no other short s-f. Short stories are not natural writing for me and I have to work them over and over—seem to think only in book length plots.

As to "Andre"—just a properly ambiguous either sex name to be worn by a female who makes a living writing male adventure stories—it can be a problem with readers unless one works behind such a smoke screen—especially when one writes for teen age boys. I am very used to being "Mr. Norton" and have stunned radio program directors when acting as guest-interviewee by appearing in skirts.

Sincerely,

Andre Norton

Until we read this brief story by Andre Norton we had concluded that a generation of writers, beginning with Stanley G. Weinbaum and coming up to the present day with Ray Bradbury and Arthur C. Clarke, had just about exhausted the possibilities of Mars as a locale for science fiction. With this wholly convincing account of the weird and lovely things Terran explorers (and racketeers) may find on the Martian deserts, Miss Norton, noted hitherto for her tasteful anthologies and admirably conceived novels of the far future, not only proves us wrong but makes a proper place for herself right up there with Messrs. Clarke and Bradbury.
Make room, gentlemen!

A.B./J.F. McComas

Mousetrap
by Andre Norton

Remember that old adage about the man who built a better mousetrap and then could hardly cope with the business which beat a state highway to his door? I saw that happen once—on Mars.

Sam Levatts was politely introduced—for local color—by the tourist guides as a "desert spider." "Drunken bum" would have been the more exact term. He prospected over and through the dry lands out of Terraport and brought in Star Stones, Gormel ore, and like knickknacks to keep him sodden and mostly content. In his highly scented stupors he dreamed dreams and saw visions. At least his muttered description of the "lovely lady" was taken to be a vision, since there are no ladies in the Terraport dives he frequented and the females met there are far from lovely.

But Sam continued a peaceful dreamer until he met Len Collins and Operation Mousetrap began.

Every dumb tourist who steps into a scenic sandmobile at Terraport has heard of the "sand monsters." Those which still

282

remain intact are now all the property of the tourist bureaus. And, brother, they're guarded as if they were a part of that cache of Martian royal jewels Black Spragg stumbled on twenty years ago. Because the monsters, which can withstand the dust storms, the extremes of desert cold and heat, crumble away if so much as a human finger tip is poked into their ribs.

Nowadays you are allowed to get within about twenty feet of the "Spider Man" or the "Armed Frog" and that's all. Try to edge a little closer and you'll get a shock that'll lay you flat on your back with your toes pointing Earthwards.

And, ever since the first monster went drifting off as a puff of dust under someone's hands, the museums back home have been adding to the cash award waiting for the fellow who can cement them for transportation. By the time Len Collins met Sam that award could be quoted in stellar figures.

Of course, all the bright boys in the glue, spray and plastic business had been taking a crack at the problem for years. The frustrating answer being that when they stepped out of the rocket over here, all steamed up about the stickability of their new product, they had nothing to prove it on. Not one of the known monsters was available for testing purposes. Every one is insured, guarded, and under the personal protection of the Space Marines.

But Len Collins had no intention of trying to reach one of these treasures. Instead he drifted into Sam's favorite lapping ground and set them up for Levatts—three times in succession. At the end of half an hour Sam thought he had discovered the buddy of his heart. And on the fifth round he spilled his wild tale about the lovely lady who lived in the shelter of two red rocks— far away—a vague wave of the hand suggesting the general direction.

Len straightaway became a lover of beauty panting to behold this supreme treat. And he stuck to Sam that night closer than a Moonman to his oxy-supply. The next morning they both disappeared from Terraport in a private sandmobile hired by Len.

Two weeks later Collins slunk into town again and booked passage back to New York. He clung to the port hotel, never sticking his head out of the door until it was time to scuttle to the rocket.

Sam showed up in the Flame Bird four nights later. He had a nasty sand burn down his jaw and he could hardly keep his feet for lack of sleep. He was also—for the first time in Martian history—cold and deadly sober. And he sat there all evening drinking nothing stronger than Sparkling Canal Water. Thereby shocking some kindred souls half out of their wits.

What TV guy doesn't smell a story in a quick change like that? I'd been running the dives every night for a week—trying to pick up some local color for our 6 o'clock casting. And the most exciting and promising thing I had come across so far was Sam's sudden change of beverage. Strictly off the record—we cater to the family and tourist public mostly—I started to do a little picking and prying. Sam answered most of my feelers with grunts.

The I hit pay dirt with the casual mention that the Three Planets Travel crowd had picked up another shocked cement dealer near their pet monster, "The Ant King." Sam rolled a mouthful of the Sparkling Water around his tongue, swallowed with a face to frighten all monsters, and asked a question of his own.

"Where do these here science guys think all the monsters come from?"

I shrugged. "No explanation that holds water. They can't examine them closely without destroying them. That's one reason for the big award awaiting any guy who can glue them together so they'll stand handling."

Sam pulled something from under the pocket flap of his spacealls. It was a picture, snapped in none too good a light, but clear enough.

Two large rocks curved toward each other to form an almost perfect archway and in their protection stood a woman. At least her slender body had the distinctly graceful curves we have come to associate with the stronger half of the race. But she also had wings, outspread in a grand sweep as if she stood on tiptoe almost ready to take off. There were only the hints of features— that gave away the secret of what she really was—because none of the sand monsters ever showed clear features.

"Where—?" I began.

Sam spat. "Nowhere now." He was grim, and his features had tightened up. He looked about ten years younger and a darn sight tougher.

"I found her two years ago. And I kept going back just to look at her. She wasn't a monster like the rest of 'em. She was perfect. Then that—" Sam lapsed into some of the finest space-searing language I have ever been privileged to hear—"that Collins got me drunk enough to show him where she was. He knocked me out, sprayed her with his goo, and tried to load her into the back of the 'mobile. It didn't work. She held together for about five minutes and then—'' He snapped his fingers. "Dust just like 'em all!"

I found myself studying the picture for a second time. And I was beginning to wish I had Collins alone for about three minutes or so. Most of the sand images I had seen I could cheerfully do without—they were all nightmare material. But, as Sam had pointed out, this was no monster. And it was the only one of its type I had ever seen or heard about. Maybe there might just be another somewhere—the desert dry lands haven't been one quarter explored.

Sam nodded as if he had caught that thought of mine right out of the smoky air.

"Won't do any harm to look. I've noticed one thing about all of the monsters—they are found only near the rocks. Red rocks like these," he tapped the snapshot, "that have a sort of blue-green moss growin' on them." His eyes focused on the wall but I had an idea that he was seeing beyond it, beyond all the sand barrier walls in Terraport, out into the dry lands. And I guessed that he wasn't telling all he knew—or suspected.

I couldn't forget that picture. The next night I was back at the Flame Bird. But Sam didn't show. Instead rumor had it that he had loaded up with about two months' supplies and had gone back to the desert. And that was the last I heard of him for weeks. Only, his winged woman had crept into my dreams and I hated Collins. The picture was something—but I would have given a month's credits—interstellar at that—to have seen the original.

During the next year Sam made three long trips out, keeping quiet about his discoveries, if any. He stopped drinking and he was doing better financially. Actually brought in two green Star Stones, the sale of which covered most of his expenses for the year. And he continued to take an interest in the monsters and the eternal quest for the fixative. Two of the rocket pilots told me that he was sending to Earth regularly for everything published on the subject.

Gossip had already labeled him "sand happy." I almost believed that after I met him going out of town one dawn. He was in his prospector's crawler and strapped up in plain sight on top of his water tanks was one of the damnedest contraptions I'd ever seen—a great big wire cage!

I did a double take at the thing when he slowed down to say good-by. He saw my bug-eyes and answered their protrusion with a grin, a wicked one.

"Gonna bring me back a sand mouse, fella. A smart man can learn a lot from just watchin' a sand mouse, he sure can!"

Martian sand mice may live in the sand—popularly they're supposed to eat and drink the stuff, too—but they are nowhere near like their Terran namesakes. And nobody with any brains meddles with a sand mouse. I almost dismissed Sam as hopeless then and there and wondered what form the final crack-up would take. But when he came back into town a couple of weeks later—minus the cage—he was still grinning. If Sam had held any grudge against me, I wouldn't have cared for that grin—not one bit!

Then Len Collins came back. And he started in right away at his old tricks—hanging around the dives listening to prospectors' talk. Sam had stayed in town and I caught up with them both at the Flame Bird, as thick as thieves over one table, Sam lapping up imported rye as if it were Canal Water and Len giving him cat at the mouse hole attention.

To my surprise Sam hailed me and pulled out a third stool at the table, insisting that I join them—much to Collins' annoyance. But I'm thick-skinned when I think I'm on the track of a story and I stuck. Stuck to hear Sam spill his big secret. He had discovered a new monster, one which so far surpassed the winged woman that they couldn't be compared. And Collins sat there licking his chops and almost drooling. I tried to shut Sam up—but I might as well have tried to can a dust storm. And in the end he insisted that I come along on their expedition to view this fabulous wonder. Well, I did.

We took a wind plane instead of a sandmobile. Collins was evidently in the chips and wanted speed. Sam piloted us. I noticed then, if Collins didn't, that Sam was a lot less drunk than he had been when he spilled his guts in the Flame Bird. And, noting that, I relaxed some,—feeling a bit happier about the whole affair.

The red rocks we were hunting stood out like fangs—a whole row of them—rather nasty looking. From the air there was no sign of any image, but then those were mostly found in the shadow of such rocks and might not be visible from above. Sam landed the plane and we slipped and slid through the shin-deep sand.

Sam was skidding around more than was necessary and he was muttering. Once he sang—in a rather true baritone—just playing the souse again. However, we followed along without question.

Collins dragged with him a small tank which had a hose attachment. And he was so eager that he fairly crowded on Sam's heels all the way. When at last Sam stopped short he slid right into him. But Sam apparently didn't even notice the bump. He was pointing ahead and grinning fatuously.

I looked along the line indicated by his finger, eager to see another winged woman or something as good. But there was nothing even faintly resembling a monster—unless you could count a lump of greenish stuff puffed up out of the sand a foot or so.

"Well, where is it?" Collins had fallen to one knee and had to put down his spray gun while he got up.

"Right there." Sam was still pointing to that greenish lump.

Collins' face had been wind-burned to a tomato red but now it darkened to a dusky purple as he stared at that repulsive hump.

"You fool!" Only he didn't say "fool." He lurched forward and kicked that lump, kicked it good and hard.

At the same time Sam threw himself flat on the ground and, having planted one of his oversize paws between my shoulders, took me with him. I bit into a mouthful of grit and sand and struggled wildly. But Sam's hand held me pinned tightly to the earth—as if I were a laboratory bug on a slide.

There was a sort of muffled exclamation, followed by an odd choking sound, from over by the rocks. But, in spite of my squirming, Sam continued to keep me more or less blindfolded. When he at last released me I was burning mad and came up with my fists ready. Only Sam wasn't there to land on. He was standing over by the rocks, his hands on his hips, surveying something with an open and proud satisfaction.

Because now there *was* a monster in evidence, a featureless anthropoidic figure of reddish stuff. Not as horrible as some I'd seen, but strange enough.

"Now—let's see if his goo does work this time!"

Sam took up the can briskly, pointed the hose tip at the monster, and let fly with a thin stream of pale bluish vapor, washing it all over that half-crouched thing.

"But—" I was still spitting sand between my teeth and only beginning to realize what must have happened. "Is that—that *thing*—"

"Collins? Yeah. He shouldn't have shown his temper that way. He kicked just once too often. That's what he did to her when she started to crumple, so I counted on him doing it again. Only, disturb one of those puff balls and get the stuff that's inside them on you and—presto—a monster! I got on to it when I was being chased by a sand mouse a couple of months back. The bugger got too close to one of those things—thinking more about dinner than danger, I guess—and whamoo! Hunted me up another mouse and another puff ball—just to be on the safe side. Same thing again. So—here we are! Say, Jim, I think this *is* going to work!" He had drawn one finger along the monster's outstretched arm and nothing happened. It still stood solid.

"Then all those monsters must once have been alive!" I shivered a little, remembering a few of them.

Sam nodded. "Maybe they weren't all natives of Mars—too many different kinds have been found. Terra was probably not the first to land a rocket there. Certainly the antmen and that big frog never lived together. Some day I'm going to get me a stellar ship and go out to look for the world my lady came from. This thin air could never have supported her wings.

"Now, Jim, if you'll just give me a hand, we'll get this work of art back to Terraport. How many million credits are the science guys offering if one is brought back in one piece?"

He was so businesslike about it that I simply did as he asked. And he collected from the scientists all right—collected enough to buy his stellar ship. He's out there now, prospecting along the Milky Way, hunting his winged lady. And the unique monster is in the Interplanetary Museum to be gaped at by all the tourists. Me—I avoid red rocks, green puff balls, and never, never kick at objects of my displeasure—it's healthier that way.

Bretnor-Editors Correspondence

17 January 1952

Dear Reg:

Here is CAT, back for a little polishing.

Our feeling is something like this: It's a wondrous pastiche of a fuddy-duddy prof writing quite seriously. Occasionally, you burst the bonds of the pastiche, go overboard and become S J Perelman. The result is a JAR to the reader.

First: The names. Titwilloughby, Luigi Nudnick, Gregory Smidgeon, et al are Perelmanese, or esque, and don't belong. Please, though it's a severe wrench, change them.

We don't like such departures from the straight as: "O, Reader reproach me not!" p 1; "like some poor moth . . ." p 5; "Here was Lilith, the vain temptress etc . . ." p 8. How about just "Here was—Lilith!" There are probably more; please search carefully for such and cut.

Beowulf's name should be spelled *Yu*. And you should certainly explain why Beowulf speaks such atrocious English while his uncle (again, Chester is a poor name) speaks most properly. A line from Chester, "This dull youth who has repaid my labors in bringing him to this country by failing lamentably to learn even the rudiments of its gracious speech." Or some such.

Suggest you do a straight pastiche right out of Cal's catalog on announcement of the various Cat courses. AB says you can grab a catalog quite easily.

I love the name Furnwillie, but I'm awfully dubious.

This doesn't entail any severe rewriting, just a little cutting and inserting.

It's a truly lovely story and I think the P O has gone to NYC.

Ever,

Mick

24 January 1952

Dear Tony & Mick,

So *Cat* comes back, de-Nudniked, Witherspooned, and quite unSmidgeoned. Otherwise, you will find that I have complied with some suggestions and not with others, for reasons to be set forth hereunder.

First, re: Professor Flewkes' prose style. I had in mind a style which was badly outdated—badly enough to convey some impression, not only of impracticality, but of an actual lack of good sense. Therefore, while I have cut out a number of his worst phrases, I have left him many others.

Secondly, I have included no new technical gags. In the original writing of the story, I gave that aspect careful consideration. I made notes of all the jokes that came to mind—like the Grimalkin's Law thing—and then decided to use only the best, keeping them to a minimum so that those readers who had never heard of philology wouldn't flounder through material which was meaningless to them.

I originally wrote the *Cat* Curriculum directly from UC's Announcement of Courses—and found that it dragged too much, and that the material I was able to use wasn't funny enough.

I have retained *You* mainly because this usage keeps the reader slightly confused with Dr. Flewkes, while *Yu* immediately gives all away. Any attempt, of course, to render Chinese in Roman letters can be nothing but a barbarous approximation, for it can give no hint of the four (or, in the north, five) tones. In any case, I think that possibly You and Yu are different, the one long, as though it were pronounced Yoo; the other short. My final reason is set forth in a poetic form fit for so recondite a theme—

A Sinological And Statistical Exposition To Boucher & McComas

You who use Yu for You, you err,
Kwong You, Kee You, Joe You, and Huey You aver—[1]
Four Yous for You, for use as I prefer,
A fine Confucian crew!

1. SF phone book, Nov. '49

(I am astounded
That you'd use Yu, a usage quite ungrounded
Which only makes Confucian worse confounded.)
Hoo!
Would you, you editors, use Yu for You
Against my queued Celestial arguments if you too knew
That, four to one, my Yous outnumber Yu?
She's three too few.[1]

And now—
There remains Mr. Furnwillie. I have changed his name
from Sacheverell (because of the sad Sitwellian connota-
tions) to Sylvester.

I hope that *Cat* is acceptable in its present form.

Best regards,

Reg. (Bretnor)

1. *Ibid*. Her name is Lillian.

Certain of R. Bretnor's friends—nice people, too!—are completely unaware that he is a writer. These know only Bretnor the ailurophile and hold him in high repute as a breeder of that most delightful of all cats, the Siamese. For their especial attention, then, as well as for the general hilarity, we offer this complete, unbiased narrative of certain occurrences in the Department of Modern Languages that shook the ivy-crowned walls of Bogwood College to their ancient foundations and, alas!, led to the resignations of several eminent members of its faculty.

A.B./J.F. McComas

Cat
by R. Bretnor

I had no premonition of disaster when Smithby married Cynthia Carmichael and took her off on his sabbatical. No inner voice whispered its awful warning in my ear when it was rumored that he was spending his year of leave in research of a strangely private nature. Even as his department head, how could I know that he was bringing *Cat* into the world?

His year drew to a close, my own sabbatical began, and off I went—intending, after three therapeutic months in sunny Italy, to seek the scholarly seclusion of Scotland's National Library for the remainder of my time. But it was not to be. Scarcely a week after I arrived in Edinburgh, the letter came.

Did I say "letter"? There was no letter in the grimy envelope which had followed my wandering path from Naples north. It contained only a brief note and an enormous clipping from some cheap green newspaper.

I glanced at the curt message:

Dear Christopher,
Smithby has betrayed our tradition and our trust. Your entire
department is in turmoil. Three of us have already tendered
our resignations.

Witherspoon

For one dreadful moment, I closed my eyes; and Smithby's
face, a pallid mask of modest erudition, appeared before me.
Then, with trembling fingers, I opened up the clipping:

WIFE'S LOVE PROMPTS SCIENCE TRIUMPH!
Young Bogwood Prof Wins Plaudits For
First Cat Language Studies!

the headlines screamed with a malicious glee, above a photograph of Smithby and his spouse, each grasping a large feline.
Stupefied, I read on:

New Haven, August 5: For the first time in nearly a century
Bogwood College flashed into the limelight today as Emerson
Smithby, professor of English Literature, bared what scientists
acclaim as the outstanding discovery of the age—the language
spoken by cats.

Giving full credit to his wife, blond curvesome Cynthia
Smithby, the surprisingly youthful savant this morning out-
lined highlights of the grueling research that enabled him to
break down the hitherto insurmountable barrier between man
and the so-called lower animals.

Professor Smithby said, in part:

"Cats not only have a language—they have a complex
culture not basically dissimilar to our own. I first began to
suspect this when Mrs. Smithby and I were honeymooning;
and she assisted me untiringly, lending both her own cats for
the enquiry.

"As soon as we convinced them of the importance of the
project, we progressed rapidly. In less than two months, we
were able to prattle conversational *Cat* with some fluency."

Professor Smithby then revealed that he has already issued a
text for beginners: Cat, Its Basic Grammar, Pronunciation, and
General Usage.

He refused, however, to discuss a rumor that, through the
efforts of Gregory Morton, widely known cat fancier and

member of Bogwood's Board of Regents, courses in Cat will shortly be added to the curriculum.

Professor Christopher Flewkes, head of Dr. Smithby's department, could not be reached for comment.

I sat there staring. Lucid thought was impossible. Blind instinct told me that Bogwood was in peril—that Bogwood needed me—that I must catch the first boat back.

Nothing could have prepared me for the reception Fate had arranged in the Faculty Club on the night of my return. Perhaps the bright light over the desk in the lobby blinded me as I entered; perhaps my preoccupation with my own harried thoughts prevented me from seeing the cat. Whatever the reason, I had no inkling of its presence until its sudden scream informed the world that I had stepped upon its tail.

It was a strange tableau. The cat had fled, leaving me standing beside my fallen bag in the middle of the floor. From behind the desk, the clerk—a young Oriental hired in my absence—glared at me through a pair of those curious spectacles known, I believe, as harlequins.

"Do you, my sir," he demanded with placid insolence, "practice to come and step upon the guests? If so, go to where you belong."

I stifled my anger. "See here," I replied, "I am Dr. Flewkes—Christopher Flewkes."

The fellow smiled. "Then the stepping will be an accident. I have knowledge of you. You are Flewkes. I am You."

I thought: *The man, of course, is mad!* "Indeed?" I exclaimed. "You are me?"

Still smiling, he shook his head gravely. "It is not Mee. It is You—Beowulf You. I have named myself after an English literature. You will be glad."

"Very well," I snapped, "you are You. Is my room ready?"

You bowed, unruffled. "I am here for studying," he informed me. "At the night, I am a clerk; at the day, I am studying *Cat* with some progress. In *Cat*, I am even possible to get a passing grade."

"Is my room ready?" I repeated grimly.

"In a certainty, my sir," said You. "At a moment, I will accompany with my presence. Now I must assure your guest of your apologies—"

He went to the cat where it sat nursing its bruised appendage in a corner. "Ee-owr-r," he said, very courteously. "Meow, meeiu mr-r-ou."

The cat paid no attention whatsoever; and You, with a worried frown, hastily took a small volume from his pocket, referred to it, and repeated his original comment several times.

Finally, the animal raised its head. "Meow," it said plaintively.

You bowed. Then he turned to me happily. "You are forgiven, for it is a cultured one. Now we ascend upstairs."

I nodded feebly. As we turned toward the staircase, I saw that the lobby was full of cats. They were on the chairs, on the rugs, before the fire. They were even on the mantel under the portrait of Ebenezer Bogwood.

I entered my room. In a daze, I heard You's ungrammatical goodnight at my door. Wearily I sat down on the bed—and, in doing so, I spied the Announcement of Courses for the current semester lying on the bedside table. I fought against the urge to pick it up—but I was powerless. I reached for it, opened it, turned the pages. And I saw:

Department of Feline Languages
Emerson Smithby, Ph.D., Chairman

This was followed by a list of courses—*Cat* 100A (Elementary), *Cat* 212 (Philology), *Cat* 227 (Literature)—and by other pertinent data, including the information that all instruction was in the hands of Mr. and Mrs. Smithby.

Hopelessly, until day was breaking, I wept for Bogwood.

I did not wake until shortly before the luncheon hour, when the telephone rang to tell me that Witherspoon was awaiting me downstairs; and sad indeed were my thoughts as I forced myself to rise and dress. Witherspoon's note had mentioned resignation from the faculty; and now the impulse came to me that perhaps I should join him in this tragic withdrawal from the academic world, that perhaps we both had been outmoded by the science of a newer age. Finally, with clothing draggled and beard uncombed, I stumbled down the stairs.

I entered the lobby, and heard that familiar voice greeting me, and saw those long shapeless tweeds unfolding from a chair by the fireplace.

"Bertrand!" I cried out, and in a moment I had him by the hand.

I gaped at him in my astonishment. Was this one the gentle, melancholy Witherspoon whom I had known? He still stooped; his gray locks were as sparse as they had ever been. But I saw instantly that the old Witherspoon had vanished—that here was a man of iron!

He seemed to read my mind. Leading me to a chair, he brushed a cat aside so that I might sit there. "Christopher," he said, his high voice very firm, "I am still at my post. The time has come to fight—and fight we shall!"

At this, my heart filled with black despair for our lost cause. "How can we fight, Bertrand?" I exclaimed, pointing at the feline population of the room.

Witherspoon seated himself beside me. "Have courage, Christopher! These wretched creatures," he gestured at the cats, "are not to blame. Even Morton, vile as he is, is but a tool. Our enemy is Smithby. We must destroy him by fair means or foul!"

His eyes almost flashed as he said it. He lowered his voice to a conspiratorial whisper. "I've planned the strategy of our campaign," he hissed. "Shall I reveal it to you?"

"Do, by all means," said I, leaning forward eagerly.

But Witherspoon had no chance to answer me. Even as I spoke, his glance shifted. Fists clenched, narrow brow frowning sheer hatred, he glared past me at the lobby's entrance.

I had not noticed those who passed through to the dining room during our conversation. But now I looked about me—and behold, coming across the floor, Smithby and Cynthia Smithby, with Beowulf You trailing in their wake. A long black cat was draped over Mrs. Smithby's shoulders in startling contrast to the coiled golden hair above it. Another cat, a Siamese, was carrying on a pleasant tête-à-tête with Smithby, who bore it in his arms.

I heard Witherspoon gnash his teeth in my ear. "Look at her!" he muttered viciously. "She looks like a cross between a cream puff and a Valkyrie."

The description, I must say, surprised me—later I learned that Witherspoon had heard it from a student. Still, it was not inaccurate. But for her heroic stature—dwarfing her husband, by a half a dozen inches—Cynthia Smithby would have suited Charles II to a T. She resembled Herrick's Julia; a splendid figure rather too ample for the modern fashion, a small red mouth, a tiny rounded chin, a rolling eye.

She was the first to see me. Instantly, an elfin smile touched her lips, and she changed her course. Head high, she came toward me.

I drew myself erect, to await her with a stern and uncompromising countenance. I knew that Witherspoon was wrong. *Here* was our enemy! Here was the Lilith who had seduced a weakling from the stony path of sober scholarship! I knew at once that there must be no pretense, that I must make my attitude quite clear.

Flushed and radiant, up she came. "Dear Mr. Flewkes!" said she, her voice low and musical. "What a delightful surprise! I am most glad to find you once again among us." She lowered her lashes in mock modesty. "And so is Emerson. Are you not, Emerson?"

Smithby blushed with embarrassment, fidgeted with a thin book he was carrying, and nodded with obvious displeasure.

"So much has happened since you went away," she went on, "so much that is very wonderful. But then—" she laughed a pretty laugh. "You can catch up by attending Emerson's seminars."

I forced myself to look into her eyes. "Madam," I declared coldly, "half my life has been devoted to the service of this institution and to the preservation of its austere ideals. I can only hang my head in shame when I observe the sad decay of what was once a great tradition. Neither by word nor deed will I condone this treachery!"

Out of the corner of my eye, I saw a hurt look come over Smithby's face; I saw Beowulf You gape stupidly. For an instant, too, Cynthia Smithby pouted like some sensitive child suddenly rebuked. Then, with a toss of her head, "Mr. Flewkes," she said, "truly I am glad that you take this stand, for here—" she turned to Smithby, "here is the challenge that we need. Your genius, Emerson, will surmount this wall of classical conservatism. Our present project is certain to succeed. Then we will have proof positive and undeniable, and Mr. Flewkes will come to you with his apologies."

"Oh, not to *me*—" There was a calf-like worship in Smithby's eyes. "To *you,* Cynthia dear. The credit will be yours. The world will know that you have done it all!"

Beowulf giggled. "Then Flewkes will also make research in *Cat.*" He peered at me through his harlequins. "I can give help. *Cat* words have one nice syllable, like Cantonese."

"Why, Beowulf—" Cynthia Smithby smiled archly. "You must devote your time to learning it yourself. You've failed every other course, you know. But let's have luncheon. Come," she took Smithby's arm. "And now, dear Mr. Flewkes, we bid you—*miaow*."

As the dining room door closed behind them, I slumped back heavily into my chair. "My God, Bertrand," I muttered, "she—she mewed at me!"

"I believe," he answered, "that she was saying good-bye to you in *Cat*."

I wiped an icy perspiration from my forehead. "It is not Smithby who is the evil genius—it is she!"

"Nonsense!" snapped Witherspoon. "It's simply that she wears no brassiere—and you are too impressionable."

I flushed. "But—but what of her new project?"

"All froth and foolishness, believe me. Some silly toy her husband's given her. How could it be more? She does not even have her Ph.D."

This argument, of course, was quite unanswerable. I held my peace.

"*He* is the culprit," continued Witherspoon. "Surely you saw that small book he was carrying? It is his latest work—*Back Fence Ballads, Translated From The Original Cat*. He sings them, Christopher, to all his students, accompanying himself upon the lute. I have been told that his caterwauling is magnificent. And there's the extension course for lion tamers, conducted in the evenings. It has brought strange folk to Bogwood, I assure you."

He broke off. He pointed an apocalyptic finger to the heavens. "Do you wonder," he cried, "that I have taken desperate measures? Do you wonder that I have hired a private eye?"

"A—a private—eye?"

"Ah, to be sure," said he. "I must explain. That is what he calls himself in the vernacular. He is a sleuth, Christopher. I brought him from New York, where hardened criminals flee at the mere mention of his name."

I started to expostulate, but Witherspoon would brook no interruption. "I have arranged for you to meet him, to lunch with him. Not here, but secretly—at an establishment known, I believe, as Jakey's Java Joint."

"But Bertrand," I protested feebly, "how can this person aid us? How?"

Witherspoon uttered a fierce, triumphant laugh. "Be patient, Christopher! Soon you will know all!"

I remember little of that first guarded meeting. Hulking, unshaven fellows wolfing their food in grubby cubicles, lewd language and coarse jests, wile music from an automatic instrument—all these I can recall only vaguely. My first unfavorable impression of Luigi Hogan, though, is still distinct. Small and round and surprisingly hairy, he neither looked nor behaved like a detective.

Witherspoon and I had turned up our coat collars and pulled our hat brims down to avoid recognition, but Hogan's sharp little eyes saw us immediately we entered, and he greeted us with much pointless snickering. When he had pulled himself together, introductions were performed; and, in a moment, he and Witherspoon were plotting in undertones over thick cups of lukewarm coffee.

Hogan's diction was atrocious; his underworld argot was almost incomprehensible to me; he talked and laughed with his mouth full of salami sandwich. Even if our encounter with Cynthia Smithby had left me in full possession of my faculties, I doubt whether I could have gleaned more than occasional fragments of the conversation. I noticed that Hogan addressed Witherspoon as "Chief." I heard him say that he had been attending Smithby's extension course for animal trainers. I even caught the very words in which he recounted Smithby's advice to them: *Y' gotta show 'em you ain't afraid er nuttin', see? Y' gotta get right inner cages wit' 'em, see? Y' gotta talk t' them goddam big feelions like you was brudders*.

Witherspoon's expression became positively bloodthirsty at this point. "Hogan," he said, out of the corner of his mouth, "you go find us a circus or a zoo, see? With a good big vicious tiger, see? Heh heh! We'll challenge Mr. Smithby to go and reason with him in his cage. He can't refuse. Catch on?"

"I catch, Chief." Hogan snickered loathsomely. "Th' Press'll eat it up."

"Not just the Press," murmured Witherspoon with a ghoulish leer. "No indeed!"

As for the rest of what they said—well, he gave it to me in outline as we walked by obscure streets back to the campus. The idea of Smithby becoming an hors-d'oeuvre for a tiger was not their main plot. Hogan was to watch him constantly until he committed some dangerous indiscretion, preferably of an amorous nature. Then he was to secure photographs which we could use to disgrace Smithby, to procure his swift dismissal. As a last resort, he was to provide a person known as Marilynne, who had yet to meet failure in her career of breaking down male inhibitions.

Ordinarily, I would have been profoundly shocked by the utter ruthlessness of these methods. But now, aware only of Bogwood's dire plight, I shared Witherspoon's ferocity and felt no qualms. One thing alone perturbed me—Cynthia Smithby. True, she had no proper academic qualifications; the chance of her making any new discovery dangerous to us was remote indeed. Still, might not Smithby, after all, be nothing more than a red herring dragged by a shrewd, designing woman across our path?

Waiting for Hogan's labors to bear fruit was no easy task. Vain doubts and fears tormented me incessantly—and all the while things went from bad to worse. Against our bitter protests, a course in Feline Culture was added to the awful list. The Press, keeping *Cat* constantly in the public eye, greeted with laudatory reviews the appearance of Smithby's handbooks for zoo and circus personnel: *Basic Lion, Basic Leopard, Basic Panther,* and so on. And the columnists, meanwhile, harped on the rumored progress of Cynthia Smithby's project, the nature of which she was still keeping secret. It was, they hinted, a way of teaching *Cat* so simple that any child could learn it in an hour. Might it not, they asked, eliminate the need for baby-sitters, for kindergarten teachers? Might it not change the social and economic structure of the world?

We had our moments of encouragement. There was the day when Hogan was able to announce that he had made arrangements with a menagerie which owned a tiger, elderly and quite untameable, who had put an end to the earthly career of at least one trainer. The challenge had been mailed to Smithby. The newspapers had been informed. And you can well imagine that Witherspoon and I fairly jumped for joy when we saw the headlines. CAT PROF MAY TAME FIERCE JUNGLE LORD! they shouted.

But Smithby weaseled out of it. Chatting with any normal tiger, he announced, was most enjoyable. This was a different matter. This tiger was clearly psychopathic. "He needs a feline psychiatrist," said Smithby. "After all, even though I speak English, I would not try to reason with a human maniac armed to the teeth." And the servile Press praised him for his "hard common sense!"

The weeks dragged by, and our furtive meetings at Jakey's Java Joint brought more and more discouraging reports. Every small detail of Smithby's life was known—and irreproachable. Perversely, he insisted in behaving as a model husband. Even Marilynne, when finally we brought her from New York, found him quite unassailable. Even Marilynne, in whose hennaed presence poor Witherspoon blushed like any schoolboy, exercised her talents all in vain. With each attempt, her remarks became increasingly sarcastic, until eventually she abandoned us—leaving behind a note in which she suggested that a catnip mouse might bring us better luck.

Oddly enough, the collapse of Witherspoon's carefully contrived plans did not daunt him in the least; nor would he listen to my suggestion that henceforth we should fight Smithby on purely academic grounds. He insisted that we keep Hogan in our service; and, when I objected, he threatened to bring "goons" to "settle Smithby's hash."

Even when we learned that Smithby had complained against us to the Board of Regents, even when we were summoned to appear before that august body, he did not share my quickened fears and my despondency. "Ah, Christopher," he cried, shaking his fist, "on Friday we must go before the Board. That means we have three days! Believe me—something will turn up, and we will face the lot of them triumphantly. We will see Smithby crushed and broken yet. *Cat* will be nothing but an evil dream!"

How bitterly the jesting gods play cat-and-mouse with all that we hold dear! On Friday morning, drowned in despair, I was making my hopeless way toward the campus when, to my great astonishment, a large red cab came to a screeching stop beside me, and its door flew open to eject an exultant Witherspoon, who seized me by the arm.

"Victory is ours!" he trumpeted, pulling me to the vehicle. "Hogan just telephoned! Smithby is in our trap!" Before I could utter a word, he bundled me into the back seat ahead of him, and slammed the door. "Yip Lee's!" he shouted to the driver, and we were off.

I got nothing further from him during that mad ride, for seemingly he knew no more. "I told you so, I told you so!" was the ecstatic cry with which he answered all my questions; and, when we reached our destination, a Chinese restaurant in the commercial district, I was as mystified as ever.

Leaving the cab and entering, we were greeted by a Celestial who spoke to Witherspoon by name. We were led upstairs to a small and private room. And there, upon its threshold, I saw a sight which took my breath away. In the center of the room stood a table and five chairs. Two of the chairs were empty. Two were occupied by Luigi Hogan and a well-dressed, middle-aged Chinese. On the fifth, covering his face in shame, sat Beowulf You.

As soon as he saw us, Hogan struck an attitude. "De whole t'ing's washed up, guys!" he declared. "All dis stuff about *Cat*—its phony! Your Smit'by—he's a fake!"

I heard Witherspoon gasp; I heard a muffled sob from Beowulf You. "This is incredible!" I cried. "Why, I myself have heard him speak to cats. I've heard them answer back. Deplorable it is, yes—but surely it must be more than a mere web of fraud? Explain yourself, man."

Hogan began to quake with merriment. "It's—it's simple!" he giggled. "Shrimps!"

"Shrimps?" Witherspoon and I echoed the word with one voice.

But Hogan was too convulsed to answer. He jerked a thumb toward the Chinese gentleman beside him.

The Chinese smiled gravely. "That is correct," he said, bowing. "I, you see, am Chester You. I am the uncle of this dull youth—" With some distaste, he indicated Beowulf. "This dull youth with the absurd glasses, who has repaid me for bringing him to this country by failing to master even the rudiments of English. I am also the proprietor of the Pilgrim Fathers Seafood Market—"

He paused courteously while we took the vacant chairs. "For some time," he went on, "I had seen Professor Smithby come in regularly once a day, followed closely by Mr. Hogan. Furthermore, Professor Smithby always bought exactly ten cents worth of shrimps, refused to have them wrapped, and put them directly in his pocket. My curiosity was aroused—and, a day or so ago, I took the liberty of speaking to Mr. Hogan about it."

Hogan smirked.

"He and I compared notes. When I learned who my strange customer was, my interest redoubled. We Chinese, you know, revere learning, and my disreputable nephew's devotion to *Cat*

had caused me much distress.'' Chester You's countenance
assumed an expression of extreme severity. "Mr. Hogan and I
came to the only possible conclusion. We tested our theory with
Hwang-ho, my own pet cat; and the results were indisputable.
He immediately became vocal at a whiff of shrimp. So this
morning we took Beowulf to task. Confronted by the evidence,
he confessed all!''

Beowulf held his fingers to his ears, moaning softly.

"Yes,'' declared his uncle, "this wretched boy admitted that
he had uncovered Smithby's secret, and turned it to his own
dishonorable advantage. Smithby, you see, mewed at the cats—
and the cats mewed for shrimp. There was no more to it than
that.''

"Do you mean,'' I exclaimed, "that all those people merely
pretended to understand *Cat*?''

"Believing that Professor Smithby understood it perfectly,
they feared to reveal what they regarded as their own stupidity.''

I shook my head. "Surely no group of intelligent men and
women—''

"Come, come, Christopher,'' protested Witherspoon, "I've
seen the same sort of thing a dozen times in the Philosophy
Department.''

And I was forced to admit that he was right.

Then Witherspoon pushed his chair back and rose. "We are
grateful to you gentlemen,'' he asserted grimly, "for placing this
monstrous swindler in our power. Now we can purge dear
Bogwood of his presence, his mewing sycophants, and his nefar-
ious works.'' He showed his teeth. "It is 11 o'clock. In half an
hour the Board of Regents meets—and you have earned the right
to share our triumph, the triumph of true learning. Let us go! Let
us grind vile Smithby in the dust!''

Without another word, he turned and strode toward the door;
and we followed him, Chester You urging his weeping nephew
forward with an ungentle hand. My heart was high indeed as we
left the restaurant and entered Hogan's car.

The Board of Regents was to meet, of course, in Cruett Hall,
in the chamber dedicated by Ebenezer Bogwood to that purpose.
It is a long room, panelled in ancient walnut, full of tradition's
gentle gloom. Upon its walls hang the stern portraits of those
scholars who, through the generations, have filled our presidential chair—and, as our small procession strode down the hall

toward it, there came to me the thought of how their noble spirits would rejoice when Witherspoon and I pricked the miasmic bubble which was *Cat.*

My doubts were all dispelled. My fears had vanished. Like conquerors, we passed the bowing flunkey at the door—

Imagine, if you can, the sight which met our gaze. At the head of the great table, gaunt and gray, sat Mr. Sylvester Furnwillie, Chairman of the Board. At his right hand was seated the President of Bogwood; at his left, the loathsome Gregory Morton puffed at an opulent cigar. The six remaining Regents were ranged on either side. Beyond them, Smithby stood. Across from him, his wife reposed. And, at the table's very end, sat an enormous tomcat, staring at Mr. Furnwillie with cold green eyes.

Smithby, all unaware of our entrance, was speaking. ". . . therefore," he was saying, "we observe that the *hsss-s-s* of Old *Cat* gradually changed to *fss-t-t* in ordinary Modern *Cat.* That shows how simple the functioning of Grimalkin's Law can be—"

"Ha!" cried Witherspoon.

Smithby suddenly was still; all eyes were on us.

Mr. Furnwillie lifted his spectacles with a palsied hand. "Dear me, dear me!" he said uncertainly. "You are some minutes late, are you not? You really shouldn't keep the Board of Regents waiting, gentlemen. No, indeed. Dr. Smithby has preferred some serious charges. Oh, *very* serious. He states that you have had him followed everywhere, and that you even hired a trollop to—er—seduce him. Tsk-tsk! We can't approve such goings-on at Bogwood, gentlemen. Now can we? After all—"

He broke off. He peered at Hogan and the Yous. His lofty forehead wrinkled with distaste. "Who are these people, Witherspoon? They cannot be alumni; they do not have the Bogwood look about them. Eh? Are they relatives of yours?"

Witherspoon folded his arms across his chest, and, in an awful voice, he answered, *"They are Smithby's doom!"*

There was a frightened murmur from the Regents, Gregory Morton emitted a vulgar feline expletive. Mr. Furnwillie exclaimed distractedly.

Witherspoon silenced them with one contemptuous glance. He pointed straight at Smithby. "Yes, his *doom*! We admit his charges, Flewkes and I! *We* hired Hogan to dog his wicked steps. *We* employed Marilynne. And we are proud of it—for by our humble efforts we have saved Bogwood from degradation and the world's disdain!"

Like Jove about to hurl his thunderbolt, he seemed to grow in stature standing there.

"Smithby!" he cried. "Smithby, your hour has come! Resign. Go far away. Never again befoul this sacred air! Beowulf has confessed your villainy, and we know all. *We, Smithby, know about the shrimps!*"

He paused. A dreadful silence reigned.

"Yes, the shrimps—the shrimps which Smithby conceals about his person, gentlemen!" Like a shrill trumpet, his voice shook the room. "*Cat* is a sham, a mockery, and a hollow fraud! No one can speak a single word of *Cat!* The creatures mew for —*Shrimp!*"

He stopped. We waited for the earth to open under Smithby's feet, the heavens to fall. And—

And nothing happened.

I looked. Dumbfounded, I looked again. Several of the Regents were whispering to each other and casting the most peculiar glances in our direction. Mr. Sylvester Furnwillie was conferring with Gregory Morton. Smithby and Cynthia Smithby were exchanging smiles. The large striped tomcat was pretending to stare unconcernedly out the window.

"Wh-what does this mean?" demanded Witherspoon.

Mr. Furnwillie ignored him. He looked around. His countenance assumed an aspect of extreme displeasure. To me he said, "Professor Flewkes, though I am deeply shocked by this vindictive and absurd denunciation, it does not surprise me. It is in keeping with the questionable associates, the reprehensible activities. Such things we might expect of Witherspoon, for he is not originally a Bogwood man. But not of *you.* Tsk-tsk. I am most gravely disappointed. Indeed I am. You—well, you should be *ashamed.*"

Shocked to the core, I started to protest. He did not let me.

"Professor Flewkes, we *know* about the shrimps. Of course Professor Smithby carries them, just as some men carry cigars to give their friends. Why shouldn't he? I carry them myself. Surely you don't expect a cat to smoke cigars?"

"B-but—but Beowulf—?" I stammered.

And it was Smithby who replied. "I think I can explain that," he said, a little sadly. "Not long ago, and much against my will, I was forced to tell poor Beowulf that I was flunking him. He was emotionally upset. I fear that, faced with his inability to master *Cat,* he sought refuge in the pretense that no one could."

Mr. Furnwillie thanked him. "You make it amply clear, Dr. Smithby—and I am only sorry that this incident should have marred so bright a morning—"

Behind me I heard the voice of Chester You snap out an angry phrase in Cantonese. I heard a squeal of pain from Beowulf as he received some corporal punishment.

Mr. Furnwillie smiled. "When you have added such a glorious leaf to Bogwood's laurels." His smile disappeared. "Yes, Professor Flewkes—this morning Dr. and Mrs. Smithby proved the validity of *Cat* to our complete satisfaction. They showed us the result of Mrs. Smithby's splendid project in education and research. Their proof is absolute, beyond cavil, and quite beyond the shadow of doubt!"

"You lie!" screamed Witherspoon, livid with rage, trembling in every limb. "Don't try to tell me that this illiterate woman has taught each one of you to babble *Cat!* This is another fraud! And you are aiding and abetting it! I shall inform the Press! Hogan and I shall expose you for what you are!"

"Tsk-tsk!" Mr. Furnwillie said reprovingly. "If you behave like that, Witherspoon, you'll have to leave the room. I cannot babble *Cat*, as you so coarsely put it, but Mr. Morton can, and—"

Witherspoon whirled. "Come, Hogan, Flewkes! Let us seek the society of honest men!" He marched toward the door; and at the door he turned. "Furnwillie—" He roared defiance like a wounded lion. *"Furnwillie, I resign!"*

Then he was gone. The only sound was Hogan's foolish giggle in the corridor.

I lacked the strength to follow. Mutely, I stood before the Board, all my high hopes for Bogwood in ashes at my feet.

Mr. Furnwillie put on his spectacles and took them off again. "Dear me," he said, "how violent the man is! Even though Dr. and Mrs. Smithby, in their complaint, did ask us not to punish him, I fear that we must accept his resignation."

"Certainly," growled Gregory Morton; and the other members of the Board nodded solemnly.

Mr. Furnwillie sighed. "Ah me, this leaves us with a painful duty, doesn't it? We should do *something,* I suppose, about Professor Flewkes?"

He looked at me, and so did all the rest. Even the tomcat favored me with a fixed regard.

I summoned all my shredded dignity. "Gentlemen," I answered,

"I shall spare you this harsh necessity. I, too, shall seek a more congenial atmosphere."

And it was then that Cynthia Smithby, with a little cry, came to her feet and ran to me. "Dear Dr. Flewkes!" she pleaded, clinging to my arm. "Do not resign! Why, Emerson and I are both so fond of you—we could not bear the thought. I beg you, stay! Let us convince you—"

As the impassioned words poured forth, she drew me willy-nilly toward the table's end.

"Let us open to you our brave new world, where cats can take at last their rightful place, contributing to science, culture, and the arts. Believe me—you will see the day when cats shall vote, hold public office, and instruct our youth. Perhaps there even may be peace on earth under a parliament of Man and Cat!"

She pointed at the tomcat on his chair. "Look! Only look! This is Rabindranath. He's the living proof!"

Roughly, I shook her off. "Madam," I exclaimed, "I am no fool. You may delude your students. You may deceive Mr. Furnwillie in his senility. But you can not persuade me that you can teach a language which does not exist!"

"Oh, *please*," she implored, "I do assure you—you do not understand. I'll introduce you to Rabindranath. His interests lie within your own domain. He's starting to translate *The Aspern Papers* into *Cat*. Dear Dr. Flewkes, at least will you not speak with him? Will you not converse?"

Two tears flowed like dewdrops down her cheeks. They did not move me. "Converse?" Contemptuously, I gestured at the cat. "No, never! Never will I demean myself to—*mew*!"

And—ah, cruel gods!

Coolly, Rabindranath looked me up and down. "Mew?" he said. "That will be scarcely necessary."

And finally, the Randall Garrett G & S parody:

I've Got a Little List

I've read s.f. for many years, and here's what I have found:
   I've got a little list—I've got a little list
Of authors who take certain themes and run 'em in the ground.

They'd none of 'em be missed—They'd none of 'em be missed!
There's the fellow who is daffy on his synergic plan—
The guy who writes the tales about the latent superman—
The humorist who thinks anachronisms are such fun—
The engineer who formulates each brand-new ship or gun—
And the fellow with the bugs and stuff, the sex-biologist,
    I don't think *he'd* be missed—I'm *sure* he'd not be missed!

There's the fiendish fellow who burns up the sun or puts it out,
    The astrophysicist! I've got *him* on the list!
And the guy whose noble heroes kick the common clods about,
    The scientologist! I don't think *he'll* be missed!
And the lad who writes the tales about the interstellar tramps
Who flit about the Galaxy in king-size hobo camps—
The guy who rewrites Toynbee, with some Gibbon added, too,
And calls it "psycho-history" to sound like something new—
And the married pair who dote upon the psychoanalyst—
    They'd none of 'em be missed—They'd none of 'em be missed!

There's the lass who lifts from Omar K. and shifts the scene to Mars—
    I've got her on the list—I've got her on the list!
And the world-assassinator who keeps blowing up the stars,
    The cataclysmatist—I don't think he'd be missed!
And the chronic Martian writer with the anti-social quirks
Who thinks that human beings all are stupid, childish jerks—
And the saintly little stories of a theologic kind,
All written by the editor of—Oh, well, never mind!
And at least a dozen others I could put upon the list;
    And they'd none of 'em be missed—They'd none of 'em be missed!

                                                —RANDALL GARRETT

RECOMMENDED
READING

The most singular aspect of the recommended reading department inaugurated in the second issue of F&SF, Winter-Spring 1950, is the intensely personal aura of the writing, both in content and style. It demonstrates the editors' passion for *quality* and their insistence on integrity while losing not a whit of their liveliness and directness. Their critical acumen is voiced in the clearest layman's language. Their sense of pleasure in what they are dealing with is a constant overlay.

Valuable to the reader are the pithy, short comments on the writing of such giants of the time as Heinlein, Bradbury and Asimov. Throughout the selected sections from this department there are editorial opinions that go far beyond the field of literary criticism. Take the final piece in this section of R.R., for instance. It deals with "some shocking statistics on the publishing of the science fiction 'novel'." In addressing certain publishers of the 1950 crop the editors say in part: "Certainly, the present situation represents the rankest kind of opportunism, resulting in the promotional sale of shoddy merchandise to the helpless reader." No beating about the bush for these editors. They fought the good fight always for readers and writers against any practices they considered shoddy or underhanded.

The sections of Recommended Reading give the reader a clear historical survey, in depth, of the field of imaginative literature of this time, not only of fiction but of the best non-fiction. The reader may expect to find comments, too, on the functioning of the publishing industry. He will probably sigh over the prices: thirty-five cents for the better paperbacks, twenty-five cents for the "cheapies"!

The editors read literally everything that came out in the field, wrote each other voluminous notes, made agreements on content and divided the writing chores. I have *never* understood how they found the time.

Recommended Reading, in many ways, is like being invited

in for a beer with the editors and settling down to some satisfying, provocative talk about the field. Tony Boucher will be incessantly pacing the floor, barefoot as usual; while Mick, sprawled on a low Morris chair, rumbles his hearty laugh. They will make you welcome, and the talk will be good.

One of the pleasures of this section is to discover unusual items to explore, books rarely heard about thirty years later like Edgar Rowe Snow's SECRETS OF THE NORTH ATLANTIC ISLANDS, true marine curiosa, or perhaps, B. A. Bodkin's A TREASURY OF WESTERN FOLKLORE.

Fandom will like the references to conventions, fan publications and the like. In the June 1952 article, note William Nolan's series of pamphlets. Answers to questions about the editors and the magazine compiled for one of these pamphlets comprise part of the section labeled "The Trade: The Tricks of and the Art of."

We begin 1950—and this new department—with a brief survey of fantasy publishing in general and the best books of the last year in particular. If any statement of future reviewing policy is needed, it's simply this: we'll read everything and bring to your attention the best in our field.

Recommended Reading
by the Editors

Vol. 1, No. 2
Winter-Spring 1950

Published output of fantasy and/or science fiction for 1949 was, curiously enough, both extremely good and extremely bad. With one or two exceptions, there were at least three contenders for the top place in each category; each category also furnished an assortment of trash that had no earthly excuse for existence between covers. On the whole, though, the best was the best of a *good* lot; the competition in the field was the toughest since fantasy book publishing made its bow in the first years of the past decade.

A further good omen is the number of fantasy and science fiction books to receive an honored place on the lists of major publishers. These all had the editorial and promotional treatment accorded a potential secondary leader on the list; in other words, such publications are regarded as a sound investment.

It's not wishful thinking to predict that in 1950 the number of general publishers dipping their toes in the water will at least triple.

1: Frederic Brown: WHAT MAD UNIVERSE (Dutton)
Announced as the first of Dutton's science fiction list.—by far the most successful of the several general publishers' offerings of science fiction for the average reader. Jack Williamson's THE HUMANOIDS (Simon & Schuster) places second only because an inconsistent ending all but ruins the wonderful suspense of the paraphysicals' struggle against the Humanoids.

2: S. Fowler Wright: THE WORLD BELOW (Shasta)
The year's most notable science fiction reissue, and high time, too.
Hard on its heels comes the reissue (by Prime) of L. Sprague de
Camp's LEST DARKNESS FALL, a witty version of the Connecticut
Yankee theme, distinguished by its lore of Gothic Rome.

3: Theodore Sturgeon: WITHOUT SORCERY (Prime)
A striking volume of science fiction short stories (with a little of the
supernatural thrown in).

4: Everett F. Bleiler & T.E. Dikty, editors: THE BEST SCIENCE FIC-
TION STORIES: 1949 (Fell)
The finest of the year's science fiction anthologies, including distin-
guished stories by Leinster, Bradbury and Shiras.

5: Chesley Bonestell & Willy Ley: THE CONQUEST OF SPACE (Viking)
At once the most beautiful and most informative (and startlingly
inexpensive) volume of factual material vital to the science fiction
reader.

6: Louis Golding: HONEY FOR THE GHOST (Dial)
The year's only notable new supernatural novel.

7: James Hogg: THE PRIVATE MEMOIRS AND CONFESSIONS OF A JUSTI-
FIED SINNER (Chanticleer)
Re-issue of a forgotten classic.

8: Leon Edel, editor: THE GHOSTLY TALES OF HENRY JAMES (Rutgers)
Eighteen magnificently conceived and executed episodes, admirably
edited, established James as one of America's foremost, if most
neglected, masters of fantasy. Other important volumes of shorts
include Shirley Jackson's THE LOTTERY (Farrar, Straus).

9: James Reynolds: GALLERY OF GHOSTS (Creative Age)
A lavishly illustrated and sumptuously produced volume of non-
fiction ghost stories.

Vol. 1, No. 3
Summer 1950
As we predicted in our last issue, 1950's crop of science fiction
and/or fantasy publications is starting out as a bumper one. The
forecast that science fiction's published output will equal that of the

mystery novel is, of course, far from being realised; however at this writing (March 1st) that prophecy doesn't seem nearly as improbable as it did, say, six months ago.

To us, the outstanding books of the season to date are:

Robert A. Heinlein's SIXTH COLUMN (Gnome);

WALDO and MAGIC, INC. (Doubleday)

This revised and expanded version of SIXTH COLUMN is Heinlein at his best, an all-around model for writers of science fiction. Reprinted in its original magazine version, WALDO, while being his best concept, illustrates the basic weakness in most of Heinlein's work, a tendency to rush the ending and to shirk final developments. Had a capable editor demanded that WALDO be properly expanded the result would have been the best science fiction novel of the last twenty years; even as here presented, it has few equals. That mad, merry mixture of black magics and politics, MAGIC, INC., should have been expanded also. Still, as it is, it's a better job of plotting and execution, although not top fantasy.

S. Fowler Wright's THE THRONE OF SATURN (Arkham)

Judith Merril's SHOT IN THE DARK (Bantam)

A widely ranging anthology, mostly of science fiction but with a few supernatural stories.

Anthony West's THE VINTAGE (Houghton Mifflin)

Widely praised as a serious psychological novel and a study of man's place in the world he has shaped, this is equally distinguished as a fantasy—a brilliantly terrifying exploration of the theme that each age creates its own peculiar species of hell and Devil.

E. M. Butler's RITUAL MAGIC (Cambridge)

This inexhaustible treasurehouse of necromantic and nigromantic fact is richer in plot ideas than any dozen supernatural anthologies, and nicely blends sound scholarship with literary charm.

Vol. 1, No. 4
Fall 1950

The outstanding event of the publishing season to this date—and quite likely of the year—is the publication of Ray Bradbury's THE MARTIAN CHRONICLES (Doubleday). This superbly organized collection of Bradbury's stories about Mars, its people and its conquests by Earth leaves the reader with the sense of having read history interpreted by a poet. All of Bradbury's great qualities are here; his soaring imagination, his profound realization of people and places, his moral sense (a rare thing in science fiction!) and ironic (and sometimes grisly) humor. These stories of high adventure, mood,

character, social criticism more than justify Merle Miller's estimate
of Ray Bradbury as one of America's finest young writers in any
field.

It is indicative of the high stature science fiction and/or fantasy
publishing is attaining to note that THE MARTIAN CHRONICLES is
narrowly the leader in a superlative lot of books. The leaders in each
category follow.

SCIENCE FICTION NOVELS

Best: Fritz Leiber's GATHER, DARKNESS! (Pellegrini & Cudahy). One
of the most imaginative and compelling magazine serials seems even
better on rereading in book form—an extraordinary fusion of scientific and sociological thinking with an evocation of horror worthy of
M. R. James.

SIENCE FICTION ANTHOLOGIES

Best: BEYOND TIME AND SPACE, edited by August Derleth (Pellegrini
& Cudahy). It is pleasing to note that both this and Martin Greenberg's
MEN AGAINST THE STARS (Gnome Press) are not indiscriminate collections, but are "planned" anthologies and as such are highly recommended. Derleth has succeeded admirably in his attempt to "glance
backward over the stream of science fiction," bringing together the
much discussed classics of the field, such as Plato's *Atlantis*, Kepler's
Somnium (in a first published English translation by Everett F.
Bleiler), as well as some of the best efforts of writers like Wells,
Verne, Stockton, Weinbaum, Padgett, Heinlein and Bradbury. Of
considerably less literary quality, the Greenberg collection nevertheless presents a very convincing picture of the steps in the conquest of
space.

NON-FICTION

Best: POPUL VUH (University of Oklahoma). Around 1555 an anonymous Quiché Indian wrote down the traditions of the Mayan people, and in so doing produced what has justly been described as the
one great creative work known from a Pre-Conquest American.
Now, Delia Goetz and Sylvanus G. Morley give us, based on the
definitive Spanish version of Adrián Recinos, the first complete
English translation—which proves to be one of the most fascinating
and skillfully told fantasy narratives in all folk literature. The POPUL
VUH has become familiar in another context recently; it is frequently
quoted in Immanuel Velikovsky's extraordinary WORLDS IN COLLI-
SION (Macmillan). Frankly, your editors want no part of the extremes
of facile gullibility and scientific dogmatism that have characterized
the two sides of the controversy raging around Velikovsky, but

strongly recommend his book, whatever its defects, as the liveliest imaginative stimulus since the days of Charles Fort.

Stop press addendum: Despite all debates on dianoetics and colliding worlds, we feel that the year will not produce a factual book more important to science fiction enthusiasts (and possibly to all mankind) than Donald Keyhoe's cogent, intelligent and persuasive THE FLYING SAUCERS ARE REAL (Fawcett)—a two-bit pocketsize original deserving more serious attention than most four-dollar hardcover books. This is your *must* of the month.

Vol. 1, No. 5
December 1950

As the upswing of science fiction in book form continues, a couple of trends have developed which cause us to address an urgent plea to all publishers: When you give first book publication to serials from old magazines, *please* pick stories whose prose and technique are at least up to the lowest modern magazine standards. And when you publish a volume of short stories, *please* label it as such, without trying to con the reader into thinking he's buying a novel.

With those gripes off our chests, we can proceed to recommend some of the more pleasant recent publishing ventures:

SCIENCE FICTION NOVELS

Judith Merril's SHADOW OF THE HEARTH (Doubleday) easily leads in the last few months, and in certain respects in the last few years or even decades; an intimate study of the domestic impact of atomic war, it's a sensitively human novel, terrifying in its small-scale reflection of grand-scale catastrophe.

SCIENCE FICTION ANTHOLOGY

The laudable trend toward patterned collections continues with Donald A. Wollheim's FLIGHT INTO SPACE (Fell), an anthology so neatly constructed and well annotated, with one story to each major body in the solar system, that one wishes the writing, story by story, were up to the overall editing.

FANTASY NOVELS

At last the superlative magazine series by L. Sprague de Camp and Fletcher Pratt, recounting Harold Shea's experiences with the mathematics of magic in alternate universes, is all in print in a completely revised and expanded form. THE INCOMPLETE ENCHANTER (universes of the Norse Gods and of the Faerie Queen) has been reissued by Prime; and Gnome has brought out for the first time the fuller version of THE CASTLE OF IRON (universe of Orlando Furioso). The last is in plot much the weakest of the two; but the whole series marks a high-point in the application of sternest intellectual logic to screwball fantasy.

Vol. 2, No. 1
February 1951

Many anthologists and magazine editors, and even some readers, make quite a serious to-do about drawing a precise line between science fiction and the rest of imaginative literature. As you know, we've never felt the tremendous importance of the distinction; and only in this review department have we tried to draw any line of demarcation between science fiction and fantasy.

But if the line is to be drawn, we feel strongly that it should come at a different point than the usual one. Extrapolation of probable science, as practised notably by Heinlein and by a few other authors such as de Camp and Simak, can be legitimately called *science* fiction; space-warps, galactic drives, BEMs and time machines are as purely fantasy as werewolves or vampires.

An example in point is one of the most attractive novels yet to appear in this spate of science fiction publishing, Theodore Sturgeon's THE DREAMING JEWELS (Greenberg). Published as the first in a series of novels under the promising editorship of Ken Crossen, it makes not the faintest attempt at scientific plausibility, but simply evolves a new fantasy mythology of its own in the entrancing concept of living jewel-like creatures who can create living matter—and from this premise proceeds to build a warm and beautifully human story of a carnival, a lovely midget, and a boy who ate ants . . . and could regenerate his lost fingers. Science, no; but fresh, creative imaginative literature, strongly, yes!

SCIENCE FICTION SHORT STORIES

Oddly, the only book of science fiction short stories to show up in the past two months also happens to be the most important volume of such to come along for many a moon. This is Robert A. Heinlein's collection, THE MAN WHO SOLD THE MOON (Shasta). This, ladies and gentlemen, is a must!

Vol. 2, No. 2
April 1951

In surveying the books of 1950 we have compiled some shocking statistics on the publishing of the science fiction "novel." (Reasons for using quotes will soon be readily apparent.) During 1950 there were twenty-seven books named—and advertised—by their publishers as "science fiction novels." Of these, seven were original novels, of varying degrees of literary quality, written primarily for book publication. Eight were renditions in book form of magazine serials published within the last ten years. A few of these might have been written with hard cover book editions in mind; judging from obvious rewriting, which usually failed to improve the original version, most of them weren't. Eight were exhumations: serials dug up from the back files of old pulp magazines. Marked by crude writing, out-dated ideas, lack of any importance whatsoever, these dead had for the most part earned an undisturbed rest! Three of the twenty-seven were collections of short stories or novelets which were dubbed *novels*. One publisher capitalized on the "flying saucer" craze to give an otherwise agreeable science-fictional spy thriller a title that had nothing to do with the book itself. Another labeled the adventures of a character long renowned in fantasy-adventure as "science-fantasy." If "legendary *magic*" is science . . . oh, well. And the situation is perhaps even worse in the 25¢ paperbacks not included in this study.

If publishers of science fiction "novels" are operating solely for that small group of fanatic collectors who will buy anything between covers, hard or soft, the foregoing is of no interest save to an equally small group of purists. But if these publishers want to reach an audience as large as, say, that of the mystery novel—and they should, if only for financial reasons—then we submit it's high time that they set up a few simple standards of honest publishing.

Certainly, the present situation represents the rankest kind of opportunism, resulting in the promotion and sale of shoddy merchandise to the helpless reader. (He, poor wight, is outside the protection of the Federal Trade Commission which has no authority over the labeling of books.) Equally helpless are too many talented young writers who'd like to write books, if publishers would cease looking backward at the dated efforts of current "names" they can seemingly reprint very cheaply. It's odd that one publishing house, noted for its development of young mystery writers, has published not one new effort on its science fiction list!

However, these never-despairing reviewers have, without too much difficulty, found a few bright spots in the picture. Under the able editorship of Groff Conklin, Grosset & Dunlap has launched a line of dollar reprints called *Science Fiction Classics*. Mr. Conklin's first four selections are excellent, headed—paradoxically—by the first book appearance of Henry Kuttner's FURY, followed close after by THE ISLAND OF CAPTAIN SPARROW, by S. Fowler Wright, Jack Williamson's THE HUMANOIDS and THE WORLD OF Ā, by A. E. Van Vogt. Two books published as juveniles that will delight the adult reader are: FARMER GILES OF HAM, by J. R. R. Tolkien (remember THE HOBBIT?), with wondrous illustrations by Pauline Diana Baynes (Houghton); and THE LION, THE WITCH AND THE WARDROBE, by C. S. Lewis (Macmillan). And to show that we object to the ressurection men only when they revive bodies better left interred, we especially recommend Prime Press's fine work in rediscovering Mary Griffith's THREE HUNDRED YEARS HENCE (1836); the exquisite job of book-making—at a phenomenally low price—Doric Books did on their reprint of W. H. Hudson's THE CRYSTAL AGE (1887); and Frederick Fell's reissue, bolstered by a sound Fletcher Pratt analysis, of Hugo Gernsback's scientifically (if hardly fictionally) significant RALPH 1241C41+ (1912).

And now, before we turn to the "best of the year," we can say that if the books discussed in the first three paragraphs were unrelieved by any creative publishing at all, 1950 would still have been a noteworthy year in science fiction, if only for the publication of Dover's one volume edition of SEVEN SCIENCE FICTION NOVELS OF H. G. WELLS. It contains all of the Old Master's works that are now classics, such as THE TIME MACHINE, THE INVISIBLE MAN, THE WAR OF THE WORLDS, etc., etc. and is a must for all readers!

So, with chest relieved of gripes and with malice toward quite a few, we offer our checklist of the best works of imaginative fiction published in 1950. Titles are listed alphabetically by author. We feel that every book belongs in every collection of imaginative literature.

Charles Addams: MONSTER RALLY (Simon & Schuster). Like Lovecraft's Richard Upton Pickman, Addams obviously "was born in strange shadow" and has "found a way to unlock the forbidden gate." Here are the latest results of his eldritch and unhallowed researches, with especial emphasis on that accursed household of clearly transplanted Arkhamites in Suburbia.

Everett F. Bleiler & T. E. Dikty, editors: THE BEST SCIENCE FICTION STORIES: 1950 (Fell).

Ray Bradbury: THE MARTIAN CHRONICLES (Doubleday).

Elizabeth Cadell: BRIMSTONE IN THE GARDEN (Morrow).

August Derleth, editor: BEYOND TIME AND SPACE (Pellegrini & Cudahy).

Basil Davenport, editor: GHOSTLY TALES TO BE TOLD (Dodd, Mead).

Martin Greenberg, editor: MEN AGAINST THE STARS (Gnome).

Robert A. Heinlein: WALDO and MAGIC, INC. (Doubleday).

Robert A. Heinlein: THE MAN WHO SOLD THE MOON (Shasta).

Donald Keyhoe: THE FLYING SAUCERS ARE REAL (Fawcett).

Fritz Leiber: GATHER, DARKNESS! (Pellegrini & Cudahy).

Eric Linklater: A SPELL FOR OLD BONES (Macmillan).

Helen McCloy: THROUGH A GLASS, DARKLY (Random).

Judith Merril: SHADOW ON THE HEARTH (Doubleday).

Judith Merril, editor: SHOT IN THE DARK (Bantam).

A. N. L. Munby: THE ALABASTER HAND (Macmillan).

Lewis Padgett: A GNOME THERE WAS (Simon & Schuster).

Theodore Sturgeon: THE DREAMING JEWELS (Greenberg).

James Thurber: THE 13 CLOCKS (Simon & Schuster).

Anthony West: THE VINTAGE (Houghton Mifflin).

Charles Williams: THE GREATER TRUMPS (Pellegrini & Cudahy).

S. Fowler Wright: THE THRONE OF SATURN (Arkham).

Vol. 2, No. 3
June 1951
Magazine deadlines come early, and books for review come late; so inevitably much of this column must be devoted to catching up with fantasy publishing in 1950.

At least one belatedly received item should have appeared on the "Best of 1950" list in our last issue: Robert A. Heinlein's FARMER IN THE SKY (Scribner's). Published as a juvenile, this magnificently detailed study of the technological and human problems of interplanetary colonization was just about the only *mature* science fiction novel of the year. To be sure, this would have meant no less than three Heinleins on the "Best" list, but who's counting? The fact remains that Heinlein, even when writing for (but never "down to") a juvenile audience, makes most of his nominally adult competition look like continuity writers for the Buck Rogers strip.

Parts of Isaac Asimov's I, ROBOT (Gnome) are not too far from the same plane. This collection of his celebrated "positronic robot" stories, though fairly well integrated in a fresh frame, is certainly not a "novel," as the jacket claims; and much of the prose and characterization is reminiscent of the corniest space operas. But each story contains a truly striking gimmick based on the author's convincing Three Laws of Robotics; and a few, particularly *Reason* and *Liar!*, must stand among the best robot stories ever written.

NEW FICTION

It would be a pleasure, if space allowed, to detail all the respects in which Philip Wylie is intolerable; and certainly he assumes every one of his most outrageous postures in the course of THE DISAPPEARANCE (Rinehart). But previously, in numerous novels and short stories, Wylie has also proved himself one of the most ingenious and stimulating modern creators of science-fantasy; and his worst detractor (your editors are tossing a coin for the honor) must admit that he has, in these parallel stories of a world-without-women and a world-without-men, produced a masterpiece of imaginative thinking and story-telling—postures and all.

Vol. 2, No. 4
August 1951

All of us enthusiasts have for so long hailed science fiction as a typically American form that it's somewhat embarrassing to admit that the two best science fiction novels of 1951 to date (this column is being written in late March) are both imports from England.

John Wyndham's THE DAY OF THE TRIFFIDS (Doubleday) may remind you of many other novels describing the collapse of contemporary civilization; but rarely have the details of that collapse been treated with such detailed plausibility and human immediacy, and never has the collapse been attributed to such an unusual and terrifying source. You'll find a high quality of novel-writing here; and those tripodal walking plants known as *triffids* will, we guarantee, haunt your nightmares for years to come.

There's no new and startling concept in Arthur C. Clarke's PRE-LUDE TO SPACE (Galaxy); the book is merely the description of the day-by-day preparation for the launching of the first moon rocket. But Mr. Clarke knows his scientific details so well, projects them so clearly, and manages miraculously to infuse them with so sensitive a poetic understanding that this simple factual narrative is more absorbing than the most elaborately plotted intergalactic epic. And it's further distinguished by the moving theme: "We will take no frontiers into space"—a refreshing change from the narrow "practical" chauvinism of so many of our writers.

A few recent items, however, are well worth reading. John W. Campbell Jr.'s THE MOON IS HELL! (Fantasy Press) is an extraordinary short novel: the diary of a stranded lunar expedition which creates its own living conditions out of that barren satellite—a narrative with much of the fascination of a SWISS FAMILY-ROBINSON or a ROBINSON CRUSOE, and with Defoe's own dry convincing factuality. Edmond Hamilton's CITY AT WORLD'S END (Fell) is a surprising departure for the creator of Captain Future: the warm and intimate story of a small mid-western town blasted into the remote future and adjusting itself to an uninhabited earth and a vastly inhabited galaxy.

There's been only one recent volume of science fiction short stories; but that one is a *must*: Ray Bradbury's THE ILLUSTRATED MAN (Doubleday). The attempt at a unifying frame-structure is, in contrast to THE MARTIAN CHRONICLES, markedly unsuccessful; and a few of the eighteen stories seem less than wisely chosen to enhance the Bradbury reputation. But enough excellent ones remain to provide a feast for every devotee of the finest traditions in imaginative fiction.

Vol. 2, No. 5
October 1951

Anyone with the faculty of short range precognition could have picked up a nice bit of change in New York publishing circles only two or three years ago by betting that five hard-cover science fiction anthologies would appear within a two-month period in 1951.

Three of the best novels from "Unknown" have at last reached hard covers. Gnome Press offers two of L. Ron Hubbard's in one volume: TYPEWRITER IN THE SKY, an entertaining adventure-farce badly in need of editing; and the classic FEAR, which still seems a nearly perfect psychological terror novel, and by far the best writing

we've ever seen from Hubbard. L. Sprague de Camp's THE UNDE-
SIRED PRINCESS (Fantasy Publishing Company) explores a world of
strict two-value Aristotelian logic with that splendid absurd rigor-
ousness which distinguishes such other vintage de Camp items as the
Harold Shea series.

Two important new non-fiction books are both, in different ways,
slightly disappointing. Arthur C. Clarke's INTERPLANETARY FLIGHT
(Harper) is a brief but comprehensive study of astronautical problems which will prove invaluable to students and especially to
writers; but much of it is so heavily technical that the average reader
may despair. Kenneth Heuer's MEN OF OTHER PLANETS (Pellegrini &
Cudahy) is an admirably well-intentioned effort to correct the limited
anthropomorphic thinking of too many "authorities"; but its own
thinking is none too cogent, and its attempts at literary style and
grace prove rather unfortunate.

Best of recent non-fiction is Vance Randolph's uproarious WE
ALWAYS LIE TO STRANGERS (Columbia University), a grand collection
of Ozark legends and monsters, written, like his great OZARK SUPER-
STITIONS, with that blend of sound scholarship and deadpan zest
which is Randolph's copyright secret. Another university press book,
Paul Fatout's AMBROSE BIERCE: THE DEVIL'S LEXICOGRAPHER (Oklahoma) is strong in fresh source material on Bierce's peculiar life,
weak in any comprehension of his fiction (for which Fatout shows a
marked distaste). Despite its title, Sara Gerstle's FOUR GHOST STO-
RIES (Adrian Wilson) also comes under non-fiction, but adds nothing
of evidential interest to psychic research, despite a quiet pleasantness
and an extraordinarily attractive job of printing and designing.

In addition to the new books, two reprints demand your attention
if you've previously missed them: Grosset & Dunlap's reissues of
two of the finest science fiction novels of all the modern crop,
Robert A. Heinlein's BEYOND THIS HORIZON and Fritz Leiber's GATH-
ER, DARKNESS!

Vol. 2, No. 6
December 1951
The most interesting recent fictional extrapolation is L. Sprague de
Camp's ROGUE QUEEN (Doubleday), which ventures into an almost
virgin (which is perhaps not the *mot juste*) field: the interplanetary
cultural aspects of sex. Lively and unusual thinking, a vigorous plot,
and a most appealing non-human heroine make the best de Camp
novel in many years.

A. E. van Vogt is also at his best in some time in THE WEAPON

SHOPS OF ISHER (Greenberg), a surprisingly successful rewriting and integration of three of the famous "Weapon Shop" stories—possibly for postgraduate science fiction readers, with its typically grandiose and limitless van Vogt concepts, but a fine excitingly involved melodrama.

In the reprint department, there are two *musts*: That 1911 classic of factual time-travel, the Moberly-Jourdain AN ADVENTURE, is at long last back in print in America (Coward-McCann). And THE OMNI-BUS JULES VERNE (Lippincott) contains almost 300,000 words by the Master: AROUND THE WORLD IN 80 DAYS, which is not science fiction but still probably Verne's masterpiece; two of his greatest scientific romances, 20,000 LEAGUES UNDER THE SEA and FROM THE EARTH TO THE MOON (complete with its sequel); and a trashy novelet (not science fiction), THE BLOCKADE RUNNERS, which seems to have wandered in by mistake. (Appeal to all publishers: Since Verne is in the public domain, with no author's royalties, when will you realize that you could afford to commission good modern translations, which are so badly needed?)

Vol. 3, No. 1
February 1952
We've previously expressed in this department the opinion that Robert A. Heinlein knows more about the technique of writing true *science* fiction than any other contemporary author. And what is perhaps most gratifying about Heinlein's work is that he's not content to sit back and be venerated as The Old Master; he's still constantly learning, expanding the scope of his own writing and of the field itself.

The newest Heinlein marks yet another departure. In THE PUPPET MASTERS (Doubleday) he's chosen a theme which old-line aficiona-dos will consider tired and even tiresome: the invasion of earth by interplanetary parasites who fasten upon men and convert them into soulless zombies. But in the development of this theme he displays not only his usual virtues of clear logic, rigorous detail-work and mastery of indirect exposition, but also something new: a startling fertility in suspense devices, a powerful ingenuity in plotting (hith-erto his weakest point), to make this as thunderously exciting a melodrama of intrigue as you'll find outside of an early Hitchcock picture. Science fiction is said to be competing with the mystery-suspense story for popular favor; and Heinlein has brilliantly com-bined the virtues of both fields in one book.

Your editors were too closely involved in the preparation of

Raymond J. Healy's NEW TALES OF SPACE AND TIME (Holt) to give a strictly objective critique; but we can stress that it avoids completely the cannibalism of anthologists as exemplified in the Pratt. No story in the Healy collection has appeared before *in any form*; all were written specifically for this book, by such topflight science fiction names as Bradbury, Asimov, Bretnor, Neville, Heard and van Vogt.

Note to serious science fiction collectors: Donald B. Day, former editor of one of the best of all fan-zines, "The Fanscient", is compiling a complete author-title index of all American professional magazines in the field from 1926 to 1950, including over 30,000 entries and a full listing of pseudonyms. The limited edition of 2000 copies will be published in the late spring of 1952 at $6.50; advance orders at the pre-publication price of $5 may be sent now to Mr. Day at 3435 N. E. 38th Ave., Portland 13, Oregon.

Vol. 3, No. 2
April 1952

Checking back on our survey of 1950 science fiction publishing (F&SF April 1951), we find that there was plenty to complain about and that we did just that in not very pleasant terms. The principal gripes, were, as you may remember, these: alarming lack of original novels, the resurrection in book form of ancient magazine trash better left buried, and the crudest sort of mis-labeling, such as presenting adventure-fantasy as "science fiction" or a crudely strung together batch of short stories as "a novel."

Fortunately for all concerned—these practises have all but ceased; and this survey of 1951 publishing will be as mild and amiable as you please. Publishers last year issued 47 volumes which they labeled as science fiction. Of the 27 novels, there was only one case of calling a book "a novel" when it was in reality a faintly disguised series of short stories; last year there were 3. There also appeared 7 collections of an author's short stories, 10 anthologies, and 3 "two-in-one" volumes each containing two short novels.

Let's see how these originated. Of 30 books (counting the two-in-one jobs) there were 11½ novels whose book publication marked their first appearance before the public! 7 other novels were (as is normal in other fields) serialized shortly before or even simultaneously with their book publication. 8½ novels were revivals of works that first saw publication in magazines of the period 1939–1949; we're sure no one will quarrel with the permanent preservation of the best of that "Golden Age" of science fiction. Of the sludge printed before that era, confident publishers assembled 3 books and, presumably, found some market therefor.

Yes, publishers were far more enterprising in 1951. In 1950, the percentage of original books in the year's outpost was 25.9; in 1951 it was 42.6. Adding those which were serialized in contemporary magazines, the total percentage of *new* novels published in 1951 was the unprecedented figure of 68.5. No wonder we're so agreeable this year!

Yet there are annoyances. Where are the new writers in science fiction? While other types of fantasy gave us W. B. Ready (who seems to have caught the mantle of James Stephens), Kem Bennett, Carlo Beuf and a newcomer from other fields, Oscar Lewis, there hasn't been a single new writer of long straight hard-cover science fiction. In that analogous field of popular entertainment, mystery fiction, 35 first novels were published, often promptly followed by seconds. New writers accounted for 20% of 1951's output of crime-suspense novels! Let's face it: some day there aren't going to be any more Heinleins, Bradburys, van Vogts, et al; it's up to publishers to groom the men (and women) who must take their places.

Now we come to that phase of science fiction which seems to have reached mass production proportions: the anthology. There had been 10 such published in 1951 when this piece went to the printers. And at that time there were at least *fifteen* in preparation for 1952! Excluding the Healy collection of originals, NEW TALES OF SPACE AND TIME, 9 anthologies reprinted 145 stories. Add to that the volumes of their own work by individual authors and you have a grand total of 214 magazine stories considered worthy of permanent preservation between hard covers. As readers, we doubt that there are that many; as editors we know darn well there aren't.

If this spate of anthologists agrees with us on hard-cover standards, it means that they will be taking in each other's washing; each new book will be (as some now are) a rehash of its predecessors. If they disagree, the law of diminishing returns guarantees that you, the purchaser, just won't be getting your money's worth.

Now on to the alphabetical listing of 1951's top books of imaginative fiction (and occasionally fact):

Kem Bennett: THE FABULOUS WINK (Pellegrini & Cudahy).
Carlo Beuf: THE INNOCENCE OF PASTOR MÜLLER (Duell, Sloan & Pearce).
Everett F. Bleiler & T. E. Dikty, editors: THE BEST SCIENCE FICTION STORIES: 1951 (Fell).

Ray Bradbury: THE ILLUSTRATED MAN (Doubleday).

John Dickson Carr: THE DEVIL IN VELVET (Harper).

Jean Charlot: DANCE OF DEATH (Sheed & Ward).

Arthur C. Clarke: PRELUDE TO SPACE (Galaxy)

Jack Coggins & Fletcher Pratt: ROCKETS, JETS, GUIDED MISSILES AND SPACE SHIPS (Random).

John Collier: FANCIES AND GOODNIGHTS (Doubleday).

Groff Conklin, editor: POSSIBLE WORLDS OF SCIENCE FICTION (Vanguard).

L. Sprague de Camp: ROGUE QUEEN (Doubleday).

Raymond J. Healy, editor: NEW TALES OF SPACE AND TIME (Holt).

Gerald Heard: THE BLACK FOX (Harper).

Robert A. Heinlein: BETWEEN PLANETS (Scribner's)

Robert A. Heinlein: THE GREEN HILLS OF EARTH (Shasta).

Robert A. Heinlein: THE PUPPET MASTERS (Doubleday).

L. Ron Hubbard: TWO NOVELS (Gnome).

Malcolm Jameson: BULLARD OF THE SPACE PATROL (World).

Walt Kelly: POGO (Simon & Schuster).

Oscar Lewis: THE LOST YEARS (Knopf).

Willy Ley: ROCKETS, MISSILES, AND SPACE TRAVEL (Viking).

Fletcher Pratt, editor: WORLD OF WONDER (Twayne).

Vance Randolph: WE ALWAYS LIE TO STRANGERS (Columbia University).

W. B. Ready: THE GREAT DISCIPLE AND OTHER STORIES (Bruce).

A. E. van Vogt: SLAN (Simon & Schuster).

Charles Williams: THE PLACE OF THE LION (Pellegrini & Cudahy).

Philip Wylie: THE DISAPPEARANCE (Rinehart).

John Wyndham: THE DAY OF THE TRIFFIDS (Doubleday).

Vol. 3, No. 3
June 1952

Note to collectors and enthusiasts: The San Diego Science-Fantasy Society has wisely decided to issue a series of booklets on individual authors rather than an amateur magazine. The first of these, RAY BRADBURY REVIEW, displays much too much uncritical ecstasy, but contains valuable biographical material (largely from Bradbury himself) and a complete bibliography. Admirers of one of the best of the younger talents—in any field—will find this a welcome reference work now—and a valuable collector's item in the future. Copies may be ordered (at 50¢ each) from the editor, William F. Nolan, 4458 56th St., San Diego, California.

A recent publication obviously not to be reviewed in this column is THE BEST FROM FANTASY & SCIENCE FICTION, edited by Anthony

Boucher and J. Francis McComas (Little, Brown), a selection of never-anthologized stories from the first two volumes (1949–1951) of this magazine's existence.

Vol. 3, No. 4
August 1952

As it must to all reviewers, the time has come for us to confess ourselves wrong. We have vehemently argued that another original anthology of science fiction shorts simply could not be assembled. We said it couldn't be done; it *was* done and we're happy to apologize to them and to you.

Robert A. Heinlein proves himself nearly as capable an editor as he is a writer with his first anthology, TOMORROW THE STARS (Doubleday). The fourteen stories, all new to book publication, have been chosen from all possible sources and are uniformly excellent. But, for us, the best reading in the book is Heinlein's introduction, an unassuming, yet keenly perceptive discussion of just what constitutes science fiction.

Heinlein expresses deep gratitude for the help of several co-editors, including among others, Judith Merril and Frederik Pohl. Pohl has done a nice job on his own with BEYOND THE END OF TIME (Permabooks). Among other achievements, this well-rounded collection strikes a stout blow at inflation in offering nineteen stories for 35 cents.

Groff Conklin is now engaged in the likeable project of "pattern" anthologies, collections that illustrate a basic theme of science fiction. It's a difficult task but so far Conklin has succeeded admirably. His newest, INVADERS OF EARTH (Vanguard), contains twenty-one stories that concern themselves with all sorts of possible intruders on our planet. Also present is that famed radio play of Howard Koch's, INVASION FROM MARS, with which Orson Wells terrorized the citizenry a few years back.

Last in the array of good anthologies, but by no means least, especially as regards quantity, is H. L. Gold's selection of what he considers the best stories he has published, GALAXY READER OF SCIENCE FICTION, (Crown).

Out of a half-dozen science fiction novels published to date, only one can be offered to you as "recommended reading." That is James Blish's JACK OF EAGLES (Greenberg), a book that is both extraordinarily good and curiously bad. It is one of the strongest pieces of real *science* fiction to be published in years. Those who glibly label as science fiction what is, after all, pure fantasy would do well to study the thinking and logic behind Blish's postulation of the development of psi powers, ESP, psycho-kinesis and kindred potentials of the human mind. Yet, plotwise his novel is tritely melodramatic, wholly devoid of characterization and rather flatly written. But we think it is to be strongly recommended, not only for its thinking but for its brilliant understanding of the essential problem behind the superman thesis, the necessity of integrating superman with humanity.

Vol. 3, No. 6
October 1952

The International Fantasy Awards committee, expanded this year to a truly representative group of scholars, critics and writers from five countries, has chosen a splendid batch of books from those published in 1951; we'd like to add a hearty concurring opinion, urging you, if by some sad chance you've missed any of the books honored, to remedy that error without delay.

The Award for fiction went to John Collier's FANCIES AND GOOD-NIGHTS (Doubleday), which also recently received the Mystery Writers of America's Edgar for short crime stories. Both awards are precisely just; the volume contains pure masterpieces in each field. Fiction runners-up were John Wyndham's THE DAY OF THE TRIFFIDS and Ray Bradbury's THE ILLUSTRATED MAN—both also from Doubleday!

In the non-fiction division, second and third places went to two books strongly commended in the past in this column. Willy Ley's DRAGONS IN AMBER (Viking) and Jack Coggins' and Fletcher Pratt's ROCKETS, JETS, GUIDED MISSILES AND SPACE SHIPS (Random). The Award proper was bestowed, however, on a book which only now reaches the American reviewer; for these International Awards go according to the year of publication in the original country.

Arthur C. Clarke's THE EXPLORATION OF SPACE (Harper), published in England in 1951, makes American publishing history in 1952 by becoming the first work of future space travel (in fiction or fact) to be chosen by the Book-of-the-Month Club. The choice is richly deserved.

Mr. Ley himself, meanwhile, briefly abandons the topic of space travel to produce with L. Sprague de Camp a completely enchanting non-fiction work: LANDS BEYOND (Rinehart). This fascinating documentation of man's credulity concerning *terrae incognitae*, from Alantis through the Kingdom of Prester John to the Lemurian colony on Mount Shasta, is written with scholarly authority, literary grace, and an amusedly tolerant exposition of error, to make one of the season's most enjoyable items.

1952 will be a truly memorable year if it produces a stronger candidate for the International Award than Clifford Simak's CITY (Gnome). Simak's wonderful tales of the dogs who inherit the earth (after man goes to Jupiter) have been woven into a solid, self-sustaining book by the scholarly commentary of a Dog editor of the infinitely remote future. The stories will be a delight for old-timers to reread; those lucky people just discovering them will quickly realize why these tales are a high-water mark in science fiction writing. Both kinds of readers will find the notes and comment (about 6000 words of new material) of the canine editor, who isn't sure whether the chronicles are history or myth, utterly convincing. Here is a book that caused these reviewers to chuck objective detachment out the window and emit a loud, partisan "Whee!"

In full-length science fiction novels, the most interesting recent event has been the revival of a "lost" 1919 serial, Francis Stevens' THE HEADS OF CERBERUS (Polaris), a slightly dated but still originally imaginative and acutely satiric story of time travel in alternate worlds. Lloyd Arthur Eshbach plans a series of such rediscoveries, which can be ordered only directly from Polaris Press, 120 N. 9th St., Reading, Pennsylvania; as limited editions of 1500 copies, singularly well made and (aside from the illustrations) beautifully designed, they are a collector's bargain at $3.

Vol. 3, No. 7
November 1952

Many of the ablest writers of imaginative fiction have also distinguished themselves as editors and critics in the field. With the publication of TIMELESS STORIES FOR TODAY AND TOMORROW (Bantam), Bradbury has done a controversial job. All editors of anthologies face bitter argument over their choices but we think the inclusions of no anthologist will ever be challenged so virulently or defended so passionately as this result of Bradbury's research. For his research has been thorough and extensive and he has carefully examined for stray fantasies many media not usually identified with the publication of this form of fiction. Which splendid virtue may also be responsible for some of the collection's faults; in his strict avoidance of standard sources, Bradbury has selected many stories whose fantasy content is, to say the least, debatable. Still, his book adds up to a lot of unusual and pleasant reading, is a superb bargain (108,000 words for 35¢), and those who disagree with him most loudly must admit that Bradbury the editor, like Bradbury the writer, is not of common mold.

Vol. 4, No. 1
January 1953

We must report more mixed reactions to the anonymously edited anthology of short novels, WITCHES THREE (Twayne). Fritz Leiber's CONJURE WIFE is one of the best of all novels on witchcraft survivals in the enlightened modern world; and its long-delayed appearance in hard covers is highly welcome. The volume is completed by an ingeniously thought-out novelet by James Blish and a long and dreary novel nominally by Fletcher Pratt, but clearly recognizable as by George U. Fletcher, author of 1948's WELL OF THE UNICORN.

As we write this, we do not know who will be our President-elect when it is published, but we do emphatically know that the wrong man won and that we have entered into a branch of time of which we do not approve. 1952 offered one ideal candidate, incredibly rejected by both major parties; and only in an alternate universe in which he was victorious would we be completely content. At any rate we can all console ourselves by reading and rereading the major campaign biography of this or any other year, Walt Kelly's immortal I GO POGO (Simon & Schuster).

Vol. 4, No. 2
February 1953

The "little magazine" cultural school has often experimented with science-fantasy in the short story, and sometimes with first-rate results, some of which we have reprinted here. But these frequently fascinating shorter efforts had hardly prepared us for what would happen when a fashionable literary cultist goes all out on a full-length science fiction novel.

"Full-length" is indeed an understatement for Bernard Wolfe's LIMBO (Random), which is as long as three average popular novels.

This pretentious hodgepodge is dealt with at such length because it is, in a peculiar way, "recommended reading." Style, bulk and publisher's promotion will cause this gallimaufry to be taken seriously by critics who wouldn't even open a book by Robert A. Heinlein; you readers who know what science fiction is and can be should at least look at it, so that you may, like Anderson's observant child, proclaim to the credulous that the Emperor is naked.

F&SF readers and the critics of "little magazines" may meet

somewhat more easily on the subject of Franz Kafka. There still may be controversy; there is even within this office. But many of you, like one of your editors, may find the SELECTED STORIES OF FRANZ KAFKA (Modern Library) one of the year's most stimulating volumes of imaginative literature. Disregard the often unfortunate influence of Kafka on his imitators, and read the man himself for bitingly logical development of strange concepts, for a powerful ability to create convincing other worlds that serve as significant mirror-images of our own, and for (what so many devout Kafkaites overlook) a peculiar vein of individual humor.

Vol. 4, No. 3
March 1953

The upsurge in science fiction publishing seems to have leveled off to a plateau. If you want a detailed statistical analysis of the year 1952, simply look up our figures on the year 1951 (F&SF, April 1952); they're still exact almost to the last decimal point.

The one place where new talent flourished strongly was in a field which hardly existed last year: the teen-age science fiction story. There were at least seventeen nominally "juvenile" science fiction books published in 1952; and the best of these can hold their own with the year's adult fiction. Whether you're looking for moderately simple stories to introduce your children to this noble field, or simply for some first-rate entertainment for yourself, you should not miss Poul Anderson's VAULT OF THE AGES, Arthur C. Clarke's ISLANDS IN THE SKY, Raymond F. Jones's SON OF THE STARS, Chad Oliver's MISTS OF DAWN (all Winston), Andre Norton's STAR MAN'S SON (Harcourt) or Robert A. Heinlein's THE ROLLING STONES (Scribner's).

Another trend somewhat distinguishing 1952 from 1951 was an increase in reprints. By now, almost every 25¢ and 35¢ line has published some science fiction; and the better books in the field stand an excellent chance of gaining in this way thousands of new readers (and dollars). Hard cover reissues have been fewer but distinguished. The collector can at last balance his library properly with the welcome return to print of such incomparable imaginative classics as E. R. Eddison's THE WORM OUROBOROS (Dutton), H. Rider Haggard's FIVE ADVENTURE NOVELS (Dover) and H. G. Wells's 28 SCIENCE FICTION STORIES (Dover).

And now on to the books which struck us as the best, in imaginative fiction and fact, of 1952:

Everett F. Bleiler & T. E. Dikty, editors: THE BEST SCIENCE FICTION STORIES: 1952 (Fell).

L. Sprague de Camp & Willy Ley: LANDS BEYOND (Rinehart).

John W. Campbell, Jr.: CLOAK OF AESIR (Shasta).

Arthur C. Clarke: THE EXPLORATION OF SPACE (Harper).

Arthur C. Clarke: SANDS OF MARS (Gnome).

Groff Conklin, editor: INVADERS OF EARTH (Vanguard).

Richard Beale Davis, editor: CHIVERS' LIFE OF POE (Dutton).

Donald B. Day, editor: INDEX TO THE SCIENCE-FICTION MAGAZINES 1926–1950 (Perri).

Martin Gardner: IN THE NAME OF SCIENCE (Putnam).

Gerald Heard: GABRIEL AND THE CREATURES (Harper).

Robert A. Heinlein, editor: TOMORROW THE STARS (Doubleday).

Franz Kafka: SELECTED STORIES (Modern Library).

Walt Kelly: I GO POGO (Simon & Schuster).

Cyril M. Kornbluth: TAKEOFF (Doubleday).

Judith Merril, editor: BEYOND HUMAN KEN (Random).

Lewis Padgett: ROBOTS HAVE NO TAILS (Gnome).

Frederik Pohl, editor: BEYOND THE END OF TIME (Permabooks).

Cornelius Ryan, editor: ACROSS THE SPACE FRONTIER (Viking).

Clifford D. Simak: CITY (Gnome).

Francis Stevens: THE HEADS OF CERBERUS (Polaris).

Wilson Tucker: THE LONG LOUD SILENCE (Rinehart).

A. E. van Vogt: AWAY AND BEYOND and DESTINATION: UNIVERSE! (Pellegrini & Cudahy).

A. E. van Vogt: THE WEAPON MAKERS (Greenberg).

Kurt Vonnegut, Jr.: PLAYER PIANO (Scribner's).

Vol. 4, No. 4
April 1953
Recently we expressed some bitterness concerning the pretentious attempt to fuse science fiction with the "serious" novel in Bernard Wolfe's LIMBO. We're now happy to report that such an attempt has been brought off very well indeed by Kurt Vonnegut, Jr. in PLAYER PIANO (Scribner's). This novel of a collapsing civilization in the near future succeeds in blending skillfully a psychological study of the persistent human problems in a mechanistically "ideal" society, a vigorous melodramatic story-line and a sharp Voltairean satire— succeeding largely because it extrapolates trends only a little beyond their present points. As a result, much of its study of man's "logical, intelligently-arrived-at botch" has contemporary validity and it offers no glib solutions for said "botch" but contents itself with an

acute statement of problems. Isaac Asimov's THE CURRENTS OF SPACE (Doubleday) has no such immediacy, but provides first-rate entertainment; its remote Galactic-Empire plot-counter-plot has little to do with science fiction, but is so much more adroitly plotted than Asimov's previous ventures in this vein that it stands up as an intricate and constantly surprising spy-suspense story.

The major event among imaginative reprints is, of course, the reissue of E. R. Eddison's THE WORM OUROBOROS (Dutton). First published 30 years ago, this epic romance has been unknown to most readers but warmly treasured by a few who found it unique in the resonant clangor of its prose, the tremendous impetus of its story-telling, the magnificent audacity (and sternly convincing consistency) of its fantasy concepts. This reissue, it is to be hoped, will make a whole new audience aware of one of the major imaginative novels of this century—not science fiction, though it is nominally set on the planet Mercury, but the detailed creation of a vividly heroic alien history. Equally welcome is the first paperback edition of Aldous Huxley's BRAVE NEW WORLD (Bantam), with a fascinating analytical foreword by the author—a novel which has strongly influenced much science fiction thinking in the past twenty years and still stands as one of the literary highpoints in the field. Scarcely in the class with these two, but still commended as highly enjoyable fiction are the brightly written short stories of Fredric Brown, SPACE ON MY HANDS (Bantam).

Vol. 5, No. 1
July 1953
Since 1940, when Robert A. Heinlein's first serial was published, no work of fiction has caused as much pleasurable excitement among readers of science fiction as the serialization of Alfred Bester's THE DEMOLISHED MAN. Such excitement should be renewed and intensified to an even headier pitch by the appearance of that novel, extensively revised and rewritten, in hard-covers (Shasta). A taut, surrealistic melodrama, the story is a masterful compounding of science and detective fiction.

But it is no routine puzzle of *who*; reader and detective know the killer's identity from the beginning. The suspense lies in the chase, in the murderer's magnificent—one can't help but admire him!—effort to match his mind against the better endowed telepath detective. And the puzzle—most brilliantly conceived and fairly clued—is *why*; not even the murderer is consciously aware of the real motive for his crime!

Just as fascinating is Mr. Bester's setting of this criminological problem in a society, ruthless and money-mad on the surface, that is dominated and being subtly reshaped by telepaths. While his picture of that future civilization is not a perfect whole, he does state the problem of such a culture in no uncertain terms and clearly delineates its one inevitable answer. Oddly, his telepaths emerge as more convincing people than do his "normal" characters; very likely this is due to his concentration on the unassailable argument that ESP man is always, in the ultimate analysis, a *man* . . . and must live as such.

But these science and detective fictional enlargements, however perceptively done, are asides; Mr. Bester never forgets that his main job is to tell a story. The riches of his imagination are ever disciplined to his prime purpose, to carry the reader headlong from a savage, useless killing to the inescapable, curious fate of the killer.

High praise of any science fiction novel seems almost always to involve the phrase "not since Heinlein"; and in order to do justice to THE SPACE MERCHANTS by Frederik Pohl and C.M. Kornbluth (Ballantine), we must repeat ourselves. The Heinlein virtue captured here, as hardly any other author has done since Heinlein began his Future History, is the detailedly plausible projection of a complete future society, from its basic concepts down to its tiniest minutiae. The terrifying future envisioned by Messrs. Pohl and Kornbluth is one which could be the longed-for Utopia of any account executive in any advertising agency, a world in which advertising has established itself as an economic oligarchy and social aristocracy; and the authors have developed a sharp melodrama of power-conflict and revolt which manages, in its very plot-structure, to explore all the implied developments of such a society. Bitter, satiric, exciting, this is easily one of the major works of logical extrapolation in several years. (Like the Bester novel, this is extensively rewritten and somewhat abridged from its serial version as GRAVY PLANET; unlike the Bester, the alterations and particularly the cuts are largely for the better.)

Murder and fantasy alternate and blend in John Collier's FANCIES AND GOODNIGHTS (Bantam), a volume which, in its 1951 hardcover appearance, won the International Fantasy Award, received Mystery Writers of America's Edgar award for crime shorts, and left us speechlessly groping for adequate superlatives. Mr. Collier is simply The Master; that's all there is to it. If you don't buy another book all year (or even—perish the thought—another magazine), this you must get!

The whole question of the nature of scientific thought and imagination is the subject of J. Bronowski's THE COMMON SENSE OF SCIENCE (Harvard). This Polish-English statistician (research director for the National Coal Board, star radio panelist of the BBC, and author of a book on William Blake) is that fabulous rarity: a genuinely cultured man—a trained scientist with a deep knowledge of history and the arts, and with a mind capable of integrating all aspects of man's civilization—and incapable of confusing science with technology. This brief and admirably written book is a splendidly clear primer for the layman on the historic development of scientific thinking, the factors which distinguish contemporary attitudes in science, and the possible trends to come—recommended reading for the devotees of science fiction, and required reading for s.f. writers.

Vol. 5, No. 2
August 1953

Man's coming conquest of space, as has often been pointed out, has been more extensively described before the event, in fact and fiction, than any other crucial development in human history. There are advantages to this: scientifically, we may find ourselves better prepared than we were, say, for the Industrial Revolution.

But there's one serious danger, both psychological and esthetic: We may talk and write and thresh the whole damned thing out so thoroughly beforehand that we lose all sense of awe and wonder and epic adventure. To a large extent this is happening in science fiction already; very few indeed are the writers who can make the voyage of a spaceship as stirring as Gunnar Heyerdahl made the voyage of a raft in KON-TIKI. We tend to take our wonders for granted even before we possess them.

As an infinitely welcome exception to this tendency, we open our arms and hearts to Arthur C. Clarke's AGAINST THE FALL OF NIGHT (Gnome). Even in that far future men will have aspirations, undefined yearnings, intimations of immortality—and out of these Clarke shapes a beautiful novel, at once the story of the maturing of a boy who does not quite conform to his race, and of the re-maturing of that smugly decadent race itself. Here indeed is poetry and awe and wonder—and a fine gradual leading of the reader from the small and immediate to the universal and vast.

A word here about those editions dubbed variously "softcover editions," "two-bit reprints," or "pocket books" (albeit Pocket Books, Inc. deeply resents such generic appellation . . . as does General Motors when you refer to your Gibson electric refrigerator as a "Frigidaire!"). There was a time when the serious collector of science and/or fantasy fiction faced a spate of publications (at prices anywhere from $2 to $3.95) that simply overwhelmed his pocketbook. Now, those two-bit, soft cover, pocket book reprints have solved that problem. Just be patient, watch your newsstands and you can buy the best of currently published improbabilia, done in good format, attractively covered and very attractively priced. Now and again these generous publishers come up with an hitherto hard-to-get classic of the past.

Vol. 5, No. 4
October 1953

There's a legend, carefully disseminated by advocates trying to bolster the prestige of science fiction, that most s.f. writers are themselves highly trained and informed scientists. We've even been guilty of this exaggeration ourselves, and we're sorry; the legend's unfortunate in that it scares off a great many good writers who become overaware of their own inadequacy and form the notion that it takes at least an M.S. to sell a science fiction story.

Now the actual facts are that, most s.f. writers are plucky and adventury, but with technical knowledge that has hardly been brought down to the beginning of the century. We are constantly amazed at the flagrant technical howlers that turn up in manuscripts submitted by well-established professionals, and even in the published books which we read as reviewers.

By which we do *not* mean to imply that we ourselves are paragons of scientific knowledge. To be honest, we have, between us, the barest minimum adequate to an educated man in this century—so that it's particularly startling that any should have even less. But we do know, as do the best of the writers who have never been near MIT or Caltech, how and where to look up the facts we may need.

Science fiction writers have been exceedingly fortunate—as have the readers who like to keep up with or even a step ahead of their favorite storytellers—in the wealth of recent factual books on the scientific and technological probabilities of the future, books that should stand at the right hand of every honest author as he writes and of every sceptical enthusiast as he reads.

Arthur C. Clarke, whose name probably appears in this column twice as often as any other, turns up this month as a fiction writer, with his most ambitious novel to date, CHILDHOOD'S END (Ballantine), and we're honestly not quite sure what to make of it. It's a history of the human race from the late Twentieth to the mid-Twenty-second

Century and its extraordinary development under the benevolent
supervision of invisible alien Overlords; to tell more would be to
spoil some neatly arranged surprises. Stapledonian is the word for
the scope of its historic concepts and also for the quality of its prose
and thinking; but as a novel it hangs in curious imbalance between its
large-scale history and a number of episodic small-scale stories—as
though LAST AND FIRST MEN were interspersed with fragmentary
chapters from ODD JOHN and SIRIUS. Let's say an awkward and
imperfect book, but still contributory evidence that Clarke is one of
the few major novelists in science fiction.

Ayn Rand's ANTHEM (Caxton) is also a thesis-novel (or rather a
short novelet), using the overworked theme of individual-revolt-
against-future-regimented-state to advance the notion that brotherly
love and social obligation are a poison and that man's only hope lies
in complete selfishness. The story was published in England in
1938, and Miss Rand implies that a sinister conspiracy of purveyors
of brotherhood has prevented its American hardcover publication
until now. One can only regret that the conspiracy finally broke
down.

Vol. 5, No. 6
December 1953

The news of the month—and indeed, for many readers, the news of
the year—is the publication of Ray Bradbury's longest work to date:
FAHRENHEIT 451 (Ballantine, hardcover $2.50, paper 35¢), an expan-
sion to 50,000 words of his *Galaxy* novella of half that length, *The
Fireman*. There's not much doubt that the intellectuals who have
discovered Bradbury (but not Ward Moore or Theodore Sturgeon or
Robert A. Heinlein or Fritz Leiber) as Literature will acclaim this
work enthusiastically; but we're uncertain as to the reaction of the
regular science fiction reader. Frankly, we're even a little uncertain
as to our own reactions.

We *are* certain that, although the story is set in a highly mecha-
nized future civilization, it is not science fiction, and that, despite its
length, it is not a novel.

Bradbury's future here, as in most of his shorter works, is not a
self-consistent probable world logically developed from specific premises, in the tradition of Wells, Leiber, Kornbluth, Heinlein or even
Huxley. It is more closely related to the creations of Franz Kafka—a
world which is at once an irrational nightmare and a direct symbol of
our own contemporary existence. Belief (or in the familiar but
valuable phrase, suspension of disbelief) in such a world is not an

intellectual conviction enforced by the author's persuasiveness, but an act of faith imposed (if at all) by the sheer power of his writing.

The texture, again as in the shorter works, is woven of symbols rather than characters—a method that can, as we know, be strikingly effective in 5,000 words, but may leave you feeling that 50,000 seems pretty empty without the creation or development of a recognizable human individual.

We're in agreement with Mr. Bradbury that certain current cultural trends are deplorable (though we think he manages to overlook or misinterpret a good many other aspects of contemporary culture), but we don't see that he has anything to say here that he has not said more sharply before at one-tenth or one-twentieth the length. But any Bradbury work, even as questionable a one as this, is of interest and even importance to all those interested in imaginative writing. So we suppose this volume (which also includes two shorter stories, one good, one flat) must be "recommended reading"—and you may well disagree violently with our comments on it.

Traditionally, we should not review a book a major part of which has appeared in these pages, but we must at any rate call your attention (and most urgently) to TALES FROM GAVAGAN'S BAR by Fletcher Pratt and L. Sprague de Camp (Twayne, $3). The volume contains 23 stories, 9 from F&SF, 12 never before published anywhere. To our taste, they're even better *en masse* than they have been individually; and the illustrations by Inga (Mrs. Pratt) are at least as delightful as the tales.

As a solo, Mr. de Camp offers SCIENCE-FICTION HANDBOOK: THE WRITING OF IMAGINATIVE FICTION (Hermitage, $3.50), a down-to-earth study of s.f., not as a Way of Life or a New Trend in Literature, but simply as a means of commercial entertainment. The magazine field changes so rapidly that the market information is already seriously outdated, and a number of minor errors of fact convince one (somewhat to one's relief) that de Camp can be fallible after all; but the solid sensibility of the whole, enlivened by skillful parody of common flows and by an eerily accurate series of sketches of leading writers and editors, makes this not merely a textbook for writers but a useful (and entertaining) guide for the general reader.

Vol. 6, No. 2
February 1954

Next month we'll devote this column to our usual Best-of-the-Past Year list; and in the four and a half years since this magazine was founded (which roughly coincides with the recognition of science fiction by regular trade publishers), we haven't had such a plethora of first-rate books to choose from. In particular, 1953 was an astonishingly strong year in full-length science fiction novels; earlier in the year there were extraordinary novels by Alfred Bester, Arthur C. Clarke, C. M. Kornbluth (both solo and in collaboration with Frederik Pohl) and Ward Moore, any one of which could have been the single, strikingly outstanding Best Novel of a previous year—and now comes Theodore Sturgeon's MORE THAN-HUMAN (Farrar, Straus & Young, hard cover, $2; Ballantine, paper, 35¢), which ranks at least beside and possibly above those just mentioned.

This is the book which was originally announced for publication as THE FABULOUS IDIOT, a long novel of which the celebrated *Galaxy* novella BABY IS THREE forms the middle section. It may seem absurd to speak of the coming of age of an old-line master responsible for so many pure classics of science-fantasy as Sturgeon; but the truth is that this new novel represents such an advance over the previous highs of Sturgeon's work that it seems to mark the first complete fulfilment of his unique talents.

As all science fiction readers know, Sturgeon has been much obsessed for years by the concept of symbiosis—the idea that among sensitive human beings one and one can add up, not to two or even three, but to a greater One, of a different order of magnitude. Here he has finally achieved the full and definite statement of this theme, in the story of a half dozen people, curiously ranging from idiocy to genius, who became together one unit of a new race: Homo Gestalt. And on this theme Sturgeon has constructed a novel as varied as the members of this strange unit. In its crystal-clear prose, its intense human warmth and its depth of psychological probing, it is a first-rate "straight" novel; its ingenious use of telepathy, psychokinesis and other "psi" powers make it admirable science-fantasy; and the adroit plotting and ceaseless surge of action qualify it as a distinguished suspense story. Symbiotically, these factors add up to more than their sum—add up, indeed to one of the most impressive proofs yet of the possiblity of science fiction as part of mainstream literature.

You'll find most of these same Sturgeonesque qualities (including many statements of the symbiosis theme) in his second collection of short stories, E PLURIBUS UNICORN (Abelard, $2.75), but this time without any cumulative effect. The book is a hodgepodge of hitherto unreprinted Sturgeon (much of it non-fantasy), which adds up only to evidence of a distinctive talent shooting off in random directions. The unicorn of the title is, of course, the beautiful *The Silken Swift* (F&SF, November, 1953) and there are a number of other Grade A

Sturgeon stories . . . along with a good many one can see no particular reason for collecting. It's still a book belonging in any fantasy library; but more selective editing could have produced a far better volume.

Vol. 6, No. 3
March, 1954

The impact of science fiction on general trade book publishing was more marked in 1953 than in any other year since New York publishers first recognized the existence of such literature.

Six years ago science fiction simply did not exist, so far as trade publishers were concerned. There'd been a midget's handful of pioneer anthologies and the early experimental ventures of the specialized presses, and that was all. In 1949 the major houses began to discover s.f.; and in that first year's rush 38 books appeared. The impetus continued into 1950, which produced 54 books, and then leveled off, with 51 in 1951 and 52 in 1952.

With a plateau of 50-odd books per year over a three-year period, one might have thought that this indicated a fixed consumer-capacity; but abruptly, in 1953, the number of s.f. books published zoomed up to 71—an increase of 36% over the preceding year!

These figures represent predominantly hardcover publishing; in any of these years the number of paperback originals has been insignificant (though all indications are that it will mount sharply in 1954 and years to come). In comparable fields of popular entertainment, hardcover publishing has fallen off markedly; mysteries, for instance, were down 15% from 1952 to 1953 in hardcovers, with paperback original publication rising strongly, and, though we don't have such precise figures, much the same has been true of westerns.

The section of the science fiction field which accounted for most of this striking rise was the original novel—the novel which has not appeared in magazine form or which is serialized only shortly before its book publication. In the beginning, most novels were revivals of five- or ten-year-old pulp serials. There were only nine new novels in the 1949 crop, 14 in 1950, 19 in 1951, 18 in 1952 . . . and 34 in 1953—or almost as many as in the previous two years combined! Not only the number, but the quality of new novels took an abrupt turn upward—so much so that we have at the moment no idea of how we will cast our ballot as judges of the International Fantasy Award; 1953 produced at least a half dozen novels better than the best of many a previous year.

This 1953 expansion of science fiction in the general market was further evidenced by an unusual amount of writing *about* s.f. In book form alone appeared two full-length critical studies of the field. Neither Reginald Bretnor's symposium, MODERN SCIENCE FICTION (Coward-McCann, $3.75), nor L. Sprague de Camp's textbook for writers, SCIENCE-FICTION HANDBOOK (Hermitage, $3.50), is so definitive as, for instance, Howard Haycraft's books on the mystery novel; but both are valuable pioneer efforts.

And now, for a list (alphabetically by author) of the best imaginative fiction of a most productive year.

Alfred Bester: THE DEMOLISHED MAN (Shasta, $3).

Everett F. Bleiler & T. E. Dikty, editors: BEST SCIENCE-FICTION STORIES: 1953 (Fell, $3.50).

Fredric Brown: THE LIGHTS IN THE SKY ARE STARS (Dutton, $3).

Arthur C. Clarke: AGAINST THE FALL OF NIGHT (Gnome, $2.75).

Arthur C. Clarke: EXPEDITION TO EARTH (Ballantine, $2 cloth, 35¢ paper).

Groff Conklin, editor: SCIENCE-FICTION ADVENTURES IN DIMENSION (Vanguard, $2.95).

Groff & Lucy Conklin, editors: THE SUPERNATURAL READER (Lippincott, $4.95).

Guy Cullingford: POST MORTEM (Lippincott, $2.50).

Basil Davenport, editor: TALES TO BE TOLD IN THE DARK (Dodd, Mead, $3).

C. M. Kornbluth: THE SYNDIC (Doubleday, $2.95).

Fritz Leiber: THE GREEN MILLENNIUM (Abelard, $2.75).

Ward Moore: BRING THE JUBILEE (Farrar, Straus, & Young, $2, Ballantine, 35¢).

Frederik Pohl, editor: STAR SCIENCE FICTION STORIES (Ballantine, $1.50 cloth, 35¢ paper).

Frederik Pohl & C. M. Kornbluth: THE SPACE MERCHANTS (Ballantine, $1.50 cloth, 35¢ paper).

Fletcher Pratt & L. Sprague de Camp: TALES FROM GAVAGAN'S BAR (Twayne, $3).

Bertrand Russell: SATAN IN THE SUBURBS (Simon & Schuster, $3).

Theodore Sturgeon: MORE THAN HUMAN (Farrar, Straus, & Young, $2, Ballantine, 35¢).

William Tenn, editor: CHILDREN OF WONDER (Simon & Schuster, $2.95).

John Wyndham: OUT OF THE DEEPS (Ballantine, cloth $2, paper, 35¢).

Vol. 6, No. 6
June 1954

Both of your editors have long shared an intense admiration for the work of Hal Clement—to be precise, for exactly twelve years; it was in June, 1942, that our eyes popped as we read, in *Astounding*, his first published story, *Proof*. It was not only an unusually good first story, even in that Golden Age when John Campbell was discovering, month by month, most of today's best established writers; it brought off a feat we would not have thought possible: the creation of a wholly believable civilization of non-solid beings evolved in the photosphere of the Sun itself.

Clement, like most brilliant debutantes, has not always been that good in later years. Both of his book-length novels—NEEDLE (Doubleday, 1950) and ICEWORLD (Gnome, 1953) seemed overwordy and pretty heavy going. But even these were redeemed by the great and almost unique Clement virtue: the meticulously detailed and convincing presentation of a wholly alien form of life.

Our scientists, in talking of life on other worlds, stubbornly stick to the conservatism of discussing ''life as we know it''—which can, of course, exist only on a world pretty much ''as we know it.'' We have never been able to see why the creative force of the universe should be so monotonously lacking in versatility. William Blake stood in awe of One who could make both the Lamb and the Tyger; surely that immortal hand or eye has, in the endless reaches of Space, framed symmetries more fearful (to us) than we can imagine.

Many science fiction writers, particularly since the days of Stanley Weinbaum, have invented ingenious forms of life as we cannot know it; but none has succeeded so well as Clement in making this invention an act, not of abstract imagination, but of pure scientific reason. And now Clement has brought forth his most impressive long piece, the novel MISSION OF GRAVITY (Doubleday, $2.95).

The postulate here is that Mesklin, the planet of a double sun some eleven lightyears from our Sol, is not spherical but almost disc-shaped, so that its gravity ranges from a mere three times that of Earth at the equator to an overpowering 700 g at the poles. There are other factors involved, too—oceans of methane, an atmosphere largely of hydrogen, exceedingly low surface temperatures and high atmospheric pressures, a period of rotation so rapid that a ''day'' is only some twenty of our minutes; and the fictional question posed is: granted all of these factors, what type of intelligent life will have evolved, and what sort of civilization, culture, and psychological attitudes will it possess? It is a splendid specimen of *science* fiction in the grandest of grand manners.

Vol. 7, No. 2
August 1954

We just don't understand the anthology situation. We've heard publishers admit that some, even some of the best, have been commercial failures; we've heard readers say that they're sick of them; we know that reviewers are becoming completely numb—and still they come . . . !

But recent years are producing new authors quite as exciting as Golden Age giants, as is evidenced by three books of short stories. Robert Sheckley's UNTOUCHED BY HUMAN HANDS (Ballantine, $2.50 and 35¢) is as brightly individual and entrancing a group of science fantasies as we've seen in some time—and from an author who has only barely begun his career! Richard Matheson's BORN OF MAN AND WOMAN (Chamberlain, $3) evinces an equally striking young talent in a more unevenly edited volume, containing too many familiar stories and a clinker or two—but still a book well worth owning. F&SF readers, who know Matheson and Sheckley well, should welcome discovering another splendidly off-beat mind in Roald Dahl's SOMEONE LIKE YOU (Knopf, $3.50). Winner of Mystery Writers of America's Edgar for its subtly devastating murder stories, this volume also contains two biting science-fantasies, plus a few unclassifiable gems (such as that perfect story, *Taste*)—the whole belonging on your shelves somewhere in the Beerbohm-Collier-Saki section.

ANNOUNCEMENT: *The introduction to* Brave New Word *didn't, I'll confess, tell the whole story. The sad fact is that J. Francis McComas is having such a fine time being a writer (in San Miguel de Allende, Guanajuato) that he has retired from the coeditorship of F&SF. He'll still remain on the staff as Advisory Editor, available for consultation on tricky points; but from now on I'm the solo target for your brickbats (and maybe occasional bouquets). McComas fans will continue to find his science fiction reviews in the N.Y.* Times *and, I hope, most of his new short fiction in F&SF.*

Readers have often wondered how McComas and I worked together and who did what, and we were forced to say we just didn't know. It was a perfectly fused editorial symbiosis, in which it was impossible to say, "This is obviously McComas' doing," or "There's a touch of Boucher." As a result, the character of F&SF has been so firmly fixed as a joint McComas-Boucher product that I don't think you'll notice any significant difference in the future. Certainly no changes in basic policy are even remotely contemplated; and I hope you'll find my solo efforts as satisfactory as those of the symbiotic team. And if not, please let me know at once!

ANTHONY BOUCHER

Vol. 7, No. 4
Oct. 1954

In our field, as in that of the suspense novel, it's largely the caprice of the publisher that determines which way a book is presented; and as a result students of the art of the novel overlook many a book which they would enjoy, because it is addressed to the restricted science fiction audience, and devotees of s.f. overlook many a fine work of imagination because it is issued as "a serious novel." There isn't much to be done, at the moment, about the first oversight; one can only hope that the literary arbiters will in time realize that Bradbury is not a unique phenomenon. But the second oversight can be remedied if you'll look into the following books, all published "straight" and all ranking among the best science-fantasy of the year so far:

I don't know any author, in or out of the specialized field, who has had so much pure damned fun with ESP as Geoffrey Kerr contrives in UNDER THE INFLUENCE (Lippincott, $3.50)—the tale of a bank clerk who, at precisely the right point of insobriety, becomes an involuntary telepathic detective.

Gore Vidal's MESSIAH (Dutton, $3.50) is rather more pretentious than any of these and rather less successful, but still an absorbing piece of prophetic fiction. The young and prolific Vidal here recounts the growth, in the next 50 years, of a new religion, from its beginnings as another Southern California sect to its triumph as a tyrannical church-state. It's a religion based on "our race's will to death and, worse, to a death in life made radiant by false dreams, by desperate adjurations"; and I can't recall a creed in future fiction which has been created out of so minute a knowledge of the nature of myth and of theological history. Oddly for a novel purely literary in intention, the book is weaker in such fundamentals as construction and characterization than it is extrapolated thinking, which is of the first order.

Vol. 7, No. 5
November 1954

In our survey of 1953's book-publishing (F&SF, March, 1954), McComas and I wrote of Theodore Sturgeon's MORE THAN HUMAN (Farrar, Straus & Young, $2, Ballantine, 35¢), "probably the *best* science fiction novel of 1953!"—and wondered at the time if we should even hedge with that cautious "probably."

It seemed rash to single one novel out of so rich a year as 1953—a much brighter period than 1954 has been so far; but apparently the experts are in full agreement with us, for MORE THAN HUMAN has just received the International Fantasy Award, bestowed by a panel of thirteen distinguished judges from the United States, England and France. And now, having been quite unable to get this beautifully written and sensitively conceived story of human symbiosis out of my mind for almost a year, I'll be even more rash and say that this is the finest novel yet to receive the IFA.

The runners-up are very nearly as impressive in quality of writing and thinking. Second place went to Alfred Bester's pyrotechnic ESP-detective story, THE DEMOLISHED MAN (Shasta, $3, Signet, 25¢), and third to the bitter satire on an advertising-agency future, THE SPACE MERCHANTS, by Frederik Pohl and C. M. Kornbluth (Ballantine, hardcover $1.50, paper 35¢).

Note of consolation: F&SF's BRING THE JUBILEE, by Ward Moore, (Farrar, Straus & Young, $2; Ballantine, 35¢) very nearly ran in the money, and wound up on an official fourth place, which is reasonably gratifying for the only F&SF-originated book eligible in the contest.

Most rewarding of 1954's new novels this month is Richard Matheson's I AM LEGEND (Gold Medal, 25¢), an extraordinary book which manages to do for vampirism what Jack Williamson's DARKER THAN YOU THINK did for lycanthropy: investigate an ancient legend in terms of modern knowledge of psychology and physiology, and turn the stuff of supernatural terror into strict (and still terrifying!) science fiction. Matheson has added a new variant on the Last Man theme, too, in this tale of the last normal human survivor in a world of bloodsucking nightmares, and has given striking vigor to his invention by a forceful style of storytelling which derives from the best hard-boiled crime novels. As a hard-hitting thriller or as fresh imaginative speculation, this is a book you can't miss.

Vol. 7, No. 6
December 1954

There hasn't been a Ray Bradbury book for over a year, and there's no prospect of one for another six months. (The author has been fully occupied in writing the screenplay of MOBY DICK for John Huston's production.) And yet Bradbury is, at the moment, the most newsworthy author of science-fantasy.

Within recent months Ray Bradbury has received the two most important literary prizes ever bestowed upon a writer in our field: from the National Institute of Arts and Letters, a $1,000 award for his contribution to American literature in THE MARTIAN CHRONICLES (Doubleday, $2.75; Bantam, 25¢) and THE ILLUSTRATED MAN (Doubleday, $2.75; Bantam, 25¢); and from the Commonwealth Club of California, its twenty-third annual gold medal for FAHRENHEIT 451 (Ballantine, $2.50; paper 35¢), judged the best work of fiction produced in the state in 1953.

(The latter is, to be sure, a regional award . . . but what a region! The last two recipients were H. B. Cavis and William Saroyan; this year's runners-up were Leon Uris and Ernest K. Gann.)

These distinctions mean, I think, that science-fantasy (I use the hybrid term because many critics, including me, feel that Bradbury has written little true science fiction) is moving more rapidly toward general literary acceptance than has any other specialized form of popular literature. No mystery writer, for instance, has received remotely comparable recognition for his crime writing (even though Nobel Prize winner William Faulkner writes strict formal detective stories as a side-line).

Ray Bradbury has not only achieved extraordinary (and justly earned) personal success in an incredibly short time; he has done more than any other single writer to persuade the literary pundits that imaginative literature of the future deserves serious critical consideration, and every science fiction writer, editor, and reader owes him an unrepayable debt.

Even more astonishing is the developing influence of science-fantasy-via-Bradbury upon contemporary music. The British Broadcasting Corporation has presented a symphony based upon FAHRENHEIT 451; and the Twelfth World Science Fiction Convention offered, last September in San Francisco, the world premiere of a new chamber opera by the well-established young composer Charles Hamm, based upon the Bradbury short story *A Scent of Sarsaparilla* (in which I had the honor of making my operatic debut as narrator). It's a beautifully constructed, melodic and evocative opera (and singularly faithful to the original); and I'm sure you'll be hearing it soon from some small Opera Theater in your area. At least three other Bradbury-based operas are now being written by recognized composers; and there's talk of a full-scale musical version of THE MARTIAN CHRONI-CLES for Broadway!

Frederic Brown's ANGELS AND SPACESHIPS (Dutton, $2.75) contains a little of everything, from screwball fantasy to sober science fiction, and from anthology favorites to nine brandnew short-shorts never before published anywhere. The only things that all 17 stories have in common are sparkling originality and delightfully crisp writing—qualities that you'll also find in the highly welcome reprint of Brown's hilarious 1949 novel WHAT MAD UNIVERSE (Bantam, 25¢). Of the nine stories in C. M. Kornbluth's THE EXPLORERS (Ballantine, 35¢), three have been previously reprinted and one long and admirable one is brandnew. Again themes, styles and lengths are varied; but Kornbluth's sharp observation is everywhere present, and in most of the stories his bitter insight into the hearts and souls of future men (and by implication, into our own). Eric Frank Russell's DEEP SPACE (Fantasy Press, $3) is an equally distinguished collection and an even better edited one: all nine of the stories appear for the first time in book form, and all are so chosen as to form a cohesive series of comments upon human (and extra-human) relationships in spaceflight and colonization. *The Timid Tiger* is as good an example as I know of Russell's quiet reasonableness and gentle (almost tender) humor; and the others are not unworthy of it.

ABOUT THE AUTHOR

ANNETTE MCCOMAS is the former wife of J. Francis McComas, one of the founders of THE MAGAZINE OF FANTASY & SCIENCE FICTION. She has worked as an editor for F&SF, taught science fiction as literature as a college instructor, and is active in the sf/fantasy community. She lives in Berkeley, California.

OUT OF THIS WORLD!

That's the only way to describe Bantam's great series of science fiction classics. These space-age thrillers are filled with terror, fancy and adventure and written by America's most renowned writers of science fiction. Welcome to outer space and have a good trip!